מגילת רות מסורת הרב

Megillat Ruth Mesorat HaRav

קורן ירושלים

OU PRESS

Note on the Cover Design

The front cover depicts "Ruth Gathering Wheat" by Edwin Long, oil on canvas.

Adorning the back cover is the image of a small nightingale, one of the most musical of all songbirds. This artistic motif is an allusion to the Soloveitchik family name, which in Russian means "little nightingale." The Soloveitchik family are Levites, and legend has it that the origin of the name harks back to the family's sacred role as Levites in the Beit HaMikdash, gracing the service with song that accompanied the *korbanot*.

WINTMAN FAMILY EDITION

מגילת רות מסורת הרב

MEGILLAT RUTH MESORAT HARAV

WITH COMMENTARY ON
MEGILLAT RUTH AND THE TORAH READINGS OF SHAVUOT
BASED ON THE TEACHINGS
OF

Rabbi Joseph B. Soloveitchik

COMPILED AND EDITED BY
Reuven Mohl

RESHIMOT COMPILED BY
Eliyahu Krakowski and Moshe Genack

•

OU PRESS
KOREN PUBLISHERS JERUSALEM

Megillat Ruth Mesorat HaRav
First Edition, 2025

OU Press, an imprint of the Orthodox Union (hereafter "OU")
11 Broadway, New York, NY 10004
www.oupress.org

Koren Publishers Jerusalem Ltd.
POB 4044, Jerusalem 9104001, ISRAEL
POB 8531, New Milford, CT 06776, USA

www.korenpub.com

Printed in the United States of America

Hardcover, ISBN 978-965-7813-59-1

SHATRY1

This edition of Megillat Ruth is lovingly dedicated
to the memory of our parents

Abraham and Sylvia Wintman

אברהם צבי בן יצחק חיים
שרה בלומא בת קלמן מרדכי הכהן

Our parents' lives together devoted to family,
community, and *Klal Yisrael*,
and the especially close relationship
our parents maintained with the Rav,
have been a wellspring of inspiration to our entire family

Kenny Wintman and Sandy Welkes

In Memory of

The Rav ***zt"l***

The close relationship between my family and the Rav's
was truly cherished.

Mrs. Soloveitchik was and remains my role model in life.

Dedicated by

Monique C. Katz and Family

In Loving Memory of Our Dear Parents

HaRav Yitzchok Singer and Rebbetzin Bluma Singer

הרב יצחק אהרן בן הרב ר' אליהו ז"ל

בלומא בת ר' ישראל אריה לייב ז"ל

Our father was an extraordinary *talmid chacham* and masterful orator.
He brought honor to the rabbinate, comfort to the afflicted,
and inspiration to the downtrodden.

Our mother was a quintessential *aishes Chayil,*
wise, warm, and dedicated.
She was both an equal partner with our father in his sacred work
and a credit to her distinguished *yichus.*

Dedicated by

Baruch and Susie Singer and Yitzchak Ahron
Rabbi Eli Hersh and Rivky Singer
Rabbi Nussie and Ruchy Singer
Yossie and Surie Singer Sruly Singer

In Loving Memory of Our Dear Parents

Estelle and Nysen Mael

ניסן בן יעקב צבי ז״ל
אסתר בת צבי ז״ל

Longtime, active members
of the Maimonides Kehilla in Brookline

Dedicated by

Lynn and Joel Mael and Family

In Memory of

Rabbi Joseph B. Soloveitchik

The towering rabbinic figure of the last century,
a brilliant Talmudic scholar and profound Jewish philosopher,
Rabbi Soloveitchik was a monumental personality
whose unparalleled intellectual contributions
continue to enrich the world of Jewish thought and law.

Dedicated by

Empire KOSHER

CONTENTS

PREFACE

Megillat Ruth is the stirring story of the eponymous convert whose devotion to her adopted people culminates in her becoming the "matriarch of monarchy" (*Bava Batra* 91b). Interestingly, in the dramatic speech of Ruth to her mother-in-law, Naomi, we can hear echoes of the father of all converts, Abraham, and his own journey toward the separation and distinctness that are the marks of Jewish peoplehood (Ruth 1:16–17):

> וַתֹּאמֶר רוּת אַל תִּפְגְּעִי בִי לְעָזְבֵךְ לָשׁוּב מֵאַחֲרָיִךְ כִּי אֶל אֲשֶׁר תֵּלְכִי אֵלֵךְ וּבַאֲשֶׁר תָּלִינִי אָלִין עַמֵּךְ עַמִּי וֵאלֹהַיִךְ אֱלֹהָי. בַּאֲשֶׁר תָּמוּתִי אָמוּת וְשָׁם אֶקָּבֵר כֹּה יַעֲשֶׂה ה׳ לִי וְכֹה יֹסִיף כִּי הַמָּוֶת יַפְרִיד בֵּינִי וּבֵינֵךְ.
>
> But Ruth replied, "Do not entreat me to leave you, to turn back, not to walk after you. For wherever you walk, I shall walk, and wherever you stay, there I stay. Your people is my people; your God is my God. Wherever you die, there I die, and there shall I be buried. So may the Lord do to me – and more – for death alone will separate me from you.

Ruth's words, אֶל אֲשֶׁר תֵּלְכִי אֵלֵךְ, "For wherever you walk, I shall walk," parallel God's first command to Abraham, לֶךְ לְךָ מֵאַרְצְךָ וּמִמּוֹלַדְתְּךָ וּמִבֵּית אָבִיךָ אֶל הָאָרֶץ אֲשֶׁר אַרְאֶךָּ, "Go forth from your native land and from your father's house to the land that I will show you" (Gen. 12:1). Like Abraham, Ruth performed an act of לֶךְ לְךָ – she was ready to leave and sacrifice her connection to her land, her birthplace, and her father's house, to travel to an unknown land from which emanated a mysterious force compelling her forward.

Ruth continued, וּבַאֲשֶׁר תָּלִינִי אָלִין, "and wherever you stay, there I stay," which parallels Abraham's commitment to *hakhnasat orḥim* – as reflected in his famed אֶשֶׁל, which *Ḥazal* understood to be a lodge (Gen. 21:33; Rashi, *Sotah* 10a, s.v. *pundak*). This אֶשֶׁל was not incidental to Abraham's identity but at the very core of his character. The Gemara (*Ketubot* 8b) refers to those who perform acts of kindness as "those who uphold the covenant of Abraham"; Rashi explains that Abraham's covenant refers to his acts of kindness exemplified by his אֶשֶׁל. The story of Ruth is likewise understood by *Ḥazal* as purely an expression of *ḥesed*: "This *megillah* contains neither [laws of] impurity nor purity, neither the forbidden nor the permitted; why then was it written? To teach us how great is the reward of those who perform kindness" (see Ruth Rabbah 2:14 and commentary below, p. 26). Ruth fully upheld this covenant of Abraham.

Third, Ruth stated, עַמֵּךְ עַמִּי וֵאלֹהַיִךְ אֱלֹהָי, "Your people is my people; your God is my God." This represents Ruth's embrace of both the people and the God of Abraham. As the Rav elaborates in this commentary, entry into the Jewish people constitutes a dual commitment. The convert must "enter into the magic circle of Jewish fate and, in a spirit of holiness, dedicate himself to Jewish destiny." In the Rav's words, "The devotion to *Keneset Israel*, both as ... a people with its own history, suffering, sense of mutual responsibility, and commitment to deeds of mutual aid, and as a holy nation, committed, heart and soul, to the God of Israel and to His ethico-halakhic demands – this dual yet unified devotion is the most basic foundation of Judaism and the most fundamental feature of undergoing conversion" (see p. 8). The commitment to these two covenants initiated by Abraham is so succinctly encapsulated in the words of Ruth, עַמֵּךְ עַמִּי וֵאלֹהַיִךְ אֱלֹהָי.

Fourth, Ruth pledged, בַּאֲשֶׁר תָּמוּתִי אָמוּת וְשָׁם אֶקָּבֵר, "Wherever you die, there I die, and there shall I be buried." This parallels the episode of Abraham's purchase of the *Me'arat HaMakhpelah*, which according to some was his final test (see R. Yonah's commentary on *Avot* 5:3). Even in death and burial, the Jew is separate, "a people that shall dwell alone, and shall not be reckoned among the nations" (Num. 23:9; see p. 10 below). Jewish burial symbolizes the Jew's distinct identity, as the Rav poignantly expressed in his essay "Majesty and Humility":

> The home for which man yearns attracts him like a powerful magnet; it brings him back, no matter how far he has traveled. "Home is the sailor, home from the sea, and the hunter home from the hill": these beautiful lines by Robert Louis Stevenson contain more than a nostalgic note. Occasionally, when I am at the airport, I happen to observe the loading of a double coffin, containing the body of a Jew who has lived, worked, raised children, prospered or failed, in the United States. It is being shipped for burial in the land of Abraham, Isaac and Jacob. The mystery of the origin apparently casts a spell even upon people who have few religious commitments. The modern secular Jew wants

◂ to rest

> to rest in eternal peace, in proximity to the site where the patriarchs found their rest.

Ruth experienced that same enigmatic pull toward the land, people, and God of Abraham. We read her story on Shavuot because it is the paradigmatic story of entry into the nation founded by Abraham, an experience undergone by every Jewish soul on the first Shavuot at Mount Sinai thousands of years ago.

OU Press is proud to present, together with Koren Publishers Jerusalem, *Megillat Ruth Mesorat HaRav.* As with our other *Mesorat HaRav* publications, the Rav's commentary consists of excerpts from the Rav's published writings as well as from the Rav's lectures and *shiurim* and *sefarim* written by students of the Rav. Also following the pattern of other of our *Mesorat HaRav* publications, we have included a section of *Reshimot,* more extensive presentations of the Rav's analysis of halakhic material than the discussions included in the commentary. The *Reshimot* are drawn from the Rav's published writings, in some cases translated from Hebrew, as well as lectures, *shiurim,* and classes which he conducted over the years, many of which have been transcribed by his students and others. Included as well is an adaptation of an essay about conversion by Rav Ahron Soloveichik, the Rav's youngest brother, originally published in a volume in honor of the Rav.

Many dedicated individuals were involved in the preparation of this volume. My esteemed friend Dr. Joel B. Wolowelsky provided guidance for this project and the impetus to bring it to successful fruition, as he has for so many other works of the Rav. Dr. Reuven Mohl compiled and edited the commentary on Ruth and the Torah readings, while Rabbi Moshe Genack and Rabbi Eliyahu Krakowski compiled and edited the *Reshimot.* We extend thanks to Rabbi David Schreiber, editor of *Noraos HaRav,* and Rabbi Michel Shurkin, author of *Harerei Kedem,* whose works also served as a source for sections of the commentary and the *Reshimot.* Rabbi Krakowski, executive editor of OU Press, was in charge of the meticulous review and editing of the manuscript as it went through numerous drafts. Rabbi Simon Posner, executive editor emeritus of OU Press, reviewed the manuscript and made many helpful suggestions. Thanks as well to Debra Bree of OU Press for her assistance in preparation

◂ of the manuscript

of the manuscript. I acknowledge Koren Publishers Jerusalem, our partners in this project, under the able leadership of Matthew Miller, for their outstanding work in editing, typesetting, and producing this edition. Special thanks go to Rabbi Steven Weil, who has consistently championed the dissemination of the Rav's works and the preservation of his legacy. Rabbi Weil has provided an extraordinary degree of encouragement and assistance to OU Press in its efforts to bring the Rav's writings to the public.

This project could not have been realized without the generous support of our sponsors. We are grateful to the Wintman family for their generosity, and we thank, as well, the Katz family, the Mael family, the Singer family, and Empire Kosher for their assistance. All those who participated in this project can be justifiably proud of their contribution to *Klal Yisrael* which this volume represents.

Menachem Dov Genack
General Editor
OU Press

מגילת רות

MEGILLAT RUTH

RUTH

In Israel, the book of Ruth is read on the first day of Shavuot. Elsewhere, it is read on the second day.

1 1 Once, in the days when the judges ruled, there was a famine in the
land. One man set out from Bethlehem of Judah and journeyed
to live for a while in the land of Moab, and his wife and two sons
2 came with him. This man's name was Elimelech, his wife's was
Naomi, and his two sons' names were Maḥlon and Kilyon, all
Efratites from Bethlehem of Judah. They duly arrived in the fields
3 of Moab, and there they stayed. But then Elimelech, Naomi's hus-
4 band, died, and she was left there with her two sons. Both of them
married Moabite women – the first was called Orpah, the second
5 Ruth – and they lived on there for some ten years. After that, the
two of them – Maḥlon and Kilyon – died as well, and the woman

---

What do we mourn over? We mourn over those who "are gone and not to be found," in the sense of an irretrievable loss.

This goes without saying in the case of the death of a great leader, a wondrous genius, or a rare philanthropist. Indeed, it is difficult to replace such people. But the tradition of mourning pertains to all men, not only to the noteworthy; it applies to the leader and to the led, to the learned and to the uneducated, to the charitable and to the one who was tight fisted toward his impoverished brethren. It is written: "He who stands beside the dead, when the soul departs, must rend his clothes; what does this resemble? It resembles a burnt Torah" (*Shabbat* 105b). It may be inferred from this that it is impossible to fill the place of anyone who has departed from this world. We do not say, "A cobbler has died, another will fill his place; a tailor has died, another will come in his stead; another clerk will fill the place of the one who has just departed, another shop-assistant shall come in place of the one who is dead." We do not say such things, because every man is indispensable; he is not just "one" who can be replaced by another "one"; he is an individual distinguished by something unique to him and to no one else. Sometimes a person develops his own inner potential, and sometimes it remains locked within him like an untapped treasure that never comes to light. (*On Repentance*, pp. 176–177)

רות

In ארץ ישראל*,* מגילת רות *is read on the first day of* שבועות*.*
Elsewhere, it is read on the second day.

א וַיְהִי בִּימֵי שְׁפֹט הַשֹּׁפְטִים וַיְהִי רָעָב בָּאָרֶץ וַיֵּלֶךְ אִישׁ מִבֵּית
ב לֶחֶם יְהוּדָה לָגוּר בִּשְׂדֵי מוֹאָב הוּא וְאִשְׁתּוֹ וּשְׁנֵי בָנָיו: וְשֵׁם
הָאִישׁ אֱלִימֶלֶךְ וְשֵׁם אִשְׁתּוֹ נָעֳמִי וְשֵׁם שְׁנֵי־בָנָיו ׀ מַחְלוֹן וְכִלְיוֹן
אֶפְרָתִים מִבֵּית לֶחֶם יְהוּדָה וַיָּבֹאוּ שְׂדֵי־מוֹאָב וַיִּהְיוּ־שָׁם:
ג ד וַיָּמָת אֱלִימֶלֶךְ אִישׁ נָעֳמִי וַתִּשָּׁאֵר הִיא וּשְׁנֵי בָנֶיהָ: וַיִּשְׂאוּ
לָהֶם נָשִׁים מֹאֲבִיּוֹת שֵׁם הָאַחַת עָרְפָּה וְשֵׁם הַשֵּׁנִית רוּת וַיֵּשְׁבוּ
ה שָׁם כְּעֶשֶׂר שָׁנִים: וַיָּמוּתוּ גַם־שְׁנֵיהֶם מַחְלוֹן וְכִלְיוֹן וַתִּשָּׁאֵר

וַיְהִי בִּימֵי שְׁפֹט הַשֹּׁפְטִים *Once, in the days when the judges ruled.* The word *shofet* denotes not only judicial or legal action, but points to the totality of human relationships. The Greek and Latin translations of *Sefer Shoftim* refer to the book as the "Book of Judges." But this is incorrect. The verse (Jud. 4:4) וּדְבוֹרָה ... הִיא שֹׁפְטָה אֶת־יִשְׂרָאֵל בָּעֵת הַהִיא is conventionally translated as "And Deborah ... judged Israel at that time." But if Deborah was only a judge, why did she act like a queen? Nothing in the chapter mentions judging, only acts of dedication to the nation. She chose the general to fight Sisera. Does a judge declare war? Apparently, she was more than a judge. She determined the destiny of her people. She was a guide and a teacher of her people, not simply a judge. *Shoftim* is not the Book of Judges, but the Book of Leaders. We know that Samuel "judged" (1 Sam. 7:6, 15) but he also shaped the spiritual image of the people. (*Shiurei Harav*, p. 152)

וַיָּמָת אֱלִימֶלֶךְ אִישׁ נָעֳמִי *But then Elimelech, Naomi's husband, died.* The Sages said: "As their faces do not resemble one another, so neither are their thoughts the same" (*Berakhot* 58a). Each man is not only one person in number but is also unique. He is different from others, being characterized by some original quality that no one else possesses. This singularity, this quality unique to him alone, which sets him apart from everyone else, reflects the divine spark in him. The concept of mourning in Judaism is based upon this assumption.

6 was left bereaved of both her children and her husband. She got
up, her daughters-in-law with her, to return from the land of Moab,
for word had reached her in the land of Moab that the Lord had
7 brought His people to mind and granted them bread. So she left
the place where she had been, both of her daughters-in-law with
8 her, and set off along the way back to the land of Judah. But to her
two daughters-in-law she said, "Go on now, turn back, each to your
mother's home, and may the Lord show you that kindness that
9 you have shown the dead and me. The Lord grant that you find a

---

exertions; it is not the result of a conglomeration of past events. The drive for Israel is fueled by anticipation, by something beautiful and miraculous which defies precise formulation, which hovers and beckons on the distant horizon. Even secular Zionists, who formally decry all religious terminology and motivations, often speak with Messianic overtones. Destiny, not causality, constitutes the dynamics of covenantal history. The future is responsible for the past.

The word "destiny" is etymologically related to the word "destination." What determines Jewish historical experience is not one's point of departure, but one's destination. There are two types of travelers. Some merely wander about restlessly, unable to stay put in any one place and going nowhere in particular. Circumstances dictate their movement. An experienced traveler, however, has a destination to which he is rushing, and he wants to get there as soon as possible. And that is precisely the factor that shapes Jewish history, which is unlike the histories of other nations. The Jew is rushing somewhere, and, however often he is sidetracked, he returns to resume the journey.

The Patriarchic Covenant created this new concept of historical destiny. It promised Israel a faith, a land, and a future redemption. It pledged, "And I shall make of thee a great nation, and I will bless thee and make thy name great, and thou shalt be a blessing . . . and all the families of the earth shall bless themselves through you" (Gen. 12:2–3). It forged a people with a great destination. (*Reflections of The Rav*, vol. 2, pp. 71–72)

יַעַשׂ יהוה עִמָּכֶם חֶסֶד כַּאֲשֶׁר עֲשִׂיתֶם עִם־הַמֵּתִים וְעִמָּדִי *And may the Lord show you that kindness that you have shown the dead and me.* The great experience of God's all-inclusiveness and His axiological supremacy over all other interests

ו הָאִשָּׁה מִשְּׁנֵי יְלָדֶיהָ וּמֵאִישָׁהּ׃ וַתָּקָם הִיא וְכַלֹּתֶיהָ וַתָּשָׁב
מִשְּׂדֵי מוֹאָב כִּי שָׁמְעָה בִּשְׂדֵה מוֹאָב כִּי־פָקַד יהוה אֶת־עַמּוֹ
ז לָתֵת לָהֶם לָחֶם׃ וַתֵּצֵא מִן־הַמָּקוֹם אֲשֶׁר הָיְתָה־שָׁמָּה וּשְׁתֵּי
ח כַלֹּתֶיהָ עִמָּהּ וַתֵּלַכְנָה בַדֶּרֶךְ לָשׁוּב אֶל־אֶרֶץ יְהוּדָה׃ וַתֹּאמֶר
נָעֳמִי לִשְׁתֵּי כַלֹּתֶיהָ לֵכְנָה שֹּׁבְנָה אִשָּׁה לְבֵית אִמָּהּ יעשה יהוה יַעַשׂ
ט עִמָּכֶם חֶסֶד כַּאֲשֶׁר עֲשִׂיתֶם עִם־הַמֵּתִים וְעִמָּדִי׃ יִתֵּן יהוה לָכֶם

וַתִּשָּׁאֵר הָאִשָּׁה מִשְּׁנֵי יְלָדֶיהָ וּמֵאִישָׁהּ *And the woman was left bereaved of both her children and her husband.* The longing for one who has died and is gone forever is worse than death. The soul is overcome and shattered by fierce longing. Just before Rosh Hashanah, I imagined that my father, of blessed memory, was standing beside me. He was the one and only *rebbi*, master and teacher, that I ever had. I put my life down before him and said: "My father, my teacher, I have had so many new insights concerning the laws of the Day of Atonement. Certainly there are amongst them some which would have pleased you, and also some which you would have rejected…." That was how I imagined myself speaking to my father, knowing that I would receive no response. Oh, what would I have given to be able to discuss Torah with him, if only for five minutes! But I knew that my beloved father, who had once been so close to me, was now far away, and my heart burst with the desire to talk to him for even five minutes, which had not seemed so valuable while he was still alive.

The same is true regarding my mother and my wife. Several days ago, I once again sat down to prepare my annual discourse on the subject of repentance. I always used to discuss it with my wife, and she would help me to define and crystallize my thoughts. This year, too, I prepared the discourse, while consulting her: "Could you please advise me? Should I expand upon this idea or cut down on that idea? Should I emphasize this point or that one?" I asked, but heard no reply. Perhaps there was a whispered response to my question, but it was swallowed up by the wind whistling through the trees and did not reach me. (*On Repentance*, pp. 259–260)

וַתֵּלַכְנָה בַדֶּרֶךְ לָשׁוּב אֶל־אֶרֶץ יְהוּדָה *And set off along the way back to the land of Judah.* In the hearts of most Jews, there is an awareness that Israel is a promised land. The promise, a destiny to be fulfilled, is the cause of present

place of rest, each in your husband's home." As she kissed them,
10 they wept aloud and said, "No. We shall return with you to your
11 people." Said Naomi, "Turn back, daughters; why would you come
with me? Have I still sons in my womb who could be husbands to
12 you? Turn back, my daughters – go; I am too old to be with a man.
Even were I to say, 'There is hope for me still,' were I even this night
13 to be married, even if I could bear sons again, are you to wait for
them as they grow? Would you be chained to them, never to be
with another man? No, daughters, for your presence is most bitter
14 to me now, for the hand of the LORD has beaten me." Aloud they

---

is not, at the outset, a refuge of grace and mercy for the despondent and desperate, an enchanted stream for crushed spirits, but a raging, clamorous torrent of man's consciousness with all its crises, pangs, and torments. Yes, it is true that during the third Sabbath meal at dusk, as the day of rest declines and man's soul yearns for its Creator and is afraid to depart from that realm of holiness whose name is Sabbath, into the dark and frightening, secular workaday week, we sing the psalm "The Lord is my shepherd; I shall not want. He maketh me to lie down in green pastures; He leadeth me beside the still waters" (Ps. 23), etc., etc., and we believe with our entire hearts in the words of the psalmist. However, this psalm only describes the ultimate destination of *homo religiosus,* not the path leading to that destination. For the path that eventually will lead to the "green pastures" and to the "still waters" is not the royal road, but a narrow, twisting footway that threads its course along the steep mountain slope: as the terrible abyss yawns at the traveler's feet. Many see "the Lord passing by; and a great and strong wind rending mountains and shattering rocks... and after the wind an earthquake... and after the earthquake a fire" but only a few prove worthy of hearing "the still small voice" (1 Kings 19:11–12). "Out of the straits have I called, Lord" (Ps. 118:5). "Out of the depths I have called unto Thee, O Lord" (Ps. 130:1). Out of the straits of inner oppositions and incongruities, spiritual doubts and uncertainties, out of the depths of a psyche rent with antinomies and contradictions, out of the bottomless pit of that struggles with its own torments I have called, I have called unto Thee, O Lord. (*Halakhic Man*, p. 142)

כִּי־מַר־לִי מְאֹד מִכֶּם *For your presence is most bitter to me now.* Out of the depths in which the individual finds himself, one calls upon God in seclusion and

וּמְצֶאןָ מְנוּחָה אִשָּׁה בֵּית אִישָׁהּ וַתִּשַּׁק לָהֶן וַתִּשֶּׂאנָה קוֹלָן
י יא וַתִּבְכֶּינָה׃ וַתֹּאמַרְנָה־לָּהּ כִּי־אִתָּךְ נָשׁוּב לְעַמֵּךְ׃ וַתֹּאמֶר נָעֳמִי
שֹׁבְנָה בְנֹתַי לָמָּה תֵלַכְנָה עִמִּי הַעוֹד־לִי בָנִים בְּמֵעַי וְהָיוּ לָכֶם
יב לַאֲנָשִׁים׃ שֹׁבְנָה בְנֹתַי לֵכְןָ כִּי זָקַנְתִּי מִהְיוֹת לְאִישׁ כִּי אָמַרְתִּי
יג יֶשׁ־לִי תִקְוָה גַּם הָיִיתִי הַלַּיְלָה לְאִישׁ וְגַם יָלַדְתִּי בָנִים׃ הֲלָהֵן ׀
תְּשַׂבֵּרְנָה עַד אֲשֶׁר יִגְדָּלוּ הֲלָהֵן תֵּעָגֵנָה לְבִלְתִּי הֱיוֹת לְאִישׁ אַל
יד בְּנֹתַי כִּי־מַר־לִי מְאֹד מִכֶּם כִּי־יָצְאָה בִי יַד־יהוה׃ וַתִּשֶּׂנָה קוֹלָן

---

and pursuits asserts itself in the performance of *ḥesed*. The latter implies the moment of divine absolute Lordship over creation and human tenancy. I must share with others the best I possess, because in reality I possess not anything at all. All I have is given to me by divine grace. God, in His infinite *ḥesed*, gives me all I need, but gives not anything away. Yet self-deception, which consists of seeing oneself as an omnipotent lord, is a frequent phenomenon and it becomes part of one's attitude toward his fellow man. In such a state of confusion, the individual acts as if he were the sole possessor of everything he has been privileged to enjoy, including his own self. At this point, *ḥesed* is eliminated. For *ḥesed* denotes an experience of ontic continuity, of an existence which is not encapsulated in the shell of concrete forms, but rather transcends the all-exclusive ego-consciousness and passes into a universal awareness that "every man is false" (Ps. 116:11), all men are liars, all are dishonest about themselves in claiming a status of autonomy and ontic freedom. All men are committed to a common cruel and insensate fate. From such a self-shattering experience, the bright idea of *ḥesed* rises like a distant star from the infinite depths of the universe.

If the community of which the individual is a member is bound by the common hand born out of unalterable fate or destiny, before which all men are equal, then one cannot delineate his individual sphere of existence from others' and must willy-nilly come closer to his fellow men and begin to share with them all he possesses. However, if one persists in his unbridled pretensions and self-deceptions and self-assertion as lord and master of his own destiny, then *ḥesed* is superseded by selfishness. (*Halakhic Morality*, p. 79)

יִתֵּן יהוה לָכֶם וּמְצֶאןָ מְנוּחָה *The Lord grant that you find a place of rest.* Religion

wept still more, then Orpah kissed her mother-in-law – but Ruth
15 clung to her. And Naomi said, "Your sister-in-law has turned back
16 to her people, to her gods. Turn back after your sister-in-law." But
Ruth replied, "Do not entreat me to leave you, to turn back, not to
walk after you. For wherever you walk, I shall walk, and wherever
you stay, there I stay. Your people is my people; your God is my God.

---

the lofty events of the distant past; "thine eyes shall see thy teacher." (*Divrei Hagut VeHaarakhah*, pp. 145–146; *Shiurei Harav*, p. 10)

עַמֵּךְ עַמִּי *Your people is my people.* We know that conversion requires acceptance of the yoke of the commandments, plus immersion in a *mikveh* and circumcision. In fact, immersion and circumcision are technical media, but the essence of conversion expresses itself in the unconditional and total commitment to fulfill the *mitzvot.* Of course, conversion requires both strict observance and the convert's involvement with heart and soul in the historical destiny of the Jewish people. He must share the travail, the misery, and the worry. The prototype of the convert is Ruth, who said "*Ammekh ammi,* Your people is my people, *ve-Elokayikh Elokai,* your God is my God." (*Abraham's Journey*, pp. 57–58)

עַמֵּךְ עַמִּי וֵאלֹהַיִךְ אֱלֹהָי *Your people is my people; your God is my God.* A gentile who comes to attach himself to the Jewish community must accept upon himself the yoke of two covenants, fate and destiny. He must enter into the magic circle of Jewish fate and, in a spirit of holiness, dedicate himself to Jewish destiny. Conversion consists in a person's joining himself to both the people formed by the covenant in Egypt and the holy nation formed by the covenant at Sinai. Take heed of a fundamental principle: There can be no partial conversion, and one cannot relinquish even the slightest iota of either of the two covenants. The devotion to Keneset Israel, both as a people whom God, with a strong hand, took unto Himself in Egypt, a people with its own history, suffering, sense of mutual responsibility, and commitment to deeds of mutual aid, and as a holy nation, committed, heart and soul, to the God of Israel and to His ethico-halakhic demands – this dual yet unified devotion is the most basic foundation of Judaism and the most fundamental feature of undergoing conversion.

For this reason, Halakhah dictates that a convert who has been circumcised but has not yet immersed himself in a *mikveh*, or who has immersed

טו וַתִּבְכֶּינָה עוֹד וַתִּשַּׁק עָרְפָּה לַחֲמוֹתָהּ וְרוּת דָּבְקָה בָּהּ: וַתֹּאמֶר
הִנֵּה שָׁבָה יְבִמְתֵּךְ אֶל־עַמָּהּ וְאֶל־אֱלֹהֶיהָ שׁוּבִי אַחֲרֵי יְבִמְתֵּךְ:
טז וַתֹּאמֶר רוּת אַל־תִּפְגְּעִי־בִי לְעָזְבֵךְ לָשׁוּב מֵאַחֲרָיִךְ כִּי אֶל־
אֲשֶׁר תֵּלְכִי אֵלֵךְ וּבַאֲשֶׁר תָּלִינִי אָלִין עַמֵּךְ עַמִּי וֵאלֹהַיִךְ אֱלֹהָי:

---

loneliness. The existential, passional experience is not shared by the thou, however close he is to the I, since it is an integral part of the existential awareness, which is singular, and hence inexpressible in the universal terms through which we communicate our standardized experiences. No one but the sufferer himself is involved in this deeply human anguish and conflict. It is the sufferer whose awareness oscillates between bliss and pain, in the great negation of the finite that rises out of its confrontation by the infinite. Neither spouse nor child nor parent may understand and sympathize with the lonely individual when his existential experience is at a low ebb, when trials, doubts and inhibitions abound. The prayer echoing the depth crisis of a questing soul emerges from seclusion, from out of the loneliness of the individual whom everybody save God has abandoned: "For my father and mother have abandoned me and God will take me in" (Ps. 27:10). The psalmist speaks of such suffering – the situation of the afflicted person, overwhelmed by his pain, who pours out his complaint before the Lord. (*Worship of the Heart*, p. 33)

וְרוּת דָּבְקָה בָּהּ *But Ruth clung to her.* It does not matter how many *talmidei hakhamim, gedolei Torah,* or scribes a generation is blessed with, with all the sweep and scope of their Torah creativity – it cannot be linked to the great chain of tradition unless it includes a remnant of scribes from the lofty past, bridging the gap between generations. To transmit and to receive is to fold up the generations underneath the religious present, to anchor the "now" in the "once." In every generation, miraculously, we meet the soul of the ancients planted in the present, an emanation of the aura of yore, the pulchritude of age. Tradition includes not only theoretical innovations, abstract concepts, halakhic formulae, logical principles, but also types of being, feelings, responses, a certain existential rhythm and experiential continuity. One cannot achieve a full tradition without personal attachment to a previous generation. In each and every era, we, the receivers, need at least one individual who can connect the generations, about whom we can say, this is the witness to

17 Wherever you die, there I die, and there shall I be buried. So may

---

When a candidate appears before a *beit din* and declares his intention to join the Jewish fold, he is asked two questions: "What motivates you? Do you not realize that we are a persecuted people, subject to oppression and hatred? Do you feel that your desire is reasonable or worthwhile?" The candidate responds, in effect, *Af al pi khen*, "Despite these considerations I am determined to convert." This response is similar to the daily affirmation of faith of all Jews who say in their morning prayers, *Ve'af al pi sheyitmahme'ah, im kol zeh aḥakeh lo* – "though the Messiah and Jewish salvation and vindication be slow in coming, I will nevertheless persist in believing in their imminent realization." The second question deals with the acceptance of the discipline and sovereignty of mitzvot, such as *kashrut*, Shabbat, *tefillin*, and *tzedakah*, which characterize our unique way of life. Here the convert makes a commitment to live a lonely life in the larger family of man, becoming a member of a minority people in a society which is often cynical and which in general hardly encourages our distinct way of life. The *berit milah* which a male convert undergoes is a covenant that binds him to the Jewish people; it is a sign of identity with the community of Israel. The *tevilah* (*mikveh* immersion) initiates the *kabbalat ol mitzvot* or assumption of mitzvah obligations. This duality of commitment is expressed in the famous words of Ruth: "Your people is my people; your God is my God." (*Reflections of the Rav*, pp. 107–108)

בַּאֲשֶׁר תָּמוּתִי אָמוּת וְשָׁם אֶקָּבֵר *Wherever you die, there I die, and there shall I be buried.* The historical loneliness of the Jew percolates from a feeling of compulsive fate. He is as alone in his life on earth as in his death. The concept of *kever yisrael* emphasizes the Jew's strange detachment from the world. Sociologists and psychologists may say what they wish about the inexplicable isolation of the Jew. Their explanations are nothing more than barren speculation, incapable of rationally describing the phenomenon. Jewish separateness belongs to the framework of the Covenant of Fate that was concluded in Egypt. In truth, Judaism and withdrawal from the world are synonymous. Even before the exile in Egypt, separateness descended upon our world with the appearance of the first Jew, our father Abraham. Abraham the Hebrew (*ivri*) lived apart. "The whole world was on one side (*ever*), and he on the other side" (Gen. Rabbah 42:8). Balaam, when he gazed upon the Israelite camp, understood the wonder of the experience of Jewish separateness and

יז בַּאֲשֶׁר תָּמוּתִי אָמוּת וְשָׁם אֶקָּבֵר כֹּה יַעֲשֶׂה יְהוָה לִי וְכֹה יֹסִיף

himself and has not yet been circumcised, is not fully converted until he does both. Circumcision, which was given to Abraham the Hebrew, the father of Jewish fate, and which was fulfilled in Egypt prior to the offering of the Paschal sacrifice – the symbol of the redemption from Egypt – signifies the fateful otherness of the nation, its necessary isolation and uniqueness. Circumcision is a sign sculpted into the very physical being of the Jew. It is a constant, indelible sign between the God of the Jews and His people, one that cannot be erased. If the Covenant of Fate is not sealed in the flesh, then the singularity of peoplehood is absent and the gentile remains outside the bounds of the Covenant of Egypt.

Immersion in a *mikveh,* in contrast to circumcision, represents the integration of man into his great destiny and his entry into the Covenant of Sinai. The Jews were commanded to immerse themselves prior to the giving of the Torah at Sinai. Immersion purifies and elevates from the profane to the holy, from life as it is to a life filled with a sublime vision. When the convert emerges from the waters of the *mikveh,* a new spiritual reality replete with destiny fills him, and he is endowed with the sanctity of the Jew (*kedushat yisrael*). It is not coincidental that the act of accepting the yoke of the commandments is tied to immersion. The entire essence of immersion is the re-creation of the experience of the acceptance of the Torah and the elevation of the people to the status of a holy nation through its freely given commitment to obey God's word. If the convert is circumcised and does not immerse himself, then the association of man to destiny is missing, and the gentile is fenced off from the Covenant of Sinai and from a halakhic identification with a holy nation.

The formula for conversion in the Book of Ruth contains these two aspects, and their essence lies in the four final words of Ruth to Naomi: עַמֵּךְ עַמִּי וֵאלֹהַיִךְ אֱלֹהָי, "Your people is my people; your God is my God." (*Fate and Destiny,* pp. 60–61)

A religious Jew makes two commitments: to observe the mitzvot of the Torah and also to identify with the historical destiny of his people. Both require a leap of faith which is impelled by the *ratzon elyon,* the sovereign, unmotivated will, the essential "I." Both may be regarded as *ḥukkim* because they involve considerable suspension of one's reason and are not based on practical considerations.

the Lord do to me – and more – for death alone will separate me
18 from you." Naomi saw that Ruth was determined to come with her,
19 and she spoke to her no more. The two of them walked on until
they came to Bethlehem, and when they arrived at Bethlehem, the

---

repentance is but a reflection. Conversion is not, as many believe, a mere matter of immersion in the ritual bath. It is not a mere ceremony. Certainly, immersion is crucial to it, but it is a mistake to believe that the conversion begins and ends with this ritual. Conversion means a radical, decisive and complete change of the person's identity, and the immersion is but a symbol indicative of this transformation. A man descends into the waters to immerse himself, and when he emerges, he is a new person. If I may paraphrase Scripture, it is written: "when you lose it, you find it" – one personality is lost and a second, different one has been found.

"Go forth out of thy country, and from thy kindred, and from thy father's house" (Gen. 12:1) – as Abraham, our forefather, the father of all righteous converts, was told. "Go forth" is not a matter of geographical change from one locality to another, but a deeply human and spiritual event. As the Halakhah puts it: "A person, having converted, is like a newborn babe." Being born again means a definitive change in his style and way of life, inwardly and outwardly. Without such a change, true conversion does not take place, not even partially. (*On Repentance*, pp. 182–183)

וַתֶּחְדַּל לְדַבֵּר אֵלֶיהָ *And she spoke to her no more.* If two individuals are close friends, sharing a sense of intimacy and companionship, then one of them need not have a message to deliver in order to walk into the other's home. That is where Martin Buber made his biggest mistake. Conversation or dialogue is not the highest form of friendship. Once a conversation comes to an end, there is nothing else to do but leave the house. But the highest form of friendship does not require words. I do not have to tell my friend why I came to see him. I just come, because I like to be present in his home. This usually happens between husband and wife, between brother and sister or parent and child. Except in our halakhic studies, my father talked very little to me; he never confided in me. But he wanted me to be around, because he liked me. There was no need for words, for an exchange of remarks. Why does a mother like to have her baby sleep in her room, or in a room next to her? It is not simply because of the safety of the baby. The mere feeling that the baby is nearby gives her satisfaction. (*Abraham's Journey*, p. 160)

יח כִּ֣י הַמָּ֔וֶת יַפְרִ֖יד בֵּינִ֥י וּבֵינֶֽךָ׃ וַתֵּ֕רֶא כִּֽי־מִתְאַמֶּ֥צֶת הִ֖יא לָלֶ֣כֶת
יט אִתָּ֑הּ וַתֶּחְדַּ֖ל לְדַבֵּ֥ר אֵלֶֽיהָ׃ וַתֵּלַ֣כְנָה שְׁתֵּיהֶ֔ם עַד־בּוֹאָ֖נָה בֵּ֣ית

---

proclaimed with amazement: "Lo, it is a people that shall dwell alone, and shall not be reckoned among the nations" (Num. 23:9). Even if a Jew reaches the pinnacle of social and political accomplishment, he will not be able to free himself from the chains of isolation. This paradoxical fate has preserved both the separateness and the uniqueness of the Jew, despite his apparent integration into his non-Jewish environment. Even people of power and authority, such as Joseph, the regent of Egypt, was separated from Egyptian society and remained alone in his tent. "And they served him [Joseph] by himself... and the Egyptians... by themselves." (Gen. 43:32). Before his death, Joseph pleaded with his brothers, "When God will surely remember you and bring you out of this land, you shall carry up my bones from here" (Gen. 50:25). Despite my greatness and glory, I am tied to you and your existence both in life and in death. This singular, inexplicable phenomenon of the individual clinging to the community and feeling alienated from the outside world was forged and formed in Egypt. There Israel was elevated to the status of a nation in the sense of a unity from which arises uniqueness as well. The awareness of the Fate Covenant in all of its manifestations is an integral part of our historical-metaphysical essence. (*Fate and Destiny*, pp. 43–45)

וַתֵּרֶא כִּי־מִתְאַמֶּצֶת הִיא לָלֶכֶת אִתָּהּ *Naomi saw that Ruth was determined to come with her.* A man's chain of associations depends upon his aspirations, upon that personal supplication whispered in the hour of silence. Some seek the nearness of the Master of the Universe; some long for power or fame; others want to expand their knowledge; and there are those who seek pleasures or money. Prayer represents man in his totality. It represents everything he is and does.

Judaism has always held that it lies within man's power to renew himself, to be reborn and to redirect the course of his life. In this task, man must rely upon himself; no one can help him. He is his own creator and innovator. He is his own redeemer; he is his own messiah who has come to redeem himself from the darkness of his exile to the light of his personal redemption.

The best example of a man's ability to create himself anew, to change his life's inner prayer, is demonstrated in the act of conversion, of which

whole town crowded around as the women asked, "Can this be
20 Naomi?" She said to the women, "Call me not Naomi. Call me
21 Mara, for Shaddai has made my life bitter beyond words. I was full
when I left this place, and empty has the LORD returned me. Why
call me, 'Naomi'? the LORD has spoken up against me; Shaddai has
22 ruined me." This is how Naomi, returning from the land of Moab
with her daughter-in-law, Ruth the Moabite, returned. They arrived
2 1 at Bethlehem just as the barley harvest began. Naomi had a relative
from her husband Elimelech's family, a man of substance and great
2 strength: his name was Boaz. Ruth the Moabite said to Naomi, "I
shall go to the field and gather the fallen grains, and follow after
anyone who should show me favor." Naomi said, "Go, then, my
3 daughter," and so she went. She came and started to gather in the
field after the harvestmen, and it chanced to be the field plot of
4 Boaz that she came to – that man of Elimelech's family. And there
came Boaz himself, arriving from Bethlehem and saying to the
harvestmen, "The LORD be with you." "The LORD bless you," they

---

וַיִּקֶר מִקְרֶהָ *And it chanced to be.* There are no accidents. Judaism rejects any belief in a deterministic *mazal* or in a blind *goral,* random events in nature and human life. We do not believe in fate as did the Greeks, who saw everything affected by absurd, unalterable, and ruthless decrees which emanated from the remote unknown. Such fate often clashes with the yearnings of man and crushes his hopes and aspirations, irrespective of his ethical behavior. This, to the Greeks, was the source of human tragedy. Man becomes a helpless pawn in the hands of inexorable forces which cannot be thwarted, even by the gods.

Judaism, even as it knew and tried to comprehend catastrophic events which cruelly destroy man's dreams and hopes, could not accept the existence of the ultimately irrational in human life. Events which we label as accidents belong to a higher divine order into which man has not been initiated. Not decrees of fate, but rather reasons beyond our comprehension, operate in such instances. We have been granted the opportunity of gaining insights and of accumulating scientific knowledge about the regular course

לֶ֑חֶם וַיְהִ֗י כְּבֹאָ֙נָה֙ בֵּ֣ית לֶ֔חֶם וַתֵּהֹ֤ם כׇּל־הָעִיר֙ עֲלֵיהֶ֔ן וַתֹּאמַ֖רְנָה
כ הֲזֹ֥את נׇעֳמִֽי׃ וַתֹּ֣אמֶר אֲלֵיהֶ֔ן אַל־תִּקְרֶ֥אנָה לִ֖י נׇעֳמִ֑י קְרֶ֤אןָ לִי֙
כא מָרָ֔א כִּי־הֵמַ֥ר שַׁדַּ֛י לִ֖י מְאֹֽד׃ אֲנִי֙ מְלֵאָ֣ה הָלַ֔כְתִּי וְרֵיקָ֖ם הֱשִׁיבַ֣נִי
יהוה לָ֣מָּה תִקְרֶ֤אנָה לִי֙ נׇעֳמִ֔י וַיהוה֙ עָ֣נָה בִ֔י וְשַׁדַּ֖י הֵ֥רַֽע לִֽי׃
כב וַתָּ֣שׇׁב נׇעֳמִ֗י וְר֨וּת הַמּוֹאֲבִיָּ֤ה כַלָּתָהּ֙ עִמָּ֔הּ הַשָּׁ֖בָה מִשְּׂדֵ֣י מוֹאָ֑ב
ב א וְהֵ֗מָּה בָּ֚אוּ בֵּ֣ית לֶ֔חֶם בִּתְחִלַּ֖ת קְצִ֥יר שְׂעֹרִֽים׃ וּֽלְנׇעֳמִ֞י מידע מוֹדַ֣ע
ב לְאִישָׁ֗הּ אִ֚ישׁ גִּבּ֣וֹר חַ֔יִל מִמִּשְׁפַּ֖חַת אֱלִימֶ֑לֶךְ וּשְׁמ֖וֹ בֹּֽעַז׃ וַתֹּ֩אמֶר
ר֨וּת הַמּוֹאֲבִיָּ֜ה אֶל־נׇעֳמִ֗י אֵֽלְכָה־נָּ֤א הַשָּׂדֶה֙ וַאֲלַקֳטָ֣ה בַשִׁבֳּלִ֔ים
ג אַחַ֕ר אֲשֶׁ֥ר אֶמְצָא־חֵ֖ן בְּעֵינָ֑יו וַתֹּ֥אמֶר לָ֖הּ לְכִ֥י בִתִּֽי׃ וַתֵּ֤לֶךְ וַתָּבוֹא֙
וַתְּלַקֵּ֣ט בַּשָּׂדֶ֔ה אַחֲרֵ֖י הַקֹּצְרִ֑ים וַיִּ֣קֶר מִקְרֶ֔הָ חֶלְקַ֤ת הַשָּׂדֶה֙ לְבֹ֔עַז
ד אֲשֶׁ֖ר מִמִּשְׁפַּ֥חַת אֱלִימֶֽלֶךְ׃ וְהִנֵּה־בֹ֗עַז בָּ֚א מִבֵּ֣ית לֶ֔חֶם וַיֹּ֥אמֶר

וַתֵּהֹם כׇּל־הָעִיר עֲלֵיהֶן *The whole town crowded around.* The awareness of shared historical experience leads to the experience of shared suffering. A feeling of empathy is a basic fact in the consciousness of shared Jewish fate. The suffering of one segment of the nation is the lot of the entire community. The scattered and separated people mourns and is consoled together. Prayer, the cry, and the consolation were formulated in the plural. Supplications that emerge from the depths of travail are not confined to the suffering and affliction of the groaning individual. They encompass the needs of the entire community. When there is a sick person in one's house, one prays not only for that person but for all the sick of Israel. When one enters the house of a mourner to comfort him and to wipe the tear from the bereaved's sad face, he directs his words of condolence to "all the mourners of Zion and Jerusalem." The slightest disturbance in the state of an individual or a sector of the people should trouble all segments of the nation throughout their dispersion. It is forbidden and it is impossible for the individual to isolate himself from his fellow and not participate in his suffering. If the assumption of shared historical experience is accurate, then shared suffering is its direct corollary. (*Fate and Destiny*, pp. 47–48)

5 replied. "Whose is that young woman over there?" asked Boaz of
6 his servant in charge of the harvestmen. "That is some Moabite girl,"
replied the servant in charge of the harvestmen, "the one who came
7 back with Naomi from the land of Moab. She said, 'Let me come
gleaning, gathering among the sheaves where the harvestmen have
been,' and so she came. She has been standing out here from early
8 morning until now and hardly sat at all in the shelter." Boaz went
to Ruth and said, "Daughter, take heed. Do not go gleaning in any
other field, and do not leave this one; cling close by my young
9 women. Keep your eyes on the field they are harvesting from and
follow after them. I have instructed the young men by no means
to touch you. When you are thirsty, go to the jugs and drink of
10 the water the young men have drawn." Ruth fell upon her face,
bowing low, and she asked him, "Why is it that I have found favor
in your eyes, that you give me recognition such as this when I
11 am a stranger?" Boaz said, "I have heard of all you have done for
your mother-in-law ever since your husband died, of how you left
your father, your mother, the land of your birth, and came to a

---

to elemental evils of nature. Sympathy with one's brethren is the basis of hospitality.

Hospitality is not confined to the poor alone; it includes everybody, poor and rich alike, for it belongs to the all-inclusive class of *gemilut ḥasadim*. However, not only the principle of charity-grace was formulated, but charity-justice as well. Jewish law has always maintained that the giving of charity is not an act of benevolence for which one deserves praise and thanks, but the fulfillment of a duty governed by the principle of *mishpat*, justice: "Treat the poor as members of your household." Not only the "what" of giving is imperative, but the "how" of the performance as well. Charity should be given in the friendliest of manners. The pauper must feel at home and not be subjected to humiliation. The amount one gives is not as important as the fashion in which aid is extended. The beggar must be treated as if he were a member of your immediate family, whose support is not looked upon as an act of charity but as the most natural deed, like the maintenance of oneself. (*Halakhic Morality*, pp. 119–120)

ה לַקּוֹצְרִים יְהוָה עִמָּכֶם וַיֹּאמְרוּ לוֹ יְבָרֶכְךָ יְהוָה׃ וַיֹּאמֶר בֹּעַז
ו לְנַעֲרוֹ הַנִּצָּב עַל־הַקּוֹצְרִים לְמִי הַנַּעֲרָה הַזֹּאת׃ וַיַּעַן הַנַּעַר הַנִּצָּב
עַל־הַקּוֹצְרִים וַיֹּאמַר נַעֲרָה מוֹאֲבִיָּה הִיא הַשָּׁבָה עִם־נָעֳמִי
ז מִשְּׂדֵה מוֹאָב׃ וַתֹּאמֶר אֲלַקֳטָה־נָּא וְאָסַפְתִּי בָעֳמָרִים אַחֲרֵי
הַקּוֹצְרִים וַתָּבוֹא וַתַּעֲמוֹד מֵאָז הַבֹּקֶר וְעַד־עַתָּה זֶה שִׁבְתָּהּ
ח הַבַּיִת מְעָט׃ וַיֹּאמֶר בֹּעַז אֶל־רוּת הֲלֹא שָׁמַעַתְּ בִּתִּי אַל־תֵּלְכִי
לִלְקֹט בְּשָׂדֶה אַחֵר וְגַם לֹא תַעֲבוּרִי מִזֶּה וְכֹה תִדְבָּקִין עִם־
ט נַעֲרֹתָי׃ עֵינַיִךְ בַּשָּׂדֶה אֲשֶׁר־יִקְצֹרוּן וְהָלַכְתְּ אַחֲרֵיהֶן הֲלוֹא
צִוִּיתִי אֶת־הַנְּעָרִים לְבִלְתִּי נָגְעֵךְ וְצָמִת וְהָלַכְתְּ אֶל־הַכֵּלִים
י וְשָׁתִית מֵאֲשֶׁר יִשְׁאֲבוּן הַנְּעָרִים׃ וַתִּפֹּל עַל־פָּנֶיהָ וַתִּשְׁתַּחוּ
אָרְצָה וַתֹּאמֶר אֵלָיו מַדּוּעַ מָצָאתִי חֵן בְּעֵינֶיךָ לְהַכִּירֵנִי וְאָנֹכִי
יא נָכְרִיָּה׃ וַיַּעַן בֹּעַז וַיֹּאמֶר לָהּ הֻגֵּד הֻגַּד לִי כֹּל אֲשֶׁר־עָשִׂית אֶת־
חֲמוֹתֵךְ אַחֲרֵי מוֹת אִישֵׁךְ וַתַּעַזְבִי אָבִיךְ וְאִמֵּךְ וְאֶרֶץ מוֹלַדְתֵּךְ

---

of events and physical nature, but we are excluded from the realm of *goral* understanding. The relationship between the individual and his environment eludes our grasp. To God there are no accidents, though they often appear so to us. There is no deterministic fate; all operates on a transcendental plane which is beyond the grasp of man's finite mind. (*Reflections of the Rav*, p. 48)

הֲלֹא שָׁמַעַתְּ בִּתִּי אַל־תֵּלְכִי לִלְקֹט בְּשָׂדֶה אַחֵר *Daughter, take heed. Do not go gleaning in any other field.* "Yose ben Yoḥanan of Jerusalem says: Let your house be open wide; treat the poor as members of your household..." (*Avot* 1:5). One should not consider his house as his castle or fortress, which is destined to separate him from the multitudes. One should not retreat from the community into the sheltered confines of one's magnificent home. On the contrary, one's house should be open wide to all guests, itinerants and paupers, without discriminating between friend and enemy. A person cannot find shelter within the impregnable walls of his castle while others are exposed

12 people you knew not the day before. May the LORD repay your labors; may your reward be full at the hand of the LORD, God of

---

Nevertheless, he came out of Egypt not only retaining his identity, but also spiritually more powerful. He grew to new heights. Adversity and opposition made him appreciate his own worldview all the more. (*Abraham's Journey*, pp. 119–120)

יְשַׁלֵּם יהוה פָּעֳלֵךְ וּתְהִי מַשְׂכֻּרְתֵּךְ שְׁלֵמָה מֵעִם יהוה אֱלֹהֵי יִשְׂרָאֵל *May the Lord repay your labors; may your reward be full at the hand of the Lord, God of Israel.* Boaz acknowledged the great courage of this pagan girl in casting her lot with a people she did not previously know. When we read these words thanking Ruth for joining a people which she knew not, we willy-nilly think of the question that is addressed to any non-Jew who applies for *gerut*: "What prompts you to convert? Do you not know that the Jews at this time are persecuted and oppressed, despised, harassed and overcome by afflictions?" (*Yevamot* 47a). Of course, Boaz did not say it explicitly; but the meaning of his words points toward the same truth: only a hero joins our strange and lonely people.

It is amazing! The words of Boaz were spoken at the dawn of Jewish history, at a time when the tension between Jew and non-Jew was as yet unknown. This episode preceded Haman's hatred and indictment of the Jews, the Alexandrian hate literature, and the Gospels. The world knew nothing of the Jew's uniqueness, his so-called isolationism and egocentrism. Nevertheless, Boaz admired Ruth's fortitude for daring to join a strange and misunderstood people.

We Jews have been a strange people since the very birth of our nation. It has always taken courage, the ability to do something bold, to defy public resentment and identify with this unknown, mysterious people. What was mysterious about the Jews in early biblical times? The mere fact that they were not pagans, that they believed in one invisible and incorporeal God, was puzzling to pagans. Moreover, the Jews served their God by preaching morality, whereas the pagans worshipped their idols by giving gifts to them, by intoxicating themselves with orgiastic pleasure, by living like voluptuaries.

Ruth was a heroic woman; she joined a people alien to her, and committed herself to a way of life she did not understand. She came from a pagan

יב וַתֵּלְכִי אֶל־עַם אֲשֶׁר לֹא־יָדַעַתְּ תְּמוֹל שִׁלְשׁוֹם׃ יְשַׁלֵּם יְהוָה
פָּעֳלֵךְ וּתְהִי מַשְׂכֻּרְתֵּךְ שְׁלֵמָה מֵעִם יְהוָה אֱלֹהֵי יִשְׂרָאֵל אֲשֶׁר־

וַתַּעַזְבִי אָבִיךְ וְאִמֵּךְ וְאֶרֶץ מוֹלַדְתֵּךְ וַתֵּלְכִי אֶל־עַם אֲשֶׁר לֹא־יָדַעַתְּ תְּמוֹל שִׁלְשׁוֹם *Of how you left your father, your mother, the land of your birth, and came to a people you knew not the day before.* When one lives with parents, it is impossible for a son or daughter to not be critical of them from time to time. "For there is not a just man upon earth, that does good, and does not sin" (Eccl. 7:20). The child picks up on such things, some inconsistencies. In my youth, I occasionally harbored critical feelings toward my father and even toward my grandfather. Most everyone has at some time gone through this rebellious state against parental authority. When did I realize that the life of my father, my mother, my grandfather was a beautiful life, a moral life, and a dedicated and meaningful life? It was when I went to Germany. I did not live among Nazis; I lived in an intellectual community in Germany, and I saw gentiles who were considered moral. However, when I began to compare them with my grandfather and my father, I found that there was no comparison. We must wander through many foreign lands and experience numerous alien cultures. We must meet the greats of these nations and their intellectual and cultural giants. Only then will we revise our approach to our own forebears. We must observe the lifestyles of the leaders of secular culture in order to truly appreciate the greatness of the halakhic masters and the glory of our ancestral tradition.

In Berlin, I spoke with Yaakov Gromer, an associate of Albert Einstein. He was also once *a talmid* of my grandfather, Rav Ḥayyim Brisker. But he left Brisk and went on to become a great mathematician. He was not observant, but many a time you used to find him with a Gemara. He had an excellent head and could "learn." He told me, "When I was in Brisk, I found many faults with Rav Ḥayyim, but when I came to Berlin I realized that Rav Ḥayyim was a saint. They told me Einstein was considered a moral person, and he was indeed a moral person. But Rav Ḥayyim had more kindness" – he used the word *ḥesed* – "in his little finger than Albert Einstein had in all his heart and brain." One cannot understand the beauty of Judaism without encountering people of another culture. That is why Abraham had to go to Egypt – to see what Egypt was. Perhaps Abraham sometimes wondered whether life wasn't better in this wonderful, powerful, respected, rich state.

13 Israel, under whose mantle you come to take shelter." "Sir," she said,
"I hope to find favor in your eyes, for you give me solace, for you
have spoken to your servant's heart though I am not fit to be your
14 servant." When the time came for eating, Boaz said to her, "Come
here; eat of this food and dip your bread in the vinegar." She sat
down beside the harvestmen, and he served her roasted grains, and

---

concerned with him. It is again an existential experience. He begins to doubt his ontological worth. This leads to alienation from the crowd surrounding him. Suddenly someone taps him on the shoulder and says: "Aren't you Mr. So-and-So? I have heard so much about you." In a fraction of a second his awareness changes. An alien being turns into a fellow member of an existential community (the crowd). What brought about the change? The recognition by somebody, the word! To recognize a person is not just to identify him physically. It is more than that: it is an act of identifying him existentially, as a person who has a job to do, that only he can do properly. To recognize a person means to affirm that he is irreplaceable. To hurt a person means to tell him that he is expendable, that there is no need for him. The Halakhah equated the act of publicly embarrassing a person with murder. Why? Because humiliation is tantamount to destroying an existential community and driving the individual into solitude. It is not enough for the charitable person to extend help to the needy. He must do more than that: he must try to restore to the dependent person a sense of dignity and worth. That is why Jews have developed special sensitivity regarding orphans and widows, since these persons are extremely sensitive and lose their self-confidence with the slightest provocation. The Bible warned us against afflicting an orphan or widow. Whatever affects the peace of mind of the widow or the orphan is considered affliction. A word, a gesture, a facial expression by which the widow or the orphan feels hurt; in short, whatever causes an accelerated heartbeat – that comes under affliction. ("The Community," pp. 16–17)

וַיֹּאמֶר לָה בֹעַז לְעֵת הָאֹכֶל גֹּשִׁי הֲלֹם וְאָכַלְתְּ מִן־הַלֶּחֶם וְטָבַלְתְּ פִּתֵּךְ בַּחֹמֶץ *When the time came for eating, Boaz said to her, "Come here; eat of this food and dip your bread in the vinegar."* There are many ways to practice kindness. The cruelty of Sodom is portrayed in terms of cruelty to guests and strangers; in contrast, Abraham's kindness expressed itself particularly in *hakhnasat orḥim*. Bear in

יג בָּאת לַחֲסוֹת תַּחַת־כְּנָפָיו: וַתֹּאמֶר אֶמְצָא־חֵן בְּעֵינֶיךָ אֲדֹנִי
כִּי נִחַמְתָּנִי וְכִי דִבַּרְתָּ עַל־לֵב שִׁפְחָתֶךָ וְאָנֹכִי לֹא אֶהְיֶה כְּאַחַת
יד שִׁפְחֹתֶיךָ: וַיֹּאמֶר לָה בֹעַז לְעֵת הָאֹכֶל גֹּשִׁי הֲלֹם וְאָכַלְתְּ מִן־
הַלֶּחֶם וְטָבַלְתְּ פִּתֵּךְ בַּחֹמֶץ וַתֵּשֶׁב מִצַּד הַקֹּצְרִים וַיִּצְבָּט־

---

background, where unlimited pleasure and over-indulgence were an element in worship, and she joined a religion that demands discipline, redemption of the biological call for gratification. The mere fact that the Halakhah interferes with every phase of human life, that Judaism is so concerned with the trivial, makes the commitment seem staggering and almost superhuman. (*Abraham's Journey*, pp. 179–181)

אֲשֶׁר־בָּאת לַחֲסוֹת תַּחַת־כְּנָפָיו *Under whose mantle you come to take shelter.* A person without God, a person who denies God or negates Him, who drifts from Him or is alienated from Him – such a person is homeless and uprooted. He can never rest or enjoy peace of mind. He never has a feeling of security, no matter how powerful or wealthy he may be. There is an inner sense of insecurity and other frights, a variety of phobias and fears that befall him and take possession of every fiber of his soul. Complete security and peace, full harmony and serenity can be found only in God. That is why the *Shekhinah* is like two large wings that cast shade, and in that shade a person finds a cool place and protection against the heat, against fatigue and exhaustion, against desolation and loneliness. Modern man has been alienated from God for so long; he is like a leaf carried by the wind, uprooted completely. But when he is *taḥat kanfei haShekhinah* he is very close to God. "The Lord is near to all those who call upon him" (Ps. 145:18). "Seek the Lord while He may be found; call upon Him while He is near" (Isa. 55:6). *Taḥat kanfei haShekhinah* has the connotation of restfulness, peace, serenity, rootedness and being anchored – the opposite of the feeling of homelessness. Man becomes a resident of a certain place; otherwise he is a vagabond in this world. "I have been a stranger" (Ex. 2:22). One can establish a residence only when one is close to God. (*Abraham's Journey*, pp. 58–59)

כִּי נִחַמְתָּנִי וְכִי דִבַּרְתָּ עַל־לֵב שִׁפְחָתֶךָ *For you give me solace, for you have spoken to your servant's heart.* Quite often a man finds himself in a crowd among strangers. He feels lonely. No one knows him, no one cares for him, no one is

15 she ate and had her fill with more left over. And when she stood up
to begin gleaning again, Boaz instructed his workers, "Let her glean
16 among the sheaves as well; do not disgrace her. Drop some ears
from the bundles as well; leave them, let her glean them, and do
17 not reproach her." Ruth carried on gleaning in the field until eve-
ning, then threshed what she had gleaned; it was almost an ephah
18 of barley. She lifted it up and came into the town. Her mother-
in-law saw what she had gleaned; she produced all that was left
19 after she had eaten her fill and gave it to her. "Where did you
gather today," she asked, "and where did you work? Bless whoever

---

and grief entail the transgression of a serious commandment; it follows that the reward for fulfilling the commandment of "open your hand" is erased by the donor's transgression of the prohibition against demeaning the poor person. But in 10:14, Maimonides carefully formulates the lowest degree of *tzedakah* as "giving *tzedakah* sadly." The formulation is precise, for it is not an antithetical parallel to "with a friendly countenance" used in the preceding halakhah. Had Maimonides wanted to say that the lowest degree of *tzedakah* is providing funds even in a way that insults and impairs the poor person's dignity, he would have used the antithetical parallel and formulated the lowest level as "giving with a hostile countenance." But he did not do so, instead altering the wording and using the term "sadly" to differentiate between this lowest degree of *tzedakah* and the very different situation referred to in 10:4. One who gives "sadly" fails to fulfill the commandment willingly, generously and graciously; but he does not disparage and torment the poor person in the manner suggested by "with a hostile countenance." (*Halakhic Morality*, pp. 147–148)

וַעֲזַבְתֶּם וְלִקְּטָה וְלֹא תִגְעֲרוּ־בָהּ *Leave them, let her glean them, and do not reproach her.* Halakhic man takes up his stand in the midst of the concrete world, his feet planted firmly on the ground of reality, and he looks about and sees, listens and hears, and publicly protests against the oppression of the helpless, the defrauding of the poor, the plight of the orphan. The rich are deemed as naught in his view. He is the father of orphans, the judge of widows. My uncle, R. Meir Berlin [Bar-Ilan], told me that once R. Ḥayyim of Brisk was asked what the function of a rabbi is. R. Ḥayyim replied: "To redress the

טו לָהּ קָלִי וַתֹּאכַל וַתִּשְׂבַּע וַתֹּתַר׃ וַתָּקָם לְלַקֵּט וַיְצַו בֹּעַז אֶת־
טז נְעָרָיו לֵאמֹר גַּם בֵּין הָעֳמָרִים תְּלַקֵּט וְלֹא תַכְלִימוּהָ׃ וְגַם שֹׁל־
תָּשֹׁלּוּ לָהּ מִן־הַצְּבָתִים וַעֲזַבְתֶּם וְלִקְּטָה וְלֹא תִגְעֲרוּ־בָהּ׃
יז וַתְּלַקֵּט בַּשָּׂדֶה עַד־הָעָרֶב וַתַּחְבֹּט אֵת אֲשֶׁר־לִקֵּטָה וַיְהִי כְּאֵיפָה
יח שְׂעֹרִים׃ וַתִּשָּׂא וַתָּבוֹא הָעִיר וַתֵּרֶא חֲמוֹתָהּ אֵת אֲשֶׁר־לִקֵּטָה
יט וַתּוֹצֵא וַתִּתֶּן־לָהּ אֵת אֲשֶׁר־הוֹתִרָה מִשָּׂבְעָהּ׃ וַתֹּאמֶר לָהּ
חֲמוֹתָהּ אֵיפֹה לִקַּטְתְּ הַיּוֹם וְאָנָה עָשִׂית יְהִי מַכִּירֵךְ בָּרוּךְ וַתַּגֵּד

---

mind that *hakhnasat orḥim* is often for the poor. A rich man is in no need of hospitality; he can find an inn or a place to stay. Yet *hakhnasat orḥim* differs from *tzedakah,* or material help to others, in a crucial way. When one gives *tzedakah,* it demonstrates sympathy, but not a philosophy of human equality holding that all Jews are *benei melakhim,* princes, regardless of differences in wealth or knowledge. *Hakhnasat orḥim,* however, demonstrates full human equality, the fact that every being has his own dignity and is just as important as any other. It is much easier to give someone money and send him away than to invite him under your own roof. If I invite him in, that means that no matter what his station in life, I am treating him with respect, as an equal. (*Abraham's Journey,* pp. 168–169)

וְלֹא תַכְלִימוּהָ *Do not disgrace her.* It is forbidden to embarrass the poor person or tarnish his dignity. That is an absolute prohibition. It is necessary to distinguish between a joyless, downcast psychological state and a posture that actually demeans and belittles the poor person. One who gives unhappily does not intend to insult or embarrass the poor person; he fails to fulfill the commandment in its entirety and loses out on the aspect of "sufficient for his need," but his action at least fulfills the element of "open your hand" (Deut. 15:8). But one who aggrieves the poor person and brings shame on him not only fails to fulfill the commandment, he actually violates a serious prohibition.

The wording of Maimonides in *Hilkhot Matenot Aniyim* is extremely precise. In 10:4, he writes: "He who gives *tzedakah* to a poor man with a hostile countenance and with his face averted to the ground loses his merit and forfeits it." In other words, anger and annoyance that cause embarrassment

recognized you so." So Ruth told her mother-in-law under whose
patronage she had worked: "The man's name is Boaz, with whom
20 I worked today." Said Naomi to her daughter-in-law, "The LORD
bless him, for he has not abandoned his kindness to the living or
the dead," and Naomi told her, "The man is our relative, one of our
21 redeemers." "He said to me as well," said Ruth the Moabite, "'Cling
22 by my young men until they finish all my harvest,'" and Naomi told
her daughter-in-law Ruth, "That is well, my daughter. Go out with
23 his young women; do not go and come to harm in other fields." So
it was that she clung by Boaz's young women to glean until the
barley harvest was over, and then the wheat, and after that she sat
3 1 at home with her mother-in-law. "Daughter," said her mother-in-
law Naomi to her, "do I not wish I could find you a resting place that
2 would be good for you? Now there is Boaz, our relative, whose
young women you were with, and he will be doing his winnowing
3 at the threshing floor tonight. You are going to wash yourself and
anoint yourself and put on your dress and go down to that threshing
floor. Do not let the man know that you are there until he has fin-
4 ished eating and drinking. And when he lies down, take note of the
place where he lies, and afterward go there, uncover his feet, and
5 lie down also – he will tell you what to do next." "I shall do," said
6 Ruth, "all that you tell me to do." She went down to the threshing
7 floor and did exactly as her mother-in-law had instructed her. Boaz

---

וַתַּעַשׂ כְּכֹל אֲשֶׁר־צִוַּתָּה חֲמוֹתָהּ *And did exactly as her mother-in-law had instructed her.* To outsiders, Judaism is a difficult religion. To convert to Judaism and accept an all-inclusive Judaic commitment borders on the heroic. In addition, even as early as the period of the Judges, to become a Jew has meant to be alienated from the rest of the world. The destiny of *Avraham ha-Ivri*, the lonely Abraham, has always accompanied the Jews.

In a word, *gerut* is heroic action at the level of observance and practical living, and also at the level of one's relationship with the non-Jewish world. No wonder the Talmud says that the Jews, upon responding "We shall do and obey," were called *gibborei koaḥ*, heroes (*Shabbat* 88a).

לַחֲמוֹתָהּ אֵת אֲשֶׁר־עָשְׂתָה עִמּוֹ וַתֹּאמֶר שֵׁם הָאִישׁ אֲשֶׁר
כ עָשִׂיתִי עִמּוֹ הַיּוֹם בֹּעַז׃ וַתֹּאמֶר נָעֳמִי לְכַלָּתָהּ בָּרוּךְ הוּא לַיהוָה
אֲשֶׁר לֹא־עָזַב חַסְדּוֹ אֶת־הַחַיִּים וְאֶת־הַמֵּתִים וַתֹּאמֶר לָהּ נָעֳמִי
כא קָרוֹב לָנוּ הָאִישׁ מִגֹּאֲלֵנוּ הוּא׃ וַתֹּאמֶר רוּת הַמּוֹאֲבִיָּה גַּם ׀
כִּי־אָמַר אֵלַי עִם־הַנְּעָרִים אֲשֶׁר־לִי תִּדְבָּקִין עַד אִם־כִּלּוּ אֵת
כב כָּל־הַקָּצִיר אֲשֶׁר־לִי׃ וַתֹּאמֶר נָעֳמִי אֶל־רוּת כַּלָּתָהּ טוֹב בִּתִּי
כג כִּי תֵצְאִי עִם־נַעֲרוֹתָיו וְלֹא יִפְגְּעוּ־בָךְ בְּשָׂדֶה אַחֵר׃ וַתִּדְבַּק
בְּנַעֲרוֹת בֹּעַז לְלַקֵּט עַד־כְּלוֹת קְצִיר־הַשְּׂעֹרִים וּקְצִיר הַחִטִּים
ג א וַתֵּשֶׁב אֶת־חֲמוֹתָהּ׃ וַתֹּאמֶר לָהּ נָעֳמִי חֲמוֹתָהּ בִּתִּי הֲלֹא
ב אֲבַקֶּשׁ־לָךְ מָנוֹחַ אֲשֶׁר יִיטַב־לָךְ׃ וְעַתָּה הֲלֹא בֹעַז מֹדַעְתָּנוּ
אֲשֶׁר הָיִית אֶת־נַעֲרוֹתָיו הִנֵּה־הוּא זֹרֶה אֶת־גֹּרֶן הַשְּׂעֹרִים
ג הַלָּיְלָה׃ וְרָחַצְתְּ ׀ וָסַכְתְּ וְשַׂמְתְּ שמלתך עָלַיִךְ וירדתי הַגֹּרֶן — שִׂמְלֹתַיִךְ וְיָרַדְתְּ
ד אַל־תִּוָּדְעִי לָאִישׁ עַד כַּלֹּתוֹ לֶאֱכֹל וְלִשְׁתּוֹת׃ וִיהִי בְשָׁכְבוֹ
וְיָדַעַתְּ אֶת־הַמָּקוֹם אֲשֶׁר יִשְׁכַּב־שָׁם וּבָאת וְגִלִּית מַרְגְּלֹתָיו
ה ושכבתי וְהוּא יַגִּיד לָךְ אֵת אֲשֶׁר תַּעֲשִׂין׃ וַתֹּאמֶר אֵלֶיהָ כֹּל — וְשָׁכָבְתְּ
ו אֲשֶׁר־תֹּאמְרִי ‏ אֶעֱשֶׂה׃ וַתֵּרֶד הַגֹּרֶן וַתַּעַשׂ כְּכֹל אֲשֶׁר־צִוַּתָּה — אֵלַי
ז חֲמוֹתָהּ׃ וַיֹּאכַל בֹּעַז וַיֵּשְׁתְּ וַיִּיטַב לִבּוֹ וַיָּבֹא לִשְׁכַּב בִּקְצֵה

---

grievances of those who are abandoned and alone, to protect the dignity of the poor, and to save the oppressed from the hands of his oppressor." Neither ritual decisions nor political leadership constitutes the main task of halakhic man. Far from it. The actualization of the ideals of justice and righteousness is the pillar of fire which halakhic man follows, when he, as a rabbi and teacher in Israel, serves his community. More, through the implementation of the principles of righteousness, man fulfills the task of creation imposed upon him: the perfection of the world under the dominion of Halakhah and the renewal of the face of creation. (*Halakhic Man*, pp. 90–91)

ate and drank and was happy, and he went and lay down beside the
heap of grain. Then she came to him silently, uncovered his feet,
8 and lay herself down. At midnight the man started and turned
9 over – there was a woman lying at his feet! "Who are you?" he said,
and she answered, "I am your maidservant Ruth – spread your
10 mantle over your maidservant, for you are a redeemer." And he
replied, "The LORD bless you, daughter, for this last kindness is yet
greater than your first, for you have not gone after the young men,
11 poor or rich. Now, daughter, do not be afraid. I shall do all that you
ask, for all within my people's gate know well that you are a woman
12 of great strength, and I am indeed a redeemer to you, but there is
13 a redeemer still closer than me. Stay on here tonight, and in the
morning, if he wishes to redeem you, good: let him redeem. And

---

provided it goes hand in hand with humility and loyalty. (*Abraham's Journey*, pp. 181–182)

הֵיטַבְתְּ חַסְדֵּךְ הָאַחֲרוֹן מִן־הָרִאשׁוֹן *For this last kindness is yet greater than your first.* The midrash (Ruth Rabbah 2:14) states: "This *megillah* contains neither [laws of] impurity nor purity, neither the forbidden nor the permitted; why then was it written? To teach us how great is the reward of those who perform kindness." However, the laws of conversion are derived from *Megillat Rut* (as explicated in *Yevamot* 47b); how then are we to understand the assertion of the midrash that this *megillah* does not contain the laws of the forbidden or permitted? The answer is that the laws of conversion derived from *Megillat Rut* were included not to teach us what is forbidden and what is permitted but as part of the description of Ruth's kindness. When Boaz said to Ruth, "The Lord bless you, daughter, for this last kindness is yet greater than your first," what first kindness did he have in mind? R. Yoel Sirkes, known by his work *Bayit Ḥadash*, explains in his commentary *Meshiv Nefesh* that the first kindness was Ruth's conversion; by entering under the wings of the *Shekhinah*, Ruth performed a great kindness. It is a kindness to the world that is lit up by the sanctity of her soul; it is a kindness to the Jewish people who is strengthened by the force of her commitment; and it is a kindness to herself, to her own soul which is now illuminated by the light of the Torah. (*Harerei Kedem*, vol. 2, p. 265)

ח הָעֲרֵמָה וַתָּבֹא בַלָּט וַתְּגַל מַרְגְּלֹתָיו וַתִּשְׁכָּב׃ וַיְהִי בַּחֲצִי הַלַּיְלָה
ט וַיֶּחֱרַד הָאִישׁ וַיִּלָּפֵת וְהִנֵּה אִשָּׁה שֹׁכֶבֶת מַרְגְּלֹתָיו׃ וַיֹּאמֶר מִי־
אָתְּ וַתֹּאמֶר אָנֹכִי רוּת אֲמָתֶךָ וּפָרַשְׂתָּ כְנָפֶךָ עַל־אֲמָתְךָ כִּי גֹאֵל
י אָתָּה׃ וַיֹּאמֶר בְּרוּכָה אַתְּ לַיהוה בִּתִּי הֵיטַבְתְּ חַסְדֵּךְ הָאַחֲרוֹן
מִן־הָרִאשׁוֹן לְבִלְתִּי־לֶכֶת אַחֲרֵי הַבַּחוּרִים אִם־דַּל וְאִם־עָשִׁיר׃
יא וְעַתָּה בִּתִּי אַל־תִּירְאִי כֹּל אֲשֶׁר־תֹּאמְרִי אֶעֱשֶׂה־לָּךְ כִּי יוֹדֵעַ
יב כָּל־שַׁעַר עַמִּי כִּי אֵשֶׁת חַיִל אָתְּ׃ וְעַתָּה כִּי אָמְנָם כִּי אם גֹאֵל
יג אָנֹכִי וְגַם יֵשׁ גֹּאֵל קָרוֹב מִמֶּנִּי׃ לִינִי ׀ הַלַּיְלָה וְהָיָה בַבֹּקֶר אִם־

The King Messiah must be endowed with heroic qualities, for he is coming to change the status quo, to revolutionize concepts and opinions, to transform our outlook on life. He will defy evil, oppose ruthlessness, challenge injustice, "and decide with equity for the meek of the earth; and he shall smite the land with the rod of his mouth and with the breath of his lips shall he slay the wicked" (Isa. 11:4). Messianism minus heroic action is meaningless.

The poor of biblical times used to glean and gather after the reapers. The Almighty, too, gleaned and gathered – not ears of corn but beautiful inclinations and noble virtues. From them He wove the soul of the King Messiah. God found a heroic girl in Moab. The Almighty was busy with the formation and creation of the Messiah's personality, which was to embody the finest and most beautiful elements concealed in the depths of mankind. God brought the girl to Judea so that she could collaborate with Him in creating a Messiah personality. She contributed the heroism of loneliness and acceptance of the incomprehensible.

Ruth, no matter how idealistic she was, no matter how sturdy her character, no matter how heroic and revolutionary her spirit, was in her heart deeply loyal and grateful. In fact, heroism was the consequence of her loyalty to her mother law. Her first words, "Do not entreat me to leave you" (1:16), tell a story of great humility. She revered her mother-in-law. When Naomi told her to do something odd, namely, to visit the threshing floor and uncover Boaz's feet, she did not argue with her mother-in-law. "And [she] did exactly as her mother-in-law had instructed her." Respect for the elderly, humility, and a sense of gratitude are indispensable. Heroism is important,

if he cares not to redeem you, I shall redeem you myself, as the
14 Lord lives – stay until morning." So she lay at his feet until morn-
ing and left before one person could recognize another. "Let not a
soul know there was a woman at the threshing floor," said he. And
15 then, "Give me the wrap that you are wearing; hold it out." She did,
and he measured six measures of barley into it; he placed it upon
16 her and went out into the city. She came to her mother-in-law,
"Who are you, my daughter?" she said. And Ruth told her all that
17 the man had done for her. "He gave me these six measures of barley,"
she said. "He said to me, 'Do not go back to your mother-in-law
18 empty-handed.'" Said Naomi, "Sit down now, daughter, until you
find out how the matter will fall, for that man will not rest unless
4 1 the matter is settled today." Boaz went up to the city gate and sat
down, and the very redeemer of whom he had spoken passed by.
"Peloni Almoni," said Boaz, "come here and be seated," and he
2 turned aside and sat down. Then Boaz took ten men from among
the elders of the city, "Be seated here," he said, and they too sat.
3 Then he said to the redeemer, "Naomi, who came back from the
4 land of Moab, must sell the field plot of our kinsman Elimelech. I
said I would let you know of it, inviting you to buy it in the presence
of those sitting here, in the presence of the elders of my people. If
you wish to redeem this, redeem; and if you will not redeem it, tell
me: let me know, for there is none before you to redeem, and I am
5 next in line to you." "I shall redeem," he said. "On the day you buy
that field from Naomi," said Boaz, "and from Ruth the Moabite, you
will have bought the wife of a dead man with it, to restore the dead
6 man's name on his estate." Said the redeemer, "Such a redemption
I could not perform; it could be the ruin of my estate. You redeem
7 in my place; I cannot redeem." In those long-ago days in Israel, a
redemption or exchange – anything to be officially enacted – was
completed as follows. One man would take off his shoe and would
hand it to the other: that was the bond then recognized among

יִגְאָלֵךְ טוֹב יִגְאָל וְאִם־לֹא יַחְפֹּץ לְגָאֳלֵךְ וּגְאַלְתִּיךְ אָנֹכִי חַי־יְהוָה
יד שִׁכְבִי עַד־הַבֹּקֶר׃ וַתִּשְׁכַּב מַרְגְּלוֹתָו עַד־הַבֹּקֶר וַתָּקָם בטרום בְּטֶרֶם
יַכִּיר אִישׁ אֶת־רֵעֵהוּ וַיֹּאמֶר אַל־יִוָּדַע כִּי־בָאָה הָאִשָּׁה הַגֹּרֶן׃
טו וַיֹּאמֶר הָבִי הַמִּטְפַּחַת אֲשֶׁר־עָלַיִךְ וְאֶחֳזִי־בָהּ וַתֹּאחֶז בָּהּ וַיָּמָד
טז שֵׁשׁ־שְׂעֹרִים וַיָּשֶׁת עָלֶיהָ וַיָּבֹא הָעִיר׃ וַתָּבוֹא אֶל־חֲמוֹתָהּ
וַתֹּאמֶר מִי־אַתְּ בִּתִּי וַתַּגֶּד־לָהּ אֵת כָּל־אֲשֶׁר עָשָׂה־לָהּ הָאִישׁ׃
יז וַתֹּאמֶר שֵׁשׁ־הַשְּׂעֹרִים הָאֵלֶּה נָתַן לִי כִּי אָמַר אַל־תָּבוֹאִי אֵלַי
יח רֵיקָם אֶל־חֲמוֹתֵךְ׃ וַתֹּאמֶר שְׁבִי בִתִּי עַד אֲשֶׁר תֵּדְעִין אֵיךְ יִפֹּל
ד א דָּבָר כִּי לֹא יִשְׁקֹט הָאִישׁ כִּי אִם־כִּלָּה הַדָּבָר הַיּוֹם׃ וּבֹעַז עָלָה
הַשַּׁעַר וַיֵּשֶׁב שָׁם וְהִנֵּה הַגֹּאֵל עֹבֵר אֲשֶׁר דִּבֶּר־בֹּעַז וַיֹּאמֶר סוּרָה
ב שְׁבָה־פֹּה פְּלֹנִי אַלְמֹנִי וַיָּסַר וַיֵּשֵׁב׃ וַיִּקַּח עֲשָׂרָה אֲנָשִׁים מִזִּקְנֵי
ג הָעִיר וַיֹּאמֶר שְׁבוּ־פֹה וַיֵּשֵׁבוּ׃ וַיֹּאמֶר לַגֹּאֵל חֶלְקַת הַשָּׂדֶה אֲשֶׁר
ד לְאָחִינוּ לֶאֱלִימֶלֶךְ מָכְרָה נָעֳמִי הַשָּׁבָה מִשְּׂדֵה מוֹאָב׃ וַאֲנִי
אָמַרְתִּי אֶגְלֶה אָזְנְךָ לֵאמֹר קְנֵה נֶגֶד הַיֹּשְׁבִים וְנֶגֶד זִקְנֵי עַמִּי
אִם־תִּגְאַל גְּאָל וְאִם־לֹא יִגְאַל הַגִּידָה לִּי וְאֵדְעָ כִּי אֵין זוּלָתְךָ
ה לִגְאוֹל וְאָנֹכִי אַחֲרֶיךָ וַיֹּאמֶר אָנֹכִי אֶגְאָל׃ וַיֹּאמֶר בֹּעַז בְּיוֹם־
קְנוֹתְךָ הַשָּׂדֶה מִיַּד נָעֳמִי וּמֵאֵת רוּת הַמּוֹאֲבִיָּה אֵשֶׁת־הַמֵּת
ו קניתי לְהָקִים שֵׁם־הַמֵּת עַל־נַחֲלָתוֹ׃ וַיֹּאמֶר הַגֹּאֵל לֹא אוּכַל קָנִיתָ
לגאול־לִי פֶּן־אַשְׁחִית אֶת־נַחֲלָתִי גְּאַל־לְךָ אַתָּה אֶת־גְּאֻלָּתִי לִגְאָל־
ז כִּי לֹא־אוּכַל לִגְאֹל׃ וְזֹאת לְפָנִים בְּיִשְׂרָאֵל עַל־הַגְּאוּלָּה וְעַל־
הַתְּמוּרָה לְקַיֵּם כָּל־דָּבָר שָׁלַף אִישׁ נַעֲלוֹ וְנָתַן לְרֵעֵהוּ וְזֹאת

שָׁלַף אִישׁ נַעֲלוֹ וְנָתַן לְרֵעֵהוּ *One man would take off his shoe and would hand it to the other.* Many different benedictions were instituted by the Sages to

8 Israel. Now this redeemer said to Boaz, "Take possession," and he

---

other." According to Halakhah, any article, not only the shoe, is effective, yet it is the shoe that was regularly employed. *Ḥalippin* is a symbolic exchange. In order to substantiate and validate a promise, removing the shoe and handing it to one's counterpart indicated "upon my honor." The role played by the shoe is connected with the fact that it bestows prestige on a person, much as the coat of arms in medieval times, which served as the mark of aristocracy. At the burning bush, Moses is told, "Remove your shoes from your feet, for the place on which you stand is holy ground" (Ex. 3:5). Since he is standing before God, conversing with Infinity, Moses must humble himself. That is manifested by removing his shoes. (*Blessings and Thanksgiving*, p. 23)

Perhaps the most common form of transaction appearing in halakhic sources is scripturally anchored in the Book of Ruth: "In those long-ago days in Israel, a redemption or exchange – anything to be officially enacted – was completed as follows. One man would take off his shoe and would hand it to the other." This became known as a "scarf purchase" (*kinyan sudar*). The difference between a money purchase and a "scarf purchase" lies in the fact that in the first case, though not paying the entire sum, one must at least pay a single penny, while in a "scarf purchase" acquisition is achieved without even a penny's worth changing hands. In a money transaction the penny has some monetary value, and it represents, as it were, the actual price which must be paid to finalize the deal. Though the smallest unit of capital, the penny is real money, a "token" of a whole sum as a grain of wheat is a particle of a heap of grain. It is otherwise when dealing with the scarf which is used as the instrument of exchange in a purchase that represents no value and possesses no specific worth of its own. The scarf is not even in the nature of a "particle" of money. It is not in the same category as money; it is totally worthless.

The difference between these two types of purchase is enormous. So long as we demand even a penny we are still working within the framework of the monetary system. The moment we accept something which has no real money value, we have departed from the normative economic system and have entered into the realm of the symbolic. In the purchase which takes place through symbolic exchange of a scarf, the seller receives nothing of

ח הַתְּעוּדָה בְּיִשְׂרָאֵל׃ וַיֹּאמֶר הַגֹּאֵל לְבֹעַז קְנֵה־לָךְ וַיִּשְׁלֹף

express thanksgiving for personal enjoyments and benefits. Nevertheless, most activities were still not covered by these *berakhot.* There are so many minor enjoyments in human life. One enjoys company and friendship; he wants to be loved; he enjoys music and books. Some enjoyments – breathing, talking with people, associating with people, seeing things, enjoying a landscape, reading books, walking – are not each a discrete activity which can be circumscribed so that you can be required to pronounce the *berakha* before engaging in that activity. The activities are scattered all over the day and are vague in their contours; that is why each individual activity does not require a separate blessing. Since the sages did not want to manufacture *berakhot,* they created one *berakha,* "Who has provided all my need for me," to cover every activity, just as *shehakol* covers diverse foods.

Why then does the Talmud (*Berakhot* 60b) connect this blessing with putting on shoes? I believe the reason is that in the aggadot of the sages the wearing of the shoe was a mark of distinction. Bondsmen, slaves and servants did not wear shoes; only free men did. In addition to its being a sign of status, the shoe protected its wearer from injury by snakes and other creatures. The shoe is very important, but there is no special *berakha* for it. The shoe is symptomatic of the whole realm of events and experiences that are vital to human happiness, to peace of mind, to enjoyment of life. They provide intangible benefit, and yet have not been marked by specific *berakhot,* as nothing has been mentioned in Tanakh about them. Our sages decided that when a person puts on his shoes he should say, "Who has provided all my need for me" because among all morning activities putting on shoes is the only important one that was not connected with a *berakha.*

We suggested that the enjoyment of the shoe is not the shoe itself; it is the social prestige that it confers on the wearer. Let us examine this idea further. In *ḥalitza* (Deut. 25:7–10), the childless widow removes the shoe of the brother-in-law who does not want to marry her and thus carry on his brother's line. When describing acquisition through *ḥalippin,* in which the acquisition is effected through the handing over of a symbolic object, the verse states, "One man would take off his shoe and would hand it to the

9 took off his shoe. "You are my witnesses this day," said Boaz to the
elders and to all the people present, "that I take possession of all
that was Elimelech's and all that was Kilyon's and Maḥlon's, from
10 Naomi's hand. And with it I take Ruth the Moabite, Maḥlon's wife,
to be mine, to rebuild the name of the dead on his estate. And the
dead man's name will not be cut off from among his brothers, from
11 the gate of his own city – you are my witnesses this day." And all
the people at the gate and the elders said, "We bear witness. May
the LORD make the woman who is joining your house like Rachel
and like Leah, who together built the House of Israel; may you
go from strength to strength in Efrata and your name be ever

---

and which demands at least token payment in the currency of suffering, then we might not be able to withstand it. For who knows what a "trace" of suffering in the eyes of the Almighty amounts to, or how severe it could be? The Day of Atonement comes and its measure of mercy and grace reduces the severity of the element of a "particle of something" of money purchase by adding the possibility of exchange – the "scarf transaction." Thus, not only is the amount of suffering diminished on the basis of the "particle of something"; in addition, it is weakened and reduced on the basis of the exchange of the "scarf purchase" (which is worthless in terms of money value). In the first instance, a mere penny will suffice; in the case of the scarf exchange not even a pennyworth is required. The suffering the sinner has to endure henceforward is merely symbolic as in the biblical examples of "one man would take off his shoe and would hand it to the other," or "and he offered him up for a burnt offering in the stead of his son" – the ram offered in place of Isaac. (*On Repentance*, pp. 286–288)

יִתֵּן יהוה אֶת־הָאִשָּׁה הַבָּאָה אֶל־בֵּיתֶךָ כְּרָחֵל וּכְלֵאָה אֲשֶׁר בָּנוּ שְׁתֵּיהֶם אֶת־בֵּית יִשְׂרָאֵל
May the Lord make the woman who is joining your house like Rachel and like Leah, who together built the house of Israel. The story of the biblical woman, the covenantal mother, ends with a tragic note. The very moment she brings her job to a close, the instant she completes her task, when the crisis is over, she returns quickly to her tent, draws down the curtain of anonymity and disappears. She is outside of the hustle and bustle of the male society.

ט נַעֲלוֹ׃ וַיֹּאמֶר בֹּעַז לַזְּקֵנִים וְכָל־הָעָם עֵדִים אַתֶּם הַיּוֹם כִּי קָנִיתִי
אֶת־כָּל־אֲשֶׁר לֶאֱלִימֶלֶךְ וְאֵת כָּל־אֲשֶׁר לְכִלְיוֹן וּמַחְלוֹן מִיַּד
י נָעֳמִי׃ וְגַם אֶת־רוּת הַמֹּאֲבִיָּה אֵשֶׁת מַחְלוֹן קָנִיתִי לִי לְאִשָּׁה
לְהָקִים שֵׁם־הַמֵּת עַל־נַחֲלָתוֹ וְלֹא־יִכָּרֵת שֵׁם־הַמֵּת מֵעִם אֶחָיו
יא וּמִשַּׁעַר מְקוֹמוֹ עֵדִים אַתֶּם הַיּוֹם׃ וַיֹּאמְרוּ כָּל־הָעָם אֲשֶׁר־
בַּשַּׁעַר וְהַזְּקֵנִים עֵדִים יִתֵּן יהוה אֶת־הָאִשָּׁה הַבָּאָה אֶל־בֵּיתֶךָ
כְּרָחֵל ׀ וּכְלֵאָה אֲשֶׁר בָּנוּ שְׁתֵּיהֶם אֶת־בֵּית יִשְׂרָאֵל וַעֲשֵׂה־חַיִל

value as payment for what he has sold. Nonetheless, the sale is valid, and let us not forget that the scarf purchase is perhaps the most effective type of transaction existing in the context of Jewish civil law. It is also the only type of purchase which applies to movable goods as well as to real estate. This type of purchase creates irrevocable obligations without anything concrete actually being exchanged.

Rabbenu Tam distinguished between a purchase by exchange of two valuable goods, such as a cow for a donkey, and a purchase by exchange of something valuable for something devoid of value. In the latter purchase, what is the compensation? Not a single thing. All that the seller receives is a symbolic substitute for the money or object of value. Instead of receiving money – even in its smallest denomination, a single penny – the seller receives something in lieu of money, as it was said of the *Akeidah* of Isaac: "And Abraham went and took the ram, and offered him up for a burnt offering in the stead of his son" (Gen. 22:13). Is the sacrifice of a ram indeed comparable in any way to the sacrifice of Isaac? It certainly is not equivalent, even in a partial sense. Then why was the sacrifice of the ram accepted instead of Isaac? This is due to the divine quality of mercy which is willing to make do with a substitute for the thing itself. This is the basis of the idea of redeeming one thing for something else (*pidyon*).

As the scarf serves a as a substitute for money and has only symbolic worth, even though it does not have even a "trace" of money value and is in a different category altogether, so it is regarding the suffering inflicted on the sinner. Were we to rely only on the element which is founded on money purchase

12 spoken in Bethlehem. May your house be as the house of Peretz,
whom Tamar bore to Judah, growing from the seed that the LORD
13 will give you from this young woman." And so it was that Boaz
took Ruth, and she became his wife, and he came to her; the
14 LORD granted her conception, and she bore a son. And the
women said to Naomi, "Blessed be the LORD, who has not with-
held your redeemer on this day – may the child's name be spoken
15 in all Israel. May he restore your spirit and sustain your old age, for
your daughter-in-law, who loves you, she has borne him, she who
16 is better to you than seven sons could be." Naomi took the child

---

וְיִקָּרֵא שְׁמוֹ בְּיִשְׂרָאֵל *May the child's name be spoken in all Israel.* Only when the individual joins the community which is claimed by God may he lay claim to a deathless existence. Only through identification with the origin may one gain eternal life. It is interesting that the term *karet,* cutting off – which, according to *Ḥazal,* our Sages, refers to severance from the transcendental order of existence – is mostly linked in the Bible with the expression "*me'adat Yisrael,* from the community of Israel" (Ex. 12:19), or "*mikerev amma,* from the midst of her nation" (Lev. 17:10). Judaism identified the termination of existence with cutting off the self from the community, for the individual strikes roots in eternity only by abiding within its confines. The great mystery involved in the relationship of child and parent is related to the fear of man vis-a-vis his short-lived sojourn as a being in the sense world and to his quest for permanence. Steadfastness can be achieved only through service which unites man with Being in eternity. This dedicated service can be realized within the community only when the individual joins the great march of *masorah* and *kabbalah,* with its perennial handing down of something great and sublime, its uninterrupted process of teaching and learning, of giving and receiving God's word, law and vision. Each individual is admitted to this fellowship only through his parents who transmitted to him the mysterious testament in order that he may forward it to his successors, thus uniting him with the abstract *makor* and *takhlit,* the source and the purpose of a metahistorical drama of gradual fulfillment of a promise and a vision. (*Family Redeemed,* pp. 156–157)

אֲשֶׁר אֲהֵבָתֶךְ *Who loves you.* Love emerges when the individual begins to no-

יב בְּאֶפְרָתָה וּקְרָא־שֵׁם בְּבֵית לָחֶם: וִיהִי בֵיתְךָ כְּבֵית פֶּרֶץ אֲשֶׁר־
יָלְדָה תָמָר לִיהוּדָה מִן־הַזֶּרַע אֲשֶׁר יִתֵּן יהוה לְךָ מִן־הַנַּעֲרָה
יג הַזֹּאת: וַיִּקַּח בֹּעַז אֶת־רוּת וַתְּהִי־לוֹ לְאִשָּׁה וַיָּבֹא אֵלֶיהָ וַיִּתֵּן
יד יהוה לָהּ הֵרָיוֹן וַתֵּלֶד בֵּן: וַתֹּאמַרְנָה הַנָּשִׁים אֶל־נָעֳמִי בָּרוּךְ
יהוה אֲשֶׁר לֹא הִשְׁבִּית לָךְ גֹּאֵל הַיּוֹם וְיִקָּרֵא שְׁמוֹ בְּיִשְׂרָאֵל:
טו וְהָיָה לָךְ לְמֵשִׁיב נֶפֶשׁ וּלְכַלְכֵּל אֶת־שֵׂיבָתֵךְ כִּי כַלָּתֵךְ אֲשֶׁר־
טז אֲהֵבַתֶךְ יְלָדַתּוּ אֲשֶׁר־הִיא טוֹבָה לָךְ מִשִּׁבְעָה בָּנִים: וַתִּקַּח

Abraham sits "in front of the tent" (Gen. 18:1). His name appears in the press and many know him; he is the leader, the father, the teacher; his lips drip honey; he enlightens the minds; he fascinates the passersby. Hardly anyone knows that there is a Sarah, humble, modest, publicly shy. Somewhere in the tent is the person who is perhaps responsible for all the accomplishments credited to Abraham, for all the glory that is bestowed upon Abraham, who is superior to him, who leads the leader and teaches the teacher and guides the master, who inspires the visionary and interprets his dreams.

It is quite interesting that although Abraham survived Sarah by thirty-eight years, his historical role came to an end with Sarah's passing. Isaac leaves the stage together with Rebecca. Jacob relinquishes his role to Joseph with the untimely death of Rachel. Without Sarah there would be no Abraham; no Isaac were it not for Rebecca; no Jacob without Rachel.

And yet, and here the tragedy manifests itself with all its impact, we say, "God of Abraham, God of Isaac, God of Jacob," but not "God of Sarah, God of Rebecca, God of Rachel and Leah," even though they had an equal share in *Borei Olam*, the Creator of the World.

The Halakhah was cognizant of the greatness of the covenantal mother when it formulated the rule that *Kedushat Yisrael*, one's status as a Jew, can be transmitted only through the woman. The Halakhah was also conscious of the loneliness and the tragic note in the feminine commitment when it accepted a contradictory rule that the child takes his father's name and family status. (*Family Redeemed*, pp. 119–120)

17 and placed him in her bosom and became his nurse. And her neigh-
bors named him, saying, "A son is born for Naomi!" They called
him Oved. And that was Oved the father of Yishai the father of
David.
18
19 This is the line of Peretz: Peretz was the father of Ḥetzron. Ḥetzron
20 was the father of Ram; Ram was the father of Aminadav. Aminadav

---

One can experience biological motherhood only in respect to one's own child. However, when motherhood was transformed into a commitment and being a mother was equated with being a teacher, an apostle of God, the carrier of God's covenant, His prophet, then motherhood, like fatherhood, was elevated to a universal spiritual level. (*Family Redeemed*, p. 108)

וַתְּהִי־לוֹ לְאֹמֶנֶת *And became his nurse.* It is not implausible to link the root **א־מ־ן** [meaning "believe"] to **אם**, "mother," since the mother is the foremost teacher of and believer in the child. A mother will never despair of her child, nor will she spare any effort to further her child's welfare, even though she does not expect to live long enough to enjoy the fruits of her toil and sacrifice. She is the most unselfish being. Her faith in her child can never be shaken. She will patiently try to do some particular thing for her child over and over again, since failure, however disappointing, does not weaken her determination to bring out the best and finest in the child. The *em* is unconditionally committed to her child, in whose capabilities she has unrestricted trust.

To believe and to bring up are identical accomplishments. The believer must be able to engage in a great educational task, to pick up the debris of a shattered world and reconstitute a harmonious creation, to seize human talent and capability in an ongoing array of deeds, suffusing these powers with meaning and integrating them into a redeemed personality. The believer is committed to the reconstruction of human society and the catharsis of the individual. All this must happen in a natural, evolutionary way, through progressive action, while man, like an infant, learns to take his first ascending steps up the steep mountain of the Lord. (*Abraham's Journey*, p. 98)

יז נָעֳמִי אֶת־הַיֶּלֶד וַתְּשִׁתֵהוּ בְחֵיקָהּ וַתְּהִי־לוֹ לְאֹמֶנֶת׃ וַתִּקְרֶאנָה
לוֹ הַשְּׁכֵנוֹת שֵׁם לֵאמֹר יֻלַּד־בֵּן לְנָעֳמִי וַתִּקְרֶאנָה שְׁמוֹ עוֹבֵד
הוּא אֲבִי־יִשַׁי אֲבִי דָוִד׃
יח יט וְאֵלֶּה תּוֹלְדוֹת פָּרֶץ פֶּרֶץ הוֹלִיד אֶת־חֶצְרוֹן׃ וְחֶצְרוֹן הוֹלִיד
כ אֶת־רָם וְרָם הוֹלִיד אֶת־עַמִּינָדָב׃ וְעַמִּינָדָב הוֹלִיד אֶת־נַחְשׁוֹן

---

tice a new truth – shocking but at the same time comforting and encouraging. I am not alone, I am not forlorn, I am not barren. The thou – despite the separateness of his individuality – merges with the I in his troubles, aspirations and quests. He becomes part of me. A new fellowship surfaces – a fellowship of destiny. This awareness redeems the individual from his bitter isolation, his individuality, and integrates him with the thou. It is here that love bursts forth from within the recesses of a frightened and perplexed soul, a love draped in gratitude to the thou, to the fellow who has joined me on my torturous path. Love sparkles and flourishes as the soul casts off the burden of barrenness and of absolute isolation; the silent monologue becomes a conversation. Love is the reaction to the wonder of individuals meeting and connecting – to the establishment of the dialogue, to a common language and words. The individual then acknowledges not only the existence of the thou but the value of his existence. This acknowledgment is not only factual, it is axiological as well. (*Halakhic Morality*, p. 162)

וַתִּקַּח נָעֳמִי אֶת־הַיֶּלֶד וַתְּשִׁתֵהוּ בְחֵיקָהּ *Naomi took the child and placed him in her bosom.* Mother's job changed into a great mission; her preoccupation with the child was endowed with ethical meaning. She not only nurses the child physically, she brings him up; she assumes the role of educator. Motherhood is not only an experience but a commitment as well. At this juncture motherhood is hallowed on account of another idea which is linked up with the spontaneous free choice of motherhood on the part of the woman in the covenantal community. As "mother-teacher," the woman is no more connected with only the fruit of her womb, with the child she bore. As long as motherhood, like fatherhood, was rooted in biological facticity, its confine was very narrow and extended only to a clan.

was the father of Naḥshon; Naḥshon was the father of Salma.
21 22 Salma was the father of Boaz; Boaz was the father of Oved. Oved
was the father of Yishai – and Yishai was the father of David.

David thought that he had just entered Jewish history, that he had entered our annals and become a historical figure when the prophet Samuel anointed him with holy oil. He did not know that the Almighty had been concerned about him centuries earlier when He saved Lot and the angels told him, "Take your wife and your two daughters who can be found."

Why were the angels so concerned about Lot's two daughters? Why did they specifically tell Lot to take the girls out of the city because of its impending destruction? The reason is that Lot's daughters were the ancestors of the Messiah. Ruth, a descendant of Moab, was the mother of the Davidic dynasty. Naamah the Ammonitess was the mother of Rehoboam (I Kings 14:21), and the King Messiah will be a descendant of David, Solomon, and Rehoboam. God did not send the angels because He was interested in Lot or in his daughters. He was interested in something else – the Messiah. The great vision of a redeemed world would have been made impossible if Lot's daughters had been destroyed in Sodom. That is why the Torah is so interested in telling us the strange story of the act of incest that took place in the cave. Why else would the Torah record such an ugly event? It is not a story of incest. It is the story of the Messiah.

The personality of the King Messiah is not monotonic. God wove the personality of the Messiah with vast amounts of multi-colored threads, like Joseph's shirt. The messianic soul is iridescent, multi-talented, rich in thought-filled volition, and will be endowed with talents that seem mutually exclusive. But everything good and fine and noble in man must be passed on to the Messiah. He will have the capacity for *gevurah* and *ḥesed*. He will be a hero with unlimited power and strength who will defend justice. He will also be a man of unlimited loving-kindness, humble and simple. All these capabilities, capacities, and talents will merge in beautiful harmony in the King Messiah. The Messiah will represent creation at its best. Apparently, then, Lot's daughters had something beautiful in them to contribute to the Messiah's rich and powerful personality. If there is something fine in the non-Jewish families of the earth, it, too, will be passed on to the Messiah. (*Abraham's Journey*, pp. 176–177)

כא וְנַחְשׁוֹן הוֹלִיד אֶת־שַׂלְמָה: וְשַׂלְמוֹן הוֹלִיד אֶת־בֹּעַז וּבֹעַז
כב הוֹלִיד אֶת־עוֹבֵד: וְעֹבֵד הוֹלִיד אֶת־יִשָׁי וְיִשַׁי הוֹלִיד אֶת־דָּוִד:

וְיִשַׁי הוֹלִיד אֶת־דָּוִד *And Yishai was the father of David.* "Moses received the Torah from Sinai, and transmitted it to Joshua," etc. (*Avot* 1:1). This is the motto of the Halakhah. The *masorah*, the process of transmission, symbolizes the Jewish people's outlook regarding the beautiful and resplendent phenomenon of time. The chain of tradition, begun millennia ago, will continue until the end of all time. Time, in this conception, is not destructive, all-consuming, and it does not simply consist of fleeting, imperceptible moments. This wondrous chain, which originated on that bright morning of the day of revelation and which stretches forward into the eschaton, represents the manner in which the Jewish people experience their own history, a history that floats upon the stormy waters of time. The consciousness of halakhic man, that master of the received tradition, embraces the entire company of the sages of the *masorah*. He lives in their midst, discusses and argues questions of Halakhah with them, delves into and analyzes fundamental halakhic principles in their company. All of them merge into one time experience. He walks alongside Maimonides, listens to R. Akiva, senses the presence of Abaye and Raba. He rejoices with them and shares in their sorrow. "David, king of Israel, yet lives and endures" [*Rosh Hashanah* 25a]; "Our father Jacob did not die" [*Taanit* 5b]; "Moses, our teacher, did not die" [Zohar I, 37b]. There can be no death and expiration among the company of the sages of tradition. Eternity and immortality reign here in unbounded fashion. Both past and future become, in such circumstances, ever-present realities. (*Halakhic Man*, p. 120)

דָּוִד *David.* There is a very strange and puzzling Talmudic passage:

> Rava said: What is the meaning of the verse "Then said I: Lo, I am come with the scroll of a book which is prescribed for me" (Ps. 40:8)? David said [when he became king], "I thought that I have come only now, but I did not know that in the scroll of the book it was already written about me. For there (Gen. 19:15) it is written, '[The angels hastened Lot, saying: Take your wife and your two daughters] who can be found, *ha-nimtza'ot*,' and here (Ps. 89:21) it is written, 'I have found, *matzati*, David My servant; with My sacred oil I have anointed him'" (*Yevamot* 77a).

קריאת התורה לשבועות

TORAH READINGS FOR SHAVUOT

The Readings of the Torah for the first and second day of Shavuot

REMOVING THE TORAH FROM THE ARK

אֵין־כָּמְוֹךָ There is none like You among the heavenly powers, LORD, *Ps. 86*
and there are no works like Yours.
Your kingdom is an eternal kingdom, *Ps. 145*
and Your dominion is for all generations.

The LORD is King, the LORD was King,
the LORD shall be King for ever and all time.
The LORD will give strength to His people; *Ps. 29*
the LORD will bless His people with peace.

Father of compassion,
favor Zion with Your goodness; rebuild the walls of Jerusalem. *Ps. 51*
For we trust in You alone, King, God,
high and exalted, Master of worlds.

The Ark is opened and the congregation stands. All say:

וַיְהִי בִּנְסֹעַ Whenever the Ark set out, Moses would say, *Num. 10*
"Arise, LORD, and may Your enemies be scattered.
May those who hate You flee before You."
For the Torah shall come forth from Zion, *Is. 2*
and the word of the LORD from Jerusalem.
Blessed is He who, in His holiness,
gave the Torah to His people Israel.

If the second day of Shavuot falls on Shabbat,
continue with "Blessed is the name" on page 44.

Say the following verses three times:

יהוה The LORD, the LORD, compassionate and gracious God, *Ex. 34*
slow to anger, abounding in loving-kindness and truth,
extending loving-kindness to a thousand generations, forgiving iniquity,
rebellion and sin, and absolving [the guilty who repent].

קריאת התורה
ליום טוב ראשון ושני של שבועות

הוצאת ספר תורה

אֵין־כָּמְוֹךָ בָאֱלֹהִים, אֲדֹנָי, וְאֵין כְּמַעֲשֶׂיךָ: תהלים פו
מַלְכוּתְךָ מַלְכוּת כָּל־עֹלָמִים, וּמֶמְשַׁלְתְּךָ בְּכָל־דּוֹר וָדֹר: תהלים קמה

יהוה מֶלֶךְ, יהוה מָלָךְ, יהוה יִמְלֹךְ לְעֹלָם וָעֶד.
יהוה עֹז לְעַמּוֹ יִתֵּן, יהוה יְבָרֵךְ אֶת־עַמּוֹ בַשָּׁלוֹם: תהלים כט

אַב הָרַחֲמִים,
הֵיטִיבָה בִרְצוֹנְךָ אֶת־צִיּוֹן תִּבְנֶה חוֹמוֹת יְרוּשָׁלָםִ: תהלים נא
כִּי בְךָ לְבַד בָּטָחְנוּ, מֶלֶךְ אֵל רָם וְנִשָּׂא, אֲדוֹן עוֹלָמִים.

The ארון קודש *is opened and the* קהל *stands. All say:*

וַיְהִי בִּנְסֹעַ הָאָרֹן וַיֹּאמֶר מֹשֶׁה במדבר י
קוּמָה יהוה וְיָפֻצוּ אֹיְבֶיךָ וְיָנֻסוּ מְשַׂנְאֶיךָ מִפָּנֶיךָ:
כִּי מִצִּיּוֹן תֵּצֵא תוֹרָה וּדְבַר־יהוה מִירוּשָׁלָםִ: ישעיה ב
בָּרוּךְ שֶׁנָּתַן תּוֹרָה לְעַמּוֹ יִשְׂרָאֵל בִּקְדֻשָּׁתוֹ.

If the second day of שבועות *falls on* שבת*,*
continue with בְּרִיךְ שְׁמֵהּ *on page 45.*

Say the following verses three times:

יהוה, יהוה, אֵל רַחוּם וְחַנּוּן, אֶרֶךְ אַפַּיִם וְרַב־חֶסֶד וֶאֱמֶת: שמות לד
נֹצֵר חֶסֶד לָאֲלָפִים, נֹשֵׂא עָוֹן וָפֶשַׁע וְחַטָּאָה, וְנַקֵּה:

Each individual says silently, inserting appropriate phrase/s in parentheses:

Master of the Universe, fulfill my heart's requests for good. Satisfy my desire, grant my request, and enable me (*name*, son/daughter of *father's name*), (and my wife/ husband, and my sons/daughters) and all the members of my household to do Your will with a perfect heart. Deliver us from the evil impulse, grant us our share in Your Torah, and make us worthy that Your Presence may rest upon us. Confer on us a spirit of wisdom and understanding, and may there be fulfilled in us the verse: "The spirit of the LORD will rest upon him – a spirit of wisdom *Is. 11* and understanding, a spirit of counsel and strength, a spirit of knowledge and reverence for the LORD." So too may it be Your will, LORD our God and God of our ancestors, that we be worthy to do deeds that are good in Your sight, and to walk before You in the ways of the upright. Make us holy through Your holiness, so that we may be worthy of a good and long life, and of the World to Come. Guard us from evil deeds and bad times that threaten to bring turmoil to the world. May loving-kindness surround one who trusts in the LORD. Amen. *Ps. 32*

יִהְיוּ May the words of my mouth and the meditation of my *Ps. 19*
heart find favor before You, LORD, my Rock and Redeemer.

Say the following verse three times:

וַאֲנִי As for me, may my prayer come to You, LORD, *Ps. 69*
at a time of favor. O God, in Your great love,
answer me with Your faithful salvation.

On all days, continue:

Blessed is the name of the Master of the Universe. Blessed is Your crown and *Zohar, Vayak-hel* Your place. May Your favor always be with Your people Israel. Show Your people the salvation of Your right hand in Your Temple. Grant us the gift of Your good light, and accept our prayers in mercy. May it be Your will to prolong our life in goodness. May I be counted among the righteous, so that You will have compassion on me and protect me and all that is mine and all that is Your people Israel's. You feed all; You sustain all; You rule over all; You rule over kings, for sovereignty is Yours. I am a servant of the Holy One, blessed be He, before whom and before whose glorious Torah I bow at all times. Not in man do I trust, nor on any angel do I rely, but on the God of heaven who is the God of truth, whose Torah is truth, whose prophets speak truth, and who abounds in acts of love and truth. ▸ In Him I trust, and to His holy and glorious name I offer praises. May it be Your will to open my heart to the Torah, and to fulfill the wishes of my heart and of the hearts of all Your people Israel for good, for life, and for peace.

Each individual says silently, inserting appropriate phrase/s in parentheses:

רִבּוֹנוֹ שֶׁל עוֹלָם, מַלֵּא מִשְׁאֲלוֹת לִבִּי לְטוֹבָה, וְהָפֵק רְצוֹנִי וְתֵן שְׁאֵלָתִי, וְזַכֵּה
לִי (פלוני/ת) בֶּן/בַּת פלוני) (וְאִשְׁתִּי/בַּעֲלִי וּבָנַי וּבְנוֹתַי) וְכָל בְּנֵי בֵיתִי, לַעֲשׂוֹת
רְצוֹנְךָ בְּלֵבָב שָׁלֵם, וּמַלְּטֵנוּ מִיֵּצֶר הָרָע, וְתֵן חֶלְקֵנוּ בְּתוֹרָתֶךָ, וְזַכֵּנוּ שֶׁתִּשְׁרֶה
שְׁכִינָתְךָ עָלֵינוּ, וְהוֹפַע עָלֵינוּ רוּחַ חָכְמָה וּבִינָה. וְיִתְקַיֵּם בָּנוּ מִקְרָא שֶׁכָּתוּב:
וְנָחָה עָלָיו רוּחַ יהוה, רוּחַ חָכְמָה וּבִינָה, רוּחַ עֵצָה וּגְבוּרָה, רוּחַ דַּעַת וְיִרְאַת ישעיה יא
יהוה: וּבְכֵן יְהִי רָצוֹן מִלְּפָנֶיךָ יהוה אֱלֹהֵינוּ וֵאלֹהֵי אֲבוֹתֵינוּ, שֶׁתְּזַכֵּנוּ לַעֲשׂוֹת
מַעֲשִׂים טוֹבִים בְּעֵינֶיךָ וְלָלֶכֶת בְּדַרְכֵי יְשָׁרִים לְפָנֶיךָ, וְקַדְּשֵׁנוּ בִּקְדֻשָּׁתֶךָ כְּדֵי
שֶׁנִּזְכֶּה לְחַיִּים טוֹבִים וַאֲרוּכִים וּלְחַיֵּי הָעוֹלָם הַבָּא, וְתִשְׁמְרֵנוּ מִמַּעֲשִׂים רָעִים
וּמִשָּׁעוֹת רָעוֹת הַמִּתְרַגְּשׁוֹת לָבוֹא לָעוֹלָם, וְהַבּוֹטֵחַ בַּיהוה חֶסֶד יְסוֹבְבֶנּוּ: אָמֵן. תהלים לב

יִהְיוּ לְרָצוֹן אִמְרֵי־פִי וְהֶגְיוֹן לִבִּי לְפָנֶיךָ, יהוה צוּרִי וְגוֹאֲלִי: תהלים יט

Say the following verse three times:

וַאֲנִי תְפִלָּתִי־לְךָ יהוה, עֵת רָצוֹן, אֱלֹהִים בְּרָב־חַסְדֶּךָ תהלים סט
עֲנֵנִי בֶּאֱמֶת יִשְׁעֶךָ:

On all days, continue:

בְּרִיךְ שְׁמֵהּ דְּמָרֵא עָלְמָא, בְּרִיךְ כִּתְרָךְ וְאַתְרָךְ. יְהֵא רְעוּתָךְ עִם עַמָּךְ יִשְׂרָאֵל זוהר ויקהל
לְעָלַם, וּפֻרְקַן יְמִינָךְ אַחֲזֵי לְעַמָּךְ בְּבֵית מַקְדְּשָׁךְ, וּלְאַמְטוּיֵי לַנָא מִטּוּב נְהוֹרָךְ,
וּלְקַבֵּל צְלוֹתַנָא בְּרַחֲמִין. יְהֵא רַעֲוָא קֳדָמָךְ דְּתוֹרִיךְ לַן חַיִּין בְּטִיבוּ, וְלֶהֱוֵי אֲנָא
פְּקִידָא בְּגוֹ צַדִּיקַיָּא, לְמִרְחַם עֲלַי וּלְמִנְטַר יָתִי וְיַת כָּל דִּי לִי וְדִי לְעַמָּךְ יִשְׂרָאֵל.
אַנְתְּ הוּא זָן לְכֹלָּא וּמְפַרְנֵס לְכֹלָּא, אַנְתְּ הוּא שַׁלִּיט עַל כֹּלָּא, אַנְתְּ הוּא דְּשַׁלִּיט
עַל מַלְכַיָּא, וּמַלְכוּתָא דִּילָךְ הִיא. אֲנָא עַבְדָּא דְקֻדְשָׁא בְּרִיךְ הוּא, דְּסָגֵדְנָא
קַמֵּהּ וּמִקַּמֵּי דִּיקַר אוֹרַיְתֵהּ בְּכָל עִדָּן וְעִדָּן. לָא עַל אֱנָשׁ רָחִיצְנָא וְלָא עַל בַּר
אֱלָהִין סָמִיכְנָא, אֶלָּא בֶּאֱלָהָא דִשְׁמַיָּא, דְּהוּא אֱלָהָא קְשׁוֹט, וְאוֹרַיְתֵהּ קְשׁוֹט,
וּנְבִיאוֹהִי קְשׁוֹט, וּמַסְגֵּא לְמֶעְבַּד טַבְוָן וּקְשׁוֹט. ◂ בֵּהּ אֲנָא רָחִיץ, וְלִשְׁמֵהּ
קַדִּישָׁא יַקִּירָא אֲנָא אֵמַר תֻּשְׁבְּחָן. יְהֵא רַעֲוָא קֳדָמָךְ דְּתִפְתַּח לִבַּאי בְּאוֹרַיְתָא,
וְתַשְׁלִים מִשְׁאֲלִין דְּלִבַּאי וְלִבָּא דְכָל עַמָּךְ יִשְׂרָאֵל לְטַב וּלְחַיִּין וְלִשְׁלָם.

Two Torah scrolls are removed from the Ark. The Leader takes one in his right arm and, followed by the congregation, says:

Listen, Israel: the LORD is our God, the LORD is One. *Deut. 6*

Leader then congregation:

One is our God; great is our Master;
holy is His name.

The Leader turns to face the Ark, bows and says:

Magnify the LORD with me, and let us exalt His name together. *Ps. 34*

The Ark is closed. The Leader carries the Torah scroll to the bima and the congregation says:

לְךָ Yours, LORD, are the greatness and the power, the glory and the majesty and splendor, for everything in heaven and earth is Yours. Yours, LORD, is the kingdom; You are exalted as Head over all. *1 Chr. 29*

רוֹמְמוּ Exalt the LORD our God and bow to His footstool; He is holy. Exalt the LORD our God, and bow at His holy mountain, for holy is the LORD our God. *Ps. 99*

Over all may the name of the Supreme King of kings, the Holy One blessed be He, be magnified and sanctified, praised and glorified, exalted and extolled, in the worlds that He has created – this world and the World to Come – in accordance with His will, and the will of those who fear Him, and the will of the whole house of Israel. He is the Rock of worlds, LORD of all creatures, God of all souls, who dwells in the spacious heights and inhabits the high heavens of old. His holiness is over the Ḥayyot and over the throne of glory. Therefore may Your name, LORD our God, be sanctified among us in the sight of all that lives. Let us sing before Him a new song, as it is written: "Sing to God, make music for His name, extol Him who rides the clouds – the LORD is His name – and exult before Him." And may we see Him eye to eye when He returns to His abode as it is written: "For they shall see eye to eye when the LORD returns to Zion." And it is said: "Then will the glory of the LORD be revealed, and all mankind together shall see that the mouth of the LORD has spoken." *Ps. 68* *Is. 52* *Is. 40*

Father of mercy, have compassion on the people borne by Him. May He remember the covenant with the mighty (patriarchs), and deliver us from evil times. May He reproach the evil instinct in the people by Him, and graciously grant that we be an eternal remnant. May He fulfill in good measure our requests for salvation and compassion.

Two ספרי תורה *are removed from the* ארון קודש. *The* שליח צבור *takes one in his right arm, and, followed by the* קהל*, says:*

דברים ו **שְׁמַע יִשְׂרָאֵל, יהוה אֱלֹהֵינוּ, יהוה אֶחָד:**

קהל *then* שליח ציבור*:*

אֶחָד אֱלֹהֵינוּ, גָּדוֹל אֲדוֹנֵינוּ, קָדוֹשׁ שְׁמוֹ.

The שליח ציבור *turns to face the* ארון קודש*, bows and says:*

תהלים לד **גַּדְּלוּ לַיהוה אִתִּי וּנְרוֹמְמָה שְׁמוֹ יַחְדָּו:**

The ארון קודש *is closed. The* שליח ציבור *carries the* ספר תורה *to the* בימה *and the* קהל *says:*

דברי הימים א׳ כט **לְךָ יהוה הַגְּדֻלָּה וְהַגְּבוּרָה וְהַתִּפְאֶרֶת וְהַנֵּצַח וְהַהוֹד, כִּי־כֹל בַּשָּׁמַיִם וּבָאָרֶץ, לְךָ יהוה הַמַּמְלָכָה וְהַמִּתְנַשֵּׂא לְכֹל לְרֹאשׁ:**

תהלים צט **רוֹמְמוּ יהוה אֱלֹהֵינוּ וְהִשְׁתַּחֲווּ לַהֲדֹם רַגְלָיו, קָדוֹשׁ הוּא: רוֹמְמוּ יהוה אֱלֹהֵינוּ וְהִשְׁתַּחֲווּ לְהַר קָדְשׁוֹ, כִּי־קָדוֹשׁ יהוה אֱלֹהֵינוּ:**

עַל הַכֹּל יִתְגַּדַּל וְיִתְקַדַּשׁ וְיִשְׁתַּבַּח וְיִתְפָּאַר וְיִתְרוֹמַם וְיִתְנַשֵּׂא שְׁמוֹ שֶׁל מֶלֶךְ מַלְכֵי הַמְּלָכִים הַקָּדוֹשׁ בָּרוּךְ הוּא בָּעוֹלָמוֹת שֶׁבָּרָא, הָעוֹלָם הַזֶּה וְהָעוֹלָם הַבָּא, כִּרְצוֹנוֹ וְכִרְצוֹן יְרֵאָיו וְכִרְצוֹן כָּל בֵּית יִשְׂרָאֵל. צוּר הָעוֹלָמִים, אֲדוֹן כָּל הַבְּרִיּוֹת, אֱלוֹהַּ כָּל הַנְּפָשׁוֹת, הַיּוֹשֵׁב בְּמֶרְחֲבֵי מָרוֹם, הַשּׁוֹכֵן בִּשְׁמֵי שְׁמֵי קֶדֶם, קְדֻשָּׁתוֹ עַל הַחַיּוֹת, וּקְדֻשָּׁתוֹ עַל כִּסֵּא הַכָּבוֹד. וּבְכֵן יִתְקַדַּשׁ שִׁמְךָ בָּנוּ יהוה אֱלֹהֵינוּ לְעֵינֵי כָּל חָי, וְנֹאמַר לְפָנָיו שִׁיר חָדָשׁ, כַּכָּתוּב:
תהלים סח שִׁירוּ לֵאלֹהִים זַמְּרוּ שְׁמוֹ, סֹלּוּ לָרֹכֵב בָּעֲרָבוֹת, בְּיָהּ שְׁמוֹ, וְעִלְזוּ לְפָנָיו:
ישעיה נב וְנִרְאֵהוּ עַיִן בְּעַיִן בְּשׁוּבוֹ אֶל נָוֵהוּ, כַּכָּתוּב: כִּי עַיִן בְּעַיִן יִרְאוּ בְּשׁוּב יהוה
ישעיה מ צִיּוֹן: וְנֶאֱמַר: וְנִגְלָה כְּבוֹד יהוה, וְרָאוּ כָל־בָּשָׂר יַחְדָּו כִּי פִּי יהוה דִּבֵּר:

אַב הָרַחֲמִים הוּא יְרַחֵם עַם עֲמוּסִים, וְיִזְכֹּר בְּרִית אֵיתָנִים, וְיַצִּיל נַפְשׁוֹתֵינוּ מִן הַשָּׁעוֹת הָרָעוֹת, וְיִגְעַר בְּיֵצֶר הָרָע מִן הַנְּשׂוּאִים, וְיָחֹן אוֹתָנוּ לִפְלֵיטַת עוֹלָמִים, וִימַלֵּא מִשְׁאֲלוֹתֵינוּ בְּמִדָּה טוֹבָה יְשׁוּעָה וְרַחֲמִים.

The Torah scroll is placed on the bima and the Gabbai calls a Kohen to the Torah.

וְיַעֲזֹר May He help, shield and save all who seek refuge in Him,
and let us say: Amen. Let us all render greatness to our God
and give honor to the Torah. *Let the Kohen come forward.
Arise (*name* son of *father's name*), the Kohen.

**If no Kohen is present, a Levi or Yisrael is called up as follows:*

/As there is no Kohen, arise (*name* son of *father's name*) in place of a Kohen./
Blessed is He who, in His holiness, gave the Torah to His people Israel.

The congregation followed by the Gabbai:

You who cling to the LORD your God are all alive today. *Deut. 4*

*The Reader shows the oleh the section to be read.
The oleh touches the scroll at that place with the tzitzit of his tallit,
which he then kisses. Holding the handles of the scroll, he says:*

Oleh: Bless the LORD, the blessed One.

Cong: Bless the LORD, the blessed One, for ever and all time.

Oleh: Bless the LORD, the blessed One, for ever and all time.
Blessed are You, LORD our God, King of the Universe,
who has chosen us from all peoples
and has given us His Torah.
Blessed are You, LORD, Giver of the Torah.

After the reading, the oleh says:

Oleh: Blessed are You, LORD our God, King of the Universe,
who has given us the Torah of truth,
planting everlasting life in our midst.
Blessed are You, LORD, Giver of the Torah.

One who has survived a situation of danger says:

Blessed are You, LORD our God, King of the Universe,
who bestows good on the unworthy, who has bestowed on me much good.

The congregation responds:

Amen. May He who bestowed much good on you
continue to bestow on you much good, Selah.

The ספר תורה is placed on the שולחן and the גבאי calls a כהן to the תורה.

וְיַעֲזֹר וְיָגֵן וְיוֹשִׁיעַ לְכָל הַחוֹסִים בּוֹ, וְנֹאמַר אָמֵן. הַכֹּל הָבוּ גֹדֶל לֵאלֹהֵינוּ וּתְנוּ כָבוֹד לַתּוֹרָה. *כֹּהֵן קְרָב, יַעֲמֹד (פלוני בֶּן פלוני) הַכֹּהֵן.

**If no כהן is present, a לוי or ישראל is called up as follows:*

/אֵין כָּאן כֹּהֵן, יַעֲמֹד (פלוני בֶּן פלוני) בִּמְקוֹם כֹּהֵן./

בָּרוּךְ שֶׁנָּתַן תּוֹרָה לְעַמּוֹ יִשְׂרָאֵל בִּקְדֻשָּׁתוֹ.

The קהל followed by the גבאי:

וְאַתֶּם הַדְּבֵקִים בַּיהוה אֱלֹהֵיכֶם חַיִּים כֻּלְּכֶם הַיּוֹם: דברים ד

The קורא shows the עולה the section to be read.
The עולה touches the scroll at that place with the ציצית of his טלית,
which he then kisses. Holding the handles of the scroll, he says:

עולה: בָּרְכוּ אֶת יהוה הַמְבֹרָךְ.

קהל: בָּרוּךְ יהוה הַמְבֹרָךְ לְעוֹלָם וָעֶד.

עולה: בָּרוּךְ יהוה הַמְבֹרָךְ לְעוֹלָם וָעֶד.

בָּרוּךְ אַתָּה יהוה, אֱלֹהֵינוּ מֶלֶךְ הָעוֹלָם
אֲשֶׁר בָּחַר בָּנוּ מִכָּל הָעַמִּים וְנָתַן לָנוּ אֶת תּוֹרָתוֹ.
בָּרוּךְ אַתָּה יהוה, נוֹתֵן הַתּוֹרָה.

After the קריאת התורה, the עולה says:

עולה: בָּרוּךְ אַתָּה יהוה אֱלֹהֵינוּ מֶלֶךְ הָעוֹלָם
אֲשֶׁר נָתַן לָנוּ תּוֹרַת אֱמֶת וְחַיֵּי עוֹלָם נָטַע בְּתוֹכֵנוּ.
בָּרוּךְ אַתָּה יהוה, נוֹתֵן הַתּוֹרָה.

One who has survived a situation of danger says:

בָּרוּךְ אַתָּה יהוה אֱלֹהֵינוּ מֶלֶךְ הָעוֹלָם הַגּוֹמֵל לְחַיָּבִים טוֹבוֹת שֶׁגְּמָלַנִי כָּל טוֹב.

The קהל responds:

אָמֵן. מִי שֶׁגְּמָלְךָ כָּל טוֹב הוּא יִגְמָלְךָ כָּל טוֹב, סֶלָה.

After a Bar Mitzva boy has finished the Torah blessing, his father says aloud:

Blessed is He who has released me
from the responsibility for this child.

FOR AN OLEH

May He who blessed our fathers, Abraham, Isaac and Jacob, bless (*name*, son of *father's name*) who has been called up in honor of the All-Present, in honor of the Torah, and in honor of (*On Shabbat:* the Sabbath and in honor of) the festival. As a reward for this, may the Holy One, blessed be He, protect and deliver him from all trouble and distress, all infection and illness, and send blessing and success to all the work of his hands and may he merit to go up to Jerusalem for the festivals, together with all Israel, his brethren, and let us say: Amen.

FOR A SICK MAN

May He who blessed our fathers, Abraham, Isaac and Jacob, Moses and Aaron, David and Solomon, bless and heal one who is ill, (*sick person's name*, son of *mother's name*), on whose behalf (*name of the one making the offering*) is making a contribution to charity. As a reward for this, may the Holy One, blessed be He, be filled with compassion for him, to restore his health, cure him, strengthen and revive him, sending him a swift and full recovery from heaven to all his 248 organs and 365 sinews, amongst the other sick ones in Israel, a healing of the spirit and a healing of the body – though on (*On Shabbat:* the Sabbath and) festivals it is forbidden to cry out, may healing be quick to come – now, swiftly and soon, and let us say: Amen.

FOR A SICK WOMAN

May He who blessed our fathers, Abraham, Isaac and Jacob, Moses and Aaron, David and Solomon, bless and heal one who is ill, (*sick person's name*, daughter of *mother's name*), on whose behalf (*name of the one making the offering*) is making a contribution to charity. As a reward for this, may the Holy One, blessed be He, be filled with compassion for her, to restore her health, cure her, strengthen and revive her, sending her a swift and full recovery from heaven to all her organs and sinews, amongst the other sick ones in Israel, a healing of the spirit and a healing of the body – though on (*On Shabbat:* the Sabbath and) festivals it is forbidden to cry out, may healing be quick to come – now, swiftly and soon, and let us say: Amen.

After a בר מצווה *has finished the* תורה *blessing, his father says aloud:*

בָּרוּךְ שֶׁפְּטָרַנִי מֵעָנְשׁוֹ שֶׁלָּזֶה.

מי שברך לעולה לתורה

מִי שֶׁבֵּרַךְ אֲבוֹתֵינוּ אַבְרָהָם יִצְחָק וְיַעֲקֹב, הוּא יְבָרֵךְ אֶת (פלוני בֶּן פלוני), בַּעֲבוּר שֶׁעָלָה לִכְבוֹד הַמָּקוֹם וְלִכְבוֹד הַתּוֹרָה (בשבת וְלִכְבוֹד הַשַּׁבָּת) וְלִכְבוֹד הָרֶגֶל. בִּשְׂכַר זֶה הַקָּדוֹשׁ בָּרוּךְ הוּא יִשְׁמְרֵהוּ וְיַצִּילֵהוּ מִכָּל צָרָה וְצוּקָה וּמִכָּל נֶגַע וּמַחֲלָה, וְיִשְׁלַח בְּרָכָה וְהַצְלָחָה בְּכָל מַעֲשֵׂה יָדָיו וְיִזְכֶּה לַעֲלוֹת לָרֶגֶל עִם כָּל יִשְׂרָאֵל אֶחָיו, וְנֹאמַר אָמֵן.

מי שברך לחולֶה

מִי שֶׁבֵּרַךְ אֲבוֹתֵינוּ אַבְרָהָם יִצְחָק וְיַעֲקֹב, מֹשֶׁה וְאַהֲרֹן דָּוִד וּשְׁלֹמֹה הוּא יְבָרֵךְ וִירַפֵּא אֶת הַחוֹלֶה (פלוני בֶּן פלונית) בַּעֲבוּר שֶׁ(פלוני בֶּן פלוני) נוֹדֵר צְדָקָה בַּעֲבוּרוֹ. בִּשְׂכַר זֶה הַקָּדוֹשׁ בָּרוּךְ הוּא יִמָּלֵא רַחֲמִים עָלָיו לְהַחֲלִימוֹ וּלְרַפְּאתוֹ וּלְהַחֲזִיקוֹ וּלְהַחֲיוֹתוֹ וְיִשְׁלַח לוֹ מְהֵרָה רְפוּאָה שְׁלֵמָה מִן הַשָּׁמַיִם לִרְמַ״ח אֵבָרָיו וּשְׁסָ״ה גִּידָיו בְּתוֹךְ שְׁאָר חוֹלֵי יִשְׂרָאֵל, רְפוּאַת הַנֶּפֶשׁ וּרְפוּאַת הַגּוּף. יוֹם טוֹב הוּא / בשבת: שַׁבָּת וְיוֹם טוֹב הֵם/ מִלִּזְעֹק, וּרְפוּאָה קְרוֹבָה לָבוֹא, הַשְׁתָּא בַּעֲגָלָא וּבִזְמַן קָרִיב, וְנֹאמַר אָמֵן.

מי שברך לחולָה

מִי שֶׁבֵּרַךְ אֲבוֹתֵינוּ אַבְרָהָם יִצְחָק וְיַעֲקֹב, מֹשֶׁה וְאַהֲרֹן דָּוִד וּשְׁלֹמֹה הוּא יְבָרֵךְ וִירַפֵּא אֶת הַחוֹלָה (פלונית בַּת פלונית) בַּעֲבוּר שֶׁ(פלוני בֶּן פלוני) נוֹדֵר צְדָקָה בַּעֲבוּרָהּ. בִּשְׂכַר זֶה הַקָּדוֹשׁ בָּרוּךְ הוּא יִמָּלֵא רַחֲמִים עָלֶיהָ לְהַחֲלִימָהּ וּלְרַפְּאתָהּ וּלְהַחֲזִיקָהּ וּלְהַחֲיוֹתָהּ וְיִשְׁלַח לָהּ מְהֵרָה רְפוּאָה שְׁלֵמָה מִן הַשָּׁמַיִם לְכָל אֵבָרֶיהָ וּלְכָל גִּידֶיהָ בְּתוֹךְ שְׁאָר חוֹלֵי יִשְׂרָאֵל, רְפוּאַת הַנֶּפֶשׁ וּרְפוּאַת הַגּוּף. יוֹם טוֹב הוּא / בשבת: שַׁבָּת וְיוֹם טוֹב הֵם/ מִלִּזְעֹק, וּרְפוּאָה קְרוֹבָה לָבוֹא, הַשְׁתָּא בַּעֲגָלָא וּבִזְמַן קָרִיב, וְנֹאמַר אָמֵן.

ON THE BIRTH OF A SON

May He who blessed our fathers, Abraham, Isaac and Jacob, Moses and Aaron, David and Solomon, Sarah, Rebecca, Rachel and Leah, bless the woman (*name*, daughter of *father's name*) who has given birth, and her son who has been born to her as an auspicious sign. Her husband, the child's father, is making a contribution to charity. As a reward for this, may father and mother merit to bring the child into the covenant of Abraham and to a life of Torah, to the marriage canopy and to good deeds, and let us say: Amen.

ON THE BIRTH OF A DAUGHTER

May He who blessed our fathers, Abraham, Isaac and Jacob, Moses and Aaron, David and Solomon, Sarah, Rebecca, Rachel and Leah, bless the woman (*name*, daughter of *father's name*) who has given birth, and her daughter who has been born to her as an auspicious sign; and may her name be called in Israel (*baby's name*, daughter of *father's name*). Her husband, the child's father, is making a contribution to charity. As a reward for this, may father and mother merit to raise her to a life of Torah, to the marriage canopy, and to good deeds, and let us say: Amen.

FOR A BAR MITZVA

May He who blessed our fathers, Abraham, Isaac and Jacob, bless (*name*, son of *father's name*) who has completed thirteen years and attained the age of the commandments, who has been called to the Torah to give praise and thanks to God, may His name be blessed, for all the good He has bestowed on him. May the Holy One, blessed be He, protect and sustain him and direct his heart to be perfect with God, to walk in His ways and keep the commandments all the days of his life, and let us say: Amen.

FOR A BAT MITZVA

May He who blessed our fathers, Abraham, Isaac and Jacob, Sarah, Rebecca, Rachel and Leah, bless (*name*, daughter of *father's name*) who has completed twelve years and attained the age of the commandments, and gives praise and thanks to God, may His name be blessed, for all the good He has bestowed on her. May the Holy One, blessed be He, protect and sustain her and direct her heart to be perfect with God, to walk in His ways and keep the commandments all the days of her life, and let us say: Amen.

מי שברך ליולדת בן

מִי שֶׁבֵּרַךְ אֲבוֹתֵינוּ אַבְרָהָם יִצְחָק וְיַעֲקֹב, מֹשֶׁה וְאַהֲרֹן דָּוִד וּשְׁלֹמֹה, שָׂרָה רִבְקָה רָחֵל וְלֵאָה הוּא יְבָרֵךְ אֶת הָאִשָּׁה הַיּוֹלֶדֶת (פלונית בַּת פלוני) וְאֶת בְּנָהּ שֶׁנּוֹלַד לָהּ לְמַזָּל טוֹב בַּעֲבוּר שֶׁבַּעְלָהּ וְאָבִיו נוֹדֵר צְדָקָה בַּעֲדָם. בִּשְׂכַר זֶה יִזְכּוּ אָבִיו וְאִמּוֹ לְהַכְנִיסוֹ בִּבְרִיתוֹ שֶׁל אַבְרָהָם אָבִינוּ וּלְגַדְּלוֹ לְתוֹרָה וּלְחֻפָּה וּלְמַעֲשִׂים טוֹבִים, וְנֹאמַר אָמֵן.

מי שברך ליולדת בת

מִי שֶׁבֵּרַךְ אֲבוֹתֵינוּ אַבְרָהָם יִצְחָק וְיַעֲקֹב, מֹשֶׁה וְאַהֲרֹן דָּוִד וּשְׁלֹמֹה, שָׂרָה רִבְקָה רָחֵל וְלֵאָה הוּא יְבָרֵךְ אֶת הָאִשָּׁה הַיּוֹלֶדֶת (פלונית בַּת פלוני) וְאֶת בִּתָּהּ שֶׁנּוֹלְדָה לָהּ לְמַזָּל טוֹב וְיִקָּרֵא שְׁמָהּ בְּיִשְׂרָאֵל (פלונית בַּת פלוני), בַּעֲבוּר שֶׁבַּעְלָהּ וְאָבִיהָ נוֹדֵר צְדָקָה בַּעֲדָן. בִּשְׂכַר זֶה יִזְכּוּ אָבִיהָ וְאִמָּהּ לְגַדְּלָהּ לְתוֹרָה וּלְחֻפָּה וּלְמַעֲשִׂים טוֹבִים, וְנֹאמַר אָמֵן.

מי שברך לבר מצווה

מִי שֶׁבֵּרַךְ אֲבוֹתֵינוּ אַבְרָהָם יִצְחָק וְיַעֲקֹב הוּא יְבָרֵךְ אֶת (פלוני בֶּן פלוני) שֶׁמָּלְאוּ לוֹ שְׁלֹשׁ עֶשְׂרֵה שָׁנָה וְהִגִּיעַ לְמִצְוֹת, וְעָלָה לַתּוֹרָה, לָתֵת שֶׁבַח וְהוֹדָיָה לְהַשֵּׁם יִתְבָּרַךְ עַל כָּל הַטּוֹבָה שֶׁגָּמַל אִתּוֹ. יִשְׁמְרֵהוּ הַקָּדוֹשׁ בָּרוּךְ הוּא וִיחַיֵּהוּ, וִיכוֹנֵן אֶת לִבּוֹ לִהְיוֹת שָׁלֵם עִם יהוה וְלָלֶכֶת בִּדְרָכָיו וְלִשְׁמֹר מִצְוֹתָיו כָּל הַיָּמִים, וְנֹאמַר אָמֵן.

מי שברך לבת מצווה

מִי שֶׁבֵּרַךְ אֲבוֹתֵינוּ אַבְרָהָם יִצְחָק וְיַעֲקֹב, שָׂרָה רִבְקָה רָחֵל וְלֵאָה, הוּא יְבָרֵךְ אֶת (פלונית בַּת פלוני) שֶׁמָּלְאוּ לָהּ שְׁתֵּים עֶשְׂרֵה שָׁנָה וְהִגִּיעָה לְמִצְוֹת, וְנוֹתֶנֶת שֶׁבַח וְהוֹדָיָה לְהַשֵּׁם יִתְבָּרַךְ עַל כָּל הַטּוֹבָה שֶׁגָּמַל אִתָּהּ. יִשְׁמְרֶהָ הַקָּדוֹשׁ בָּרוּךְ הוּא וִיחַיֶּהָ, וִיכוֹנֵן אֶת לִבָּהּ לִהְיוֹת שָׁלֵם עִם יהוה וְלָלֶכֶת בִּדְרָכָיו וְלִשְׁמֹר מִצְוֹתָיו כָּל הַיָּמִים, וְנֹאמַר אָמֵן.

On the second day of Shavuot, turn to page 102.

TORAH READING FOR THE FIRST DAY OF SHAVUOT

On Shavuot, after the Kohen is called up to the Torah and before he makes the blessing, the following is said responsively by the Reader and the congregation.

AKDAMUT

Leader: The beginning of words – the opening of speech:
I shall ask permission and leave to begin.

Cong: Trembling I open my mouth with two matters and three,
by leave of the One who bears us through to old age.

Leader: His are eternal mighty acts,
which could not be laid out in words,
even were all the skies parchment, and all the forests reeds;

Cong: if all the seas were ink, and all the lakes,
and the all people, scribes and clerks.

Leader: The glorious Master of Heaven, Ruler of the land,
founded His world alone, and took control of it.

Cong: Without weariness He perfected it, without tiring at all;
by the lightest of letters, something without substance.

Leader: He summoned forth all creation in those six days;
and then His shining glory rose, to sit upon His throne of fire.

---

and now that man can acquire a share in the world to come. The creation of the world does not inflict any "blemish" upon the idea of divinity, does not infringe upon infinity; on the contrary, it is the will of God that His Shekhinah, His Divine Presence, should contract and limit itself within the realm of empirical reality. The great promised destiny, "In that day shall the Lord be one, and His name one" (Zech. 14:9), instead of referring to the mystical dream of the overcoming and negation of reality, refers to the era in which the Halakhah will find its fulfillment, its total realization in this world. (*Halakhic Man*, pp. 51–52)

On the second day of שבועות*, turn to page 103.*

קריאה ליום טוב ראשון של שבועות

On שבועות*, after the* כהן *is called up to the* תורה *and before he makes the* ברכה*,*
the following is said responsively by the שליח ציבור *and the* קהל*.*

אקדמות

ש״ץ: אַקְדָּמוּת מִלִּין וְשָׁרָיוּת שׁוּתָא
אַוְלָא שָׁקֵלְנָא הַרְמָן וּרְשׁוּתָא.

קהל: בְּבָבֵי תְּרֵי וּתְלָת דְּאֶפְתַּח בְּנַקְשׁוּתָא
בְּבָרֵי דְבָרֵי וְטָרֵי עֲדֵי לְקַשִּׁישׁוּתָא.

ש״ץ: גְּבוּרָן עָלְמִין לֵהּ, וְלָא סְפֵק פְּרִישׁוּתָא
גְּוִיל אִלּוּ רְקִיעֵי, קְנֵי כָּל חֻרְשָׁתָא.

קהל: דְּיוֹ אִלּוּ יַמֵּי וְכָל מֵי כְנִישׁוּתָא
דָּיְרֵי אַרְעָא סָפְרֵי וְרָשְׁמֵי רַשְׁוָתָא.

ש״ץ: הֲדַר מָרֵי שְׁמַיָּא וְשַׁלִּיט בְּיַבֶּשְׁתָּא
הֲקֵים עָלְמָא יְחִידָאי, וְכַבְשֵׁהּ בְּכַבְשׁוּתָא.

קהל: וּבְלָא לֵאוּ שַׁכְלְלֵהּ, וּבְלָא תְשָׁשׁוּתָא
וּבְאָתָא קַלִּילָא דְּלֵית בַּהּ מְשָׁשׁוּתָא.

ש״ץ: זַמֵּן כָּל עֲבִידְתֵּהּ בְּהַךְ יוֹמֵי שִׁתָּא
זְהוֹר יְקָרֵהּ עַלִּי, עֲלֵי כָּרְסְיֵהּ דְּאֶשָּׁתָא.

AKDAMUT

וּבְלָא לֵאוּ שַׁכְלְלֵהּ, וּבְלָא תְשָׁשׁוּתָא *Without weariness He perfected it, without tiring at all.* The mystery of *tzimtzum* should not precipitate metaphysical anguish but rather gladness and joy. Man resides together with his Creator in this world, and it is only through cultivating that togetherness in the here

Cong: A heavenly host of a thousand thousands
and myriads serve Him –
created each morning anew, so great is His faithfulness.

Leader: Seraphim, covered with six wings, bow many times over,
and stand in utter silence until they have leave.

Cong: They receive leave from each other –
and at once, without pause,
His glory fills all the world, at their threefold sanctifying.

Leader: Like a voice from the Almighty, like the noise of many waters –
Cherubim raise themselves towards the Ophanim
in a roar of noise,

Cong: to see face to face what looks like sparks of the rainbow flying,
and wherever they are sent, they arrive in a flash of motion.

Leader: They bless His glory in every secret term,
from the place of the home of His Presence,
which cannot even be sought.

Cong: And all the hosts of heaven give praises in great fear,
of the sovereignty that will last through all ages, forever.

Leader: They each lay out His holiness in praise,
and when their moment has passed
it is gone forever; seven years will go by and it will not return.

Cong: His precious estate, Israel – they are more fortunate, for always
may they praise Him, dawn and dusk.

Leader: They are set apart, His portion, to perform His will,
and they will tell the wonders of His praise in speech.

Cong: He desires and values and yearns for them
to labor for Him to weariness,
and so He accepts their prayers; it is their pleas that are fulfilled.

---

it should become sweet in our mouths. The idea of passing on, of transmitting, of perpetuating *divrei Torah*, of what I call belonging to the *mesora*

קהל: חֲיַל אֱלֶף אַלְפִין וְרִבּוֹא לְשַׁמָּשׁוּתָא
חַדְתִּין נְבוֹט לְצַפְרִין, סַגִּיאָה טְרָשׁוּתָא.

ש״ץ: טְפֵי יְקִידִין שְׂרָפִין, כְּלוֹל גַּפֵּי שִׁתָּא
טְעֵם עַד יִתְיְהֵב לְהוֹן, שְׁתִיקִין בְּאַדִּישְׁתָּא.

קהל: יְקַבְּלוּן דֵּין מִן דֵּין שָׁוֵי דְּלָא בְשַׁשְׁתָּא
יְקָר מְלֵי כָל אַרְעָא לְתַלּוֹתֵי קְדֻשְׁתָּא.

ש״ץ: כְּקָל מִן קֳדָם שַׁדַּי, כְּקָל מֵי נְפִישׁוּתָא
כְּרוּבִין קֳבֵל גַּלְגִּלִּין מְרוֹמְמִין בְּאַוְשָׁתָא.

קהל: לְמֶחֱזֵי בְּאַנְפָּא עֵין כְּוָת גִּירֵי קַשְׁתָּא
לְכָל אֲתַר דְּמִשְׁתַּלְּחִין, זְרִיזִין בְּאַשְׁוָתָא.

ש״ץ: מְבָרְכִין בְּרִיךְ יְקָרֵהּ בְּכָל לִשַּׁן לְחִישׁוּתָא
מֵאֲתַר בֵּית שְׁכִינְתֵּהּ, דְּלָא צְרִיךְ בְּחִישׁוּתָא.

קהל: נְהֵם כָּל חֵיל מְרוֹמָא, מְקַלְּסִין בַּחֲשַׁשְׁתָּא
נְהִירָא מַלְכוּתֵהּ לְדָר וְדָר לְאַפְרַשְׁתָּא.

ש״ץ: סְדִירָא בְהוֹן קְדֻשְׁתָּא, וְכַד חָלְפָא שַׁעְתָּא
סִיּוּמָא דִלְעָלַם, וְאוֹף לָא לִשְׁבוּעֲתָא.

קהל: עֲדַב יְקַר אַחְסַנְתֵּהּ חֲבִיבִין, דְּבִקְבַעְתָּא
עֲבִידִין לֵהּ חֲטִיבָא בִּדְנַח וּשְׁקַעְתָּא.

ש״ץ: פְּרִישָׁן לְמָנָתֵהּ לְמֶעְבַּד לֵהּ רְעוּתָא
פְּרִישָׁתֵי שְׁבָחֵהּ יְחַוּוֹן בְּשָׁעוּתָא.

קהל: צְבֵי וְחָמֵד וְרָגֵג דְּיִלְאוֹן בְּלָעוּתָא
צְלוֹתְהוֹן בְּכֵן מְקַבֵּל, וְהָנְיָא בָעוּתָא.

צְבֵי וְחָמֵד וְרָגֵג דְּיִלְאוֹן בְּלָעוּתָא *He desires and values and yearns for them to labor for Him to weariness.* The Torah should fascinate us, it should allure us,

Leader: And those pleas are joined, with a crown and an oath,
to the One who lives forever,
and worn with the phylacteries He binds to Himself always,

Cong: which are inscribed inside with wisdom and with insight,
with the greatness of Israel, who read the Shema.

Leader: And I, in the same way, praise the Master of the Universe,
and it befits me to speak of Him to those of other nations,

Cong: who come and form crowds, like waves all around,
doubting, asking about Him, about the signs He performs –

Leader: "Where is your Beloved from, yes who is He, who is so beautiful,
that you let yourselves be killed for Him in the lions' den?

Cong: "You would be more respected, lovelier,
if you bent yourselves to our rule:
your will would be done then wherever you would be."

Leader: With wisdom I reply to them, telling them of the end –
"If you only knew, if you only truly knew Him,

---

monism. A man can know many things, but one can live only in one value system. Intellectually, man is basically a pluralist. There is no competition within the intellect, no envy or jealousy. I can know many things. However, there is great competition among values in the axiological world. I can cherish one value; I cannot cherish five values, because values are basically competitive; they are jealous of each other, if I may use this expression. Since intellectual commitment is not total commitment, I can commit myself to different fields of knowledge. But axiological commitment is a total commitment that requires full devotion. Love has the element of jealousy, like a husband jealous of his wife. It demands full attention, like a child who wants the full attention of the mother. Intellectually, we can be engaged in many things but one cannot be involved emotionally in two worlds. We cannot worship two gods. We cannot divide our emotions, our love, our sympathy, our appreciation, between two fields. Axiologically, we require a monistic attitude, and that means to be devoted to Torah alone. (*Blessings and Thanksgiving*, pp. 54–55)

ש״ץ: קְטִירָא לְחַי עָלְמָא בְּתָגָא בְּשְׁבוּעֲתָא
קָבֵל יְקַר טוֹטֶפְתָּא יְתִיבָא בִּקְבִיעֲתָא.

קהל: רְשִׁימָא הִיא גוּפָא בְּחָכְמְתָא וּבְדַעְתָּא
רְבוּתְהוֹן דְּיִשְׂרָאֵל, קָרָאֵי בִשְׁמַעְתָּא.

ש״ץ: שְׁבַח רִבּוֹן עָלְמָא, אֲמִירָא דַכְוָתָא
שְׁפַר עֲלַי לְחַוּוֹיֵהּ בְּאַפֵּי מַלְכְוָתָא.

קהל: תָּאִין וּמִתְכַּנְשִׁין כְּחֵזוּ אַדְוָתָא
תְּמֵהִין וְשָׁיְלִין לֵהּ בְּעֵסֶק אָתְוָתָא.

ש״ץ: מְנָן וּמַאן הוּא רְחִימָךְ, שַׁפִּירָא בְּרֵוָתָא
אֲרוּם בְּגִינֵהּ סְפֵית מְדוֹר אַרְיָוָתָא.

קהל: יְקָרָא וְיָאָה אַתְּ, אִין תְּעָרְבִי לְמָרְוָתָא
רְעוּתֵךְ נַעֲבֵד לִיךְ בְּכָל אַתְרְוָתָא.

ש״ץ: בְּחָכְמְתָא מְתִיבָתָא לְהוֹן, קְצָת לְהוֹדָעוּתָא
יְדַעְתּוּן חַכְּמִין לֵהּ בְּאִשְׁתְּמוֹדָעוּתָא.

---

community, is not realized through an intellectual act, but through emotional involvement. You can pass on mathematics because it is very useful for your child to know mathematics or physics. But when it is not a question of usefulness, it is impossible to pass on an axiological system without loving it, without being dedicated and devoted to it. As a matter of fact, the intellectual genius cannot be creative unless he is emotionally involved. It is the intuitive feeling which is the source of creativity; creativity does not come from having a certain discipline at one's fingertips, it does not come simply from accumulated knowledge. Of course, it is impossible to develop intuition unless you know your astronomy, or chemistry, or physics, or philosophy. But it is a great love which generates intuition, an involvement which reveals new horizons. Creativity comes from total involvement in a discipline.

We have to distinguish between cognitive pluralism and axiological

Cong: "and what your greatness is worth when compared to that glory,
or the greatness
I will be granted when my salvation comes...

Leader: "When light comes to me, and shame covers you over;
when His presence is revealed to me in might and in great pride."

Cong: He shall pay His enemies back in kind, the aggressors
of the distant isles,
and perform justice for the beloved people, rich in merit,

Leader: when He brings perfect happiness, and us as pure vessels;
when He brings the exiles back into the city of Jerusalem.

Cong: He shall cast His glory over them day and night,
as a canopy where they shall voice the splendor in
joyful songs,

Leader: for the shining of those clouds will make each canopy fine
as the actions of the one who sits in it; so will each shelter
be made.

Cong: On seats of finest gold, in seven tiers, sit the righteous
in their places before the One whose acts are manifold.

Leader: And they appear as seven tiers of joy,
like the dome of the sky in its brilliance, like stars of light.

---

rest! The benediction always signifies a moment of grace, a great, sublime moment for the utterer of the benediction, in which he attains a deep vision and acute look through the miraculous portal torn open by a hidden hand to reveal a world that is entirely good and pleasant, and entirely miraculous. The Halakhah says: Fortunate is the creature who encounters the Creator along the pathways of the world from time to time, when he takes a sip of water or tastes a bit of bread. Fortunate is the man for whom God is the Lord whenever he uses his senses and derives enjoyment from them. (*And From There You Shall Seek*, p. 21)

קהל: וְבוּתְכוֹן מֶה חֲשִׁיבָא קֳבֵל הַהִיא שְׁבַחְתָּא
וְבוּתָא דְיֵעֲבֵד לִי, כַּד מָטְיָא יְשׁוּעָתָא.

ש״ץ: בְּמֵיתֵי לִי נְהוֹרָא, וְתַחֲפֵי לְכוֹן בַּהֲתָא
יְקָרֵהּ כַּד אִתְגְּלֵי בְּתָקְפָּא וּבְגֵיוְתָא.

קהל: יְשַׁלֵּם גְּמֻלַיָּא לְשָׂנְאֵי וְנַגְוָתָא
צִדְקָתָא לְעַם חָבִיב וְסַגִּי זַכְוָתָא.

ש״ץ: חֲדוּ שְׁלֵמָא בְּמֵיתֵי, וּמָנָא דַכְוָתָא
קִרְיָתָא דִירוּשְׁלֵם כַּד יְכַנֵּשׁ גָּלְוָתָא.

קהל: יְקָרֵהּ מַטֵּל עֲלֵהּ בְּיוֹמֵי וְלֵילְוָתָא
גְּנוּנֵהּ לְמֶעְבַּד בַּהּ בְּתֻשְׁבְּחָן כְּלִילָתָא.

ש״ץ: דְּזֵהוֹר עֲנָנַיָּא לְמִשְׁפַּר כִּילָתָא
לְפֻמֵּהּ דַעֲבִידְתָּא עֲבִידָן מְטַלַּלְתָּא.

קהל: בְּתַכְתְּקֵי דְהַב פִּזָא, וּשְׁבַע מַעֲלָתָא
תְּחִימִין צַדִּיקֵי קֳדָם רַב פָּעֳלָתָא.

ש״ץ: וְרֵוֵיהוֹן דָּמֵי לְשָׂבְעָא חֶדְוָתָא
רְקִיעָא בְּזֵהוֹרֵהּ וְכוֹכְבֵי זִיוָתָא.

רְקִיעָא בְּזֵהוֹרֵהּ וְכוֹכְבֵי זִיוָתָא *Like the dome of the sky in its brilliance, like stars of light.* For the Jew there is no such thing as routine. Everything is a wondrous miracle. He is excited by everything, from the novel and unknown to the everyday and the ordinary. In everything he sees the glory of God; over everything he utters a benediction. The beloved goes out always – at each dawn with the radiance of the morning star, and at every twilight with the winking of the evening star, when her drowsy eyelids droop each night and when she opens her eyes every morning – to greet her ruddy lover who peers out from the radiant dawn and the starlight, out of exhaustion and

Cong: This is a glory no mouth can express,
glory that the prophets never heard or saw in their visions.

Leader: For no eye has ever overseen the Garden of Eden,
where the righteous circle the place of the dance, and the holy
Presence among them.

Cong: And they point to Him, saying with awe, "It is He!
"The One for whom we longed when we were captives, in our
powerful faith.

Leader: "And He will lead us in both worlds; and He will lead us dancing,
as if we were young again;
lead us to our land, set aside from the beginning of the world
for us."

Cong: He plays with the Leviathan, with the Behemoth of the
high mountain,
and when they wrestle one another in their great duel,

Leader: the horns of the great Behemoth will gore,
and the mighty Leviathan will leap out at him with his fins,

Cong: and finally, his Creator will step forward with His great sword,
and prepare a meal, a feast, of that meat, for all the righteous.

Leader: And they shall sit at tables of rubies and gems,
with rivers of balsam flowing before them,

Cong: and quench their thirst in luxury with overflowing cups
of the wondrous wine stored up for them since the first days
of creation.

Leader: My righteous listeners, as you have heard the praises in this song,
so may you be promised a place in those joyous circles.

Cong: And may you merit to sit in those heavenly rows,
for heeding God's words, which come forth in splendor.

Leader: Our God is in the highest heights, the first and the last,
desiring us and cherishing us, and giving us the Torah.

קהל: הֲדָרָא דְלָא אֶפְשַׁר לְמִפְרַט שְׁפוּתָא
וְלָא אִשְׁתְּמַע וַחֲמֵי נְבִיאָן חֶזְוָתָא.

ש״ץ: בְּלָא שָׁלְטָא בֵהּ עֵין, בְּגוֹ עֵדֶן גִּנְּתָא
מְטַיְּלֵי בֵהּ חִנְגָּא לְבַהֲדֵי דְשְׁכִינְתָא.

קהל: עֲלֵהּ רָמְזֵי דֵין הוּא, בְּרַם בְּאֵימְתָנוּתָא
שַׂבְרְנָא לֵהּ בְּשִׁבְיַן, תְּקוֹף הֵמָנוּתָא.

ש״ץ: יַדְבֵּר לַן עָלְמִין, עָלְמִין מְדַמּוּתָא
מְנָת דִּילַן דְּמִלְּקַדְמִין פָּרֵשׁ בַּאֲרָמוּתָא.

קהל: טְלוּלָא דְלִוְיָתָן וְתוֹר טוּר רָמוּתָא
וְחַד בְּחַד כִּי סָבֵךְ וְעָבֵד קְרָבוּתָא.

ש״ץ: בְּקַרְנוֹהִי מְנַגַּח בְּהֵמוֹת בִּרְבוּתָא
יְקַרְטַע נוּן לְקִבְלֵהּ בְּצִיצוֹי בִּגְבוּרְתָא.

קהל: מְקָרֵב לֵהּ בָּרְיֵהּ בְּחַרְבֵּהּ בְּרַבְרְבוּתָא
אֲרִסְטוֹן לְצַדִּיקֵי יְתַקֵּן, וְשֵׁרוּתָא.

ש״ץ: מְסַחֲרִין עֲלֵי תַכֵּי דְּכַדְכֹּד וְגוּמַרְתָּא
נְגִידִין קָמֵיהוֹן אֲפַרְסְמוֹן נַהֲרָתָא.

קהל: וּמִתְפַּנְּקִין וְרָווֹ בְּכָסֵי רְוָיָתָא
חֲמַר מְרַת דְּמִבְּרֵאשִׁית נְטִיר בֵּי נַעֲוָתָא.

ש״ץ: זַכָּאִין, כַּד שְׁמַעְתּוּן שְׁבַח דָּא שִׁירָתָא
קְבִיעִין כֵּן תֶּהֱווּן בְּהַנְהוּ חֲבוּרָתָא.

קהל: וְתִזְכּוּן דִּי תֵיתְּבוּן בְּעֵלָּא דָרָתָא
אֲרֵי תְצִיתוּן לְמִלּוֹי, דְּנָפְקִין בְּהַדְרָתָא.

ש״ץ: מְרוֹמַם הוּא אֱלָהִין בְּקַדְמְתָא וּבַתְרַיְתָא
צְבִי וְאִתְרְעִי בַן, וּמְסַר לַן אוֹרַיְתָא.

TORAH READING FOR THE FIRST DAY OF SHAVUOT

19 1 On the first day of the third month after the Israelites had left *Exodus*
2 Egypt they came to the Sinai Desert. Setting out from Refidim they
had arrived at the Sinai Desert, encamping in the wilderness, and
3 there Israel camped, facing the mountain, while Moses went up
to God. And the Lord called to him from the mountain: "This
is what you shall say to the House of Jacob, what you shall tell
4 the people of Israel: You yourselves have seen what I did to the

---

such, and the *beit din* acted only as the agent and representative of the people. The *sefer Torah* symbolizes the community as one entity. (A reminder of this practice is found in our custom of announcing the new month. While holding the *sefer Torah* in his embrace, the cantor demonstratively makes the solemn proclamation, *"Ḥaverim kol Yisrael,* All Israel is united in fellowship.") (*Halakhic Morality*, pp. 184–185)

וּמֹשֶׁה עָלָה אֶל־הָאֱלֹהִים *While Moses went up to God.* Halakhic man received the Torah from Sinai not as a simple recipient but as a creator of worlds, as a partner with the Almighty in the act of creation. The power of creative interpretation (*ḥiddush*) is the very foundation of the received tradition. When Moses ascended on high, he found the Holy One, blessed be He, sitting there tying crowns to the letters that future generations should, by virtue of their powers of creative interpretation, discover heaps upon heaps contained in every tittle (see *Menaḥot* 29b). All new, creative insights that a bright student will glean are an integral part of the Oral Law (see Y. *Peah* 2:6; Lev. Rabbah 22:1). "Only man is capable of creative interpretation (*ḥiddush*), something which is beyond the power of angels, for since the Holy One, blessed be He, created them in a state of perfection, they need not and, therefore, cannot develop and progress. But this is not the case with man, for he progresses and his intellect gains ever-increasing strength. Thus the sages have added fences and guards [around the law] which would not be possible had the Torah been given to the angels. For in that case it would remain forever unchanged, without addition or diminution" (R. Ḥayyim Volozhin, *Ruaḥ Ḥayyim*, on *Avot* 6:1). The essence of the Torah is intellectual creativity. (*Halakhic Man*, pp. 81–82)

כֹּה תֹאמַר לְבֵית יַעֲקֹב וְתַגֵּיד לִבְנֵי יִשְׂרָאֵל *This is what you shall say to the House of Jacob, what you shall tell the people of Israel.* People are mistaken in thinking

קריאת התורה ליום טוב ראשון של שבועות

יט א בַּחֹ֙דֶשׁ֙ הַשְּׁלִישִׁ֔י לְצֵ֥את בְּנֵֽי־יִשְׂרָאֵ֖ל מֵאֶ֣רֶץ מִצְרָ֑יִם בַּיּ֣וֹם הַזֶּ֔ה שמות
ב בָּ֖אוּ מִדְבַּ֥ר סִינָֽי׃ וַיִּסְע֣וּ מֵרְפִידִ֗ים וַיָּבֹ֙אוּ֙ מִדְבַּ֣ר סִינַ֔י וַֽיַּחֲנ֖וּ בַּמִּדְבָּ֑ר
ג וַיִּֽחַן־שָׁ֥ם יִשְׂרָאֵ֖ל נֶ֥גֶד הָהָֽר׃ וּמֹשֶׁ֥ה עָלָ֖ה אֶל־הָאֱלֹהִ֑ים וַיִּקְרָ֨א
אֵלָ֤יו יְהוָה֙ מִן־הָהָ֣ר לֵאמֹ֔ר כֹּ֤ה תֹאמַר֙ לְבֵ֣ית יַעֲקֹ֔ב וְתַגֵּ֖יד לִבְנֵ֥י
ד יִשְׂרָאֵֽל׃ אַתֶּ֣ם רְאִיתֶ֔ם אֲשֶׁ֥ר עָשִׂ֖יתִי לְמִצְרָ֑יִם וָאֶשָּׂ֤א אֶתְכֶם֙

TORAH READING FOR THE FIRST DAY

וַיִּחַן־שָׁם יִשְׂרָאֵל נֶגֶד הָהָר *And there Israel camped, facing the mountain.* We are individuals, unique and different from each other; our notions, emotions, aspirations and visions are incompatible. As such, we are floating on the tide of ceaseless change and continuous passing away in the play of perpetual movement. But we are also representatives of *Keneset Yisrael,* an idealized, hypostatized, invisible entity that lays claim to sameness at all times and for all subjects – a covenantal community, bound to God and eternity. A subjective, changing, evanescent community could not keep a rendezvous with God. If this community would change with each generation – or if we ourselves change at different moments – how could it assume commitments to God forever?

The Jew is a history-minded being with a wealth and variety of radical differences dividing generations at a historical level and individuals at a psychological one. The Jew continually sheds old identities and appears in new roles, steadily witnessing the outburst of new thoughts and changing views, values and commitments. Therefore, the fulfillment of the mitzvot was considered a unifying factor, as it emphasizes what is universal in all members of the covenantal community. It consolidates many individuals who are different in temper, habits and modes of thinking and feeling into one uniform body whose duties, as well as whose ways of implementing these duties, are identical. No wonder that wherever the unity and identity of the Jewish people has to be demonstrated, a *sefer Torah* serves as the symbol of this identical, undifferentiated community. *Pirkei DeRabbi Eliezer* (chap. 7) tells us that the *beit din,* the court which was charged with the task of fixing an additional month, would pronounce the leap year while holding a *sefer Torah.* The authority to fix the calendar was conferred upon the people as

Egyptians: how I lifted you up on eagles' wings and brought you
5 to Me. Now, if you faithfully heed My voice and keep My cov-
enant, you will be My treasure among all the peoples, although

---

The laws of Shabbat, for instance, were passed on to me by my father; they are a part of *mussar avikha*. The Shabbat as a living entity, as a queen, was revealed to me by my mother; it is a part of *torat imekha*. The fathers knew much about the Shabbat; the mothers lived the Shabbat, experienced her presence, and perceived her beauty and splendor. The fathers taught generations how to observe the Shabbat; mothers taught generations how to greet the Shabbat and how to enjoy her twenty-four-hour presence. ("A Tribute to the Rebbitzen of Talne," p. 5)

וִהְיִיתֶם לִי סְגֻלָּה מִכָּל־הָעַמִּים *You will be My treasure among all the peoples.* The word "singular" means "being only one," "exceptional," "extraordinary" and "separate." The word *segulah* in Hebrew similarly connotes singularity. The Torah enunciates the doctrine of the election of Israel as a cardinal tenet of our faith. "You will be My *segulah* among all the peoples." The word *segulah* is interpreted by Rashi as referring to "a cherished treasure, comparable to costly vessels and precious stones for which a king has a special regard." *Segulah* may also describe relationships between people. For example, Jacob loved Rachel but he did not hate Leah, despite the verse, "And the Eternal saw that Leah was unloved" (*senu'ah*) (Gen. 29:31). His bond to her merely suffered by comparison with Rachel, as in the verse, "And he [Jacob] loved Rachel more than Leah" (ibid. v. 30). He had no reason to feel any animosity toward her. But his relationship with Rachel was singular. Similarly, Jacob loved Joseph and Benjamin, Rachel's children, differently than he loved his other sons. Judah described this succinctly: "his [Jacob's] soul is bound up with the lad's soul" (ibid. 44:30). There was a *segulah* dimension in these special loves. It involved an intertwining of souls, a union beyond verbal description. It was more than emotional love; it was a oneness achieved, which is the highest rung of identification. A *segulah* love is an ontological merger.

Similarly, the people of Israel are a *segulah* people, singularly valued by God; this involves no denigration of other nations. It is a specialness – a nation, one of its kind, which God has designated to preserve and disseminate His divine teachings. (*Reflections of the Rav*, pp. 119–120)

ה עַל־כַּנְפֵי נְשָׁרִים וָאָבִא אֶתְכֶם אֵלָי׃ וְעַתָּה אִם־שָׁמוֹעַ תִּשְׁמְעוּ
בְּקֹלִי וּשְׁמַרְתֶּם אֶת־בְּרִיתִי וִהְיִיתֶם לִי סְגֻלָּה מִכָּל־הָעַמִּים

---

that there is only one *masorah* and one *masorah* community, the community of the fathers. It is not true. We have two *masorot,* two traditions, two communities, two *shalshelot hakabbalah* – the *masorah* community of the fathers and that of the mothers. "This is what you shall say to the House of Jacob [the women], what you shall tell the people of Israel [the men]." "Hear my son the instruction of thy father (*mussar avikha*) and forsake not the teaching of thy mother (*torat imekha*)" (Prov. 1:8), counseled the old king. What is the difference between those two *masorot*? What is the distinction between *mussar avikha* and *torat imekha*? Let us explore what one learns from the father and what one learns from the mother. One learns much from father: how to read a text – the Bible or the Talmud – how to comprehend, how to analyze, how to conceptualize, how to classify, how to infer, how to apply, etc. One also learns from father what to do and what not to do, what is morally right and what is morally wrong. Father teaches the son the discipline of thought as well as the discipline of action. Father's tradition is an intellectual-moral one. That is why it is identified with *mussar,* which is the biblical term for discipline.

What is *torat imekha*? What kind of a Torah does the mother pass on? I admit that I am not able to define precisely the masoretic role of the Jewish mother. Only by circumscription I hope to be able to explain it. Permit me to draw upon my own experiences. I used to have long conversations with my mother. In fact, it was a monologue rather than a dialogue. She talked and I "happened" to overhear. What did she talk about? I must use a halakhic term in order to answer this question: she talked *me'inyana deyoma.* I used to watch her arranging the house in honor of a holiday. I used to see her recite prayers; I used to watch her recite the *sidra* every Friday night and I still remember the nostalgic tune. I learned from her very much. Most of all I learned that Judaism expresses itself not only in formal compliance with the law but also in a living experience. She taught me that there is a flavor, a scent and warmth to mitzvot. I learned from her the most important thing in life – to feel the presence of the Almighty and the gentle pressure of His hand resting upon my frail shoulders. Without her teachings, which quite often were transmitted to me in silence, I would have grown up a soulless being, dry and insensitive.

6 the whole earth is Mine. A kingdom of priests and a holy nation
you shall be to Me. These are the words you must speak to the
7 Israelites." So Moses came and summoned the elders of the peo- LEVI
ple, and set before them all that the LORD had commanded him.

---

kingdom of priests and a holy nation. This promise is new. Abraham was never told of a *mamlekhet kohanim*, "a kingdom of priests." He was promised a great nation – "and I will make of you a great nation" (Gen. 12:2) – yet never was the future priestly role of his children mentioned. This indicates a new phase in the covenant; however, this does not convey to us the idea of an entirely new covenant.

We may say that the new aspect in the Sinaitic covenant is the idea of *mamlekhet kohanim,* a "divine-human kingdom." God speaking from the flame had anticipated this hour: "And I will take you to Me as a people, and I will be to you a God" (Ex. 6:7). Now He proclaims that the moment has come, and the idea of the kingdom may be realized. (*The Emergence of Ethical Man*, pp. 193–195)

וְגוֹי קָדוֹשׁ *And a holy nation. Kedushah* fascinates; man in all his aspirations, hopes, visions, dreams, and yearning is out to realize the idea of holiness, to find God and cling to him. *Kedushah* has a strange quality; it frightens people, but it also pulls and attracts them. It is daunting with regard to those who refuse to think, to feel, to delve within themselves, to understand the mystery of man and his strange destiny. However, for those blessed with sweep of imagination, depth of perception, breadth of thought, and boldness of character, *kedushah* is the most fascinating experience, pulling them unconsciously and instinctually to the Creator. At times, it is hard to protect oneself against the onslaught of *kedushah*; it is hard to run away from the Creator, who trails behind man and challenges him to come back. (*Abraham's Journey*, pp. 60–61)

וַיָּבֹא מֹשֶׁה וַיִּקְרָא לְזִקְנֵי הָעָם וַיָּשֶׂם לִפְנֵיהֶם אֵת כָּל־הַדְּבָרִים הָאֵלֶּה אֲשֶׁר צִוָּהוּ יהוה *So Moses came and summoned the elders of the people, and set before them all that the Lord had commanded him.* Moses was not immortalized as a political hero or a strategist. Moses was immortalized as a teacher. We do not say *Moshe Go'alenu*, or *Moshe Moshi'enu*, or *Moshe Meshiḥenu*; we say *Moshe Rabbenu*. Calling him *Moshe Go'alenu*, Moses our Redeemer, would be blasphemy. Man cannot usurp God's attributes of power. A man who calls himself powerful is

ו כִּֽי־לִ֖י כׇּל־הָאָֽרֶץ׃ וְאַתֶּ֧ם תִּהְיוּ־לִ֛י מַמְלֶ֥כֶת כֹּהֲנִ֖ים וְג֣וֹי קָד֑וֹשׁ
ז אֵ֚לֶּה הַדְּבָרִ֔ים אֲשֶׁ֥ר תְּדַבֵּ֖ר אֶל־בְּנֵ֥י יִשְׂרָאֵֽל׃ *וַיָּבֹ֣א מֹשֶׁ֔ה וַיִּקְרָ֖א לוי
לְזִקְנֵ֣י הָעָ֑ם וַיָּ֣שֶׂם לִפְנֵיהֶ֗ם אֵ֚ת כׇּל־הַדְּבָרִ֣ים הָאֵ֔לֶּה אֲשֶׁ֥ר צִוָּ֖הוּ

כִּי־לִי כׇּל־הָאָרֶץ *Although the whole earth is Mine.* When God gave the Law to the people at Mount Sinai, he said, "Now if you faithfully heed My voice and keep My covenant, you will be My treasure among all the peoples, כִּי לִי כׇּל הָאָרֶץ, although the whole earth is Mine." God meant to say: I am giving the Law to you, and you will become My firstborn. You will be My precious child, but don't think for a single moment that I am going to abandon the world or abolish humanity. Yes, you will be elected. I will be on intimate terms with you. You will be My messengers, My priests. But the rest of the world will not be abandoned, כִּי לִי כׇּל הָאָרֶץ. (*Festival of Freedom*, p. 146)

מַמְלֶכֶת כֹּהֲנִים *A kingdom of priests.* The Bible critics, advocates of the "Kenite Hypothesis," claim that "If God had been the God of Israel even before Moses, a covenant would have been superfluous" (Buber, *Moses*, p. 42). The covenant concluded with the patriarchs would have been sufficient for the constitution of Israel's relationship with God. For this reason, they maintain, Israel and God did not hitherto know each other. Apparently, these scholars interpreted the covenant episode at Sinai as the conclusion of a new agreement. Yet, reading the chapters in Exodus which deal with the covenant, we do not discover that the Bible conceives it as something new. On the contrary, the narrative emphasizes the historical character of the occurrence. It never mentions that this was a surprise performance on the part of God.

The first divine message to Israel begins with the following words: "This is what you shall say to the House of Jacob, what you shall tell the people of Israel." God addresses Himself not to a new people, to strangers, but to the house of Jacob and to the children of Israel. A historical reference to an old bond of companionship is quite obvious. The middle part of the speech (the conditional part) – "Now if you faithfully heed My voice and keep My covenant, you will be My treasure among all the peoples" – does not make a new offer of a covenant, but speaks of an old agreement which has been in existence for a long time. The only new element in this message is the closing sentence: "...you will be My treasure among all the peoples... A kingdom of priests and a holy nation you shall be to Me."

By observing the covenant, the people will be a unique treasure and a

8 And the people answered as one – "All that the LORD has spoken
9 we will do." Moses brought their answer back to the LORD. Then
the LORD said to Moses, "I will come to you in a dense cloud, that
the people may hear Me speaking to you. They will then believe
you forever." When Moses reported the words of the people to
10 the LORD, the LORD said to Moses, "Go to the people and con-
secrate them today and tomorrow; let them wash their clothes
11 and be ready for the third day, for on that third day the LORD will

---

my youngest brother. And there are hundreds of memories like that. This common past is a tremendous bond. The fraternal experience also includes a common future, a common destiny. This common future is more of a depth experience than a surface experience. We have to dig into the recesses of our awareness in order to discover the element of common destiny.

As Jews, we have a living memory which spans centuries and millennia. We also have an awareness of a common destiny. The past is real to us; the future is also real – as real as the past. Basically, this memory of the past together with anticipation of the future are two experiences of brothers. And since Jews are brothers, "our brethren all the house of Israel," that is what unites us: the common past and the common future. (*Vision and Leadership*, pp. 3–4)

וְהָיוּ נְכֹנִים לַיּוֹם הַשְּׁלִישִׁי *And be ready for the third day.* When the man of destiny stands before the Almighty, he envisions the God of Israel who reveals Himself only with man's approval and invitation. The God of Israel is united with the finite creature only after man has sanctified and cleansed himself from all pollution, and longingly and agitatedly awaits this wondrous encounter. The revelation of the God of Israel does not come, in any event, in all conditions and circumstances. It demands a special state of spirit and soul, in the manner of "and be ready for the third day." Without the readiness of man, the God of Israel will not reveal Himself. He does not surprise His creatures. He responds to man's urgent petition. However, when man does not actively long for God with spiritual intensity, then the God of Israel shows no interest in him. When the God of the Hebrews chases after man against his will, He does not ask him for his opinion or desires. The God of Israel, however, consults with a person before an encounter. Already in Egypt the Holy One revealed Himself to Moses not only as the God of the Hebrews but also as the God of Israel who waits for man and invites him to His

ח יְהוָה: וַיַּעֲנוּ כָל־הָעָם יַחְדָּו וַיֹּאמְרוּ כֹּל אֲשֶׁר־דִּבֶּר יְהוָה נַעֲשֶׂה
ט וַיָּשֶׁב מֹשֶׁה אֶת־דִּבְרֵי הָעָם אֶל־יְהוָה: וַיֹּאמֶר יְהוָה אֶל־מֹשֶׁה
הִנֵּה אָנֹכִי בָּא אֵלֶיךָ בְּעַב הֶעָנָן בַּעֲבוּר יִשְׁמַע הָעָם בְּדַבְּרִי
עִמָּךְ וְגַם־בְּךָ יַאֲמִינוּ לְעוֹלָם וַיַּגֵּד מֹשֶׁה אֶת־דִּבְרֵי הָעָם אֶל־
י יְהוָה: וַיֹּאמֶר יְהוָה אֶל־מֹשֶׁה לֵךְ אֶל־הָעָם וְקִדַּשְׁתָּם הַיּוֹם
יא וּמָחָר וְכִבְּסוּ שִׂמְלֹתָם: וְהָיוּ נְכֹנִים לַיּוֹם הַשְּׁלִישִׁי כִּי ׀ בַּיּוֹם

---

nothing but an idiot. A malignant little cell kills the most powerful man, and nothing can stop it. It is ridiculous to speak of man as powerful.

Moses was not the political architect of the Jewish people, but he was the architect of our spiritual history. Why is it permissible to say that Moses is our teacher, and wrong to say that he is our liberator and redeemer? The teacher of mankind, and particularly of the Jewish community, is the Almighty. Behind every teacher, every *melammed,* every *rosh yeshivah,* stands God. The attributes of wisdom, knowledge, kindness, and grace belong exclusively to God, but man has a right – even a duty – to usurp them, to take something of God's attributes for himself. He is duty-bound to imitate God – not regarding power, but regarding teaching. (*Festival of Freedom,* pp. 155–156)

וַיַּעֲנוּ כָל־הָעָם יַחְדָּו *And the people answered as one.* A nation is not a clan. It is an entity *per se,* a personality, an individuality. It is not a collective thing integrated of the many, but an aboriginal unity. *Keneset Yisrael,* corporate Israel, is a being. It exists in the same manner as I, you and he exist. For instance, we believe that the Promised Land belongs to us. To whom? To me, to you, to him? To all of us? No! It belongs not to one of us, nor to all of us in partnership! It belongs to *Keneset Yisrael* as an individuality, an original being. *Keneset Yisrael* may encompass all of mankind, since everybody can join through *gerut,* conversion. No racial legitimation is required. (*Family Redeemed,* p. 124)

בַּעֲבוּר יִשְׁמַע הָעָם בְּדַבְּרִי עִמָּךְ וְגַם־בְּךָ יַאֲמִינוּ לְעוֹלָם *That the people may hear Me speaking to you. They will then believe you forever.* Brotherhood involves a common past and common memories. I remember when I was seven or eight, I saved up money to buy ice cream (which was a paradisiacal treat because we were very poor) and I shared it with my brother. This is a memory that unites me with him. It did not unite me with my sisters, nor did it unite me with

12 descend on Mount Sinai before all the people's eyes. Set a bound-
ary for the people around the mountain; tell them to take care
not to ascend to it, nor even touch its edge. Anyone who touches
13 the mountain must be put to death. No hand shall touch him: he
shall be stoned or shot with arrows; beast or man, he shall not live.
When the ram's horn sounds a long blast – only then may they go
14 up on the mountain." So Moses came down from the mountain to SHELISHI
15 the people; he consecrated them and they cleansed their clothes.
"Be ready for the third day," he told them, "and do not draw close
16 to your wives." The third day came; and that morning there was
thunder and lightning and a dense cloud on the mountain and
the sound of a ram's horn, intensely loud, and all the people in the
17 camp shook. Then Moses led the people out of the camp to meet

---

is fulfilled by coming closer to God. The spirit that longs for its divine lover wraps itself in the grandeur of His might. It turns, fades, and disappears into the terrible Infinity that fills everything and surrounds everything, that causes everything and outlasts everything.

"Set a boundary for the people around the mountain; tell them to take care not to ascend it, not even touch its edge"; "Let them not go inside and look at the sacred objects as they are being covered, lest they die" (Num. 4:20). The people of Bet Shemesh peeked and died (I Sam. 6:19). Man must not come too close to God. "You cannot see My face" (Ex. 33:20). Vision of God annihilates everything. "He is not to come at will into the Sanctuary... for I appear in the cloud" (Lev. 16:2). A priest who enters the *Heikhal,* the Sanctuary, is flogged, but if he enters the Holy of Holies he is punishable by death at the hands of God. He must not enter the place where the *Shekhinah* is located. One who utters the holy name of God in vain has transgressed a negative commandment. One who pronounces an unnecessary benediction has also transgressed a negative commandment. The Halakhah, in its sober, simple way, expresses a sublime metaphysical idea. Sometimes it is necessary for there to be a tension of great fear that is manifested in retreat. (*And From There You Shall Seek*, pp. 63–64)

וַיֶּחֱרַד כָּל־הָעָם אֲשֶׁר בַּמַּחֲנֶה *And all the people in the camp shook.* At Sinai, *mattan Torah* was an isolated event whose purpose was to confirm the covenant between the Almighty and the descendants of Abraham, Isaac, and

יב הַשְּׁלִשִׁי יֵרֵד יְהוָה לְעֵינֵי כָל־הָעָם עַל־הַר סִינָי: וְהִגְבַּלְתָּ אֶת־
הָעָם סָבִיב לֵאמֹר הִשָּׁמְרוּ לָכֶם עֲלוֹת בָּהָר וּנְגֹעַ בְּקָצֵהוּ כָּל־
יג הַנֹּגֵעַ בָּהָר מוֹת יוּמָת: לֹא־תִגַּע בּוֹ יָד כִּי־סָקוֹל יִסָּקֵל אוֹ־יָרֹה
יִיָּרֶה אִם־בְּהֵמָה אִם־אִישׁ לֹא יִחְיֶה בִּמְשֹׁךְ הַיֹּבֵל הֵמָּה יַעֲלוּ
יד בָהָר: *וַיֵּרֶד מֹשֶׁה מִן־הָהָר אֶל־הָעָם וַיְקַדֵּשׁ אֶת־הָעָם וַיְכַבְּסוּ שלישי
טו שִׂמְלֹתָם: וַיֹּאמֶר אֶל־הָעָם הֱיוּ נְכֹנִים לִשְׁלֹשֶׁת יָמִים אַל־תִּגְּשׁוּ
טז אֶל־אִשָּׁה: וַיְהִי בַיּוֹם הַשְּׁלִישִׁי בִּהְיֹת הַבֹּקֶר וַיְהִי קֹלֹת וּבְרָקִים
וְעָנָן כָּבֵד עַל־הָהָר וְקֹל שֹׁפָר חָזָק מְאֹד וַיֶּחֱרַד כָּל־הָעָם אֲשֶׁר
יז בַּמַּחֲנֶה: וַיּוֹצֵא מֹשֶׁה אֶת־הָעָם לִקְרַאת הָאֱלֹהִים מִן־הַמַּחֲנֶה

---

service to do His work. "So said the Lord, the God of Israel: Let my people go, that they shall make a feast unto Me in the wilderness" (Ex. 5:1). (*Fate and Destiny*, pp. 56–57)

לְעֵינֵי כָל־הָעָם עַל־הַר סִינָי *On Mount Sinai before all the people's eyes. Mattan Torah,* the giving of the Torah, initiated the messianic process of redeeming the world from its crudity and profanity. The Torah was given to the Jew, who was told to disseminate the word of God among pagans, atheists, agnostics, and hedonists, thereby bringing them to their Maker. It is a piecemeal, slow movement. Nevertheless, it will be consummated in the messianic era, when "the mountain of the Lord's house shall be established on the top of the mountains" (Isa. 2:2). *Mattan Torah* is bound up with the Messiah, who will possess the heroism of his grandmothers whom the Almighty found in the non-Jewish world. They represented the heroism of loneliness, the heroism of universal commitment, and the heroism of faith and waiting. The ideal of *mattan Torah* will be fully realized only in the time of the Messiah. (*Abraham's Journey*, p. 183)

וְהִגְבַּלְתָּ אֶת־הָעָם סָבִיב *Set a boundary for the people.* The creation's cleaving to the Creator involves the abrogation of the self as well as of the world's independence. It is a submerging of the finite in the infinite. The world exists when it folds up inside itself. It loses its existence when it breaks out of its circle (and moves) toward God. The fear of the annihilation of being is interwoven with the yearning for the elevation of being, a yearning that

18 God, and they stood at the foot of the mountain. Mount Sinai was
enveloped in smoke because the LORD had descended on it in fire.
Smoke billowed up from it as if from a furnace, and the mountain
19 shook violently as one. As the sound of the ram's horn grew louder
20 and louder, Moses spoke and God answered him aloud. And the REVI'I
LORD descended on Mount Sinai, to the top of the mountain,

---

smoke because the Lord had descended on it in fire. Torah cannot be taught at a low temperature: "Is not My word like fire? says the Lord" (Jer. 23:29). Fire symbolizes passion, emotional excitement, involvement, dedication and consecration. "And the mountain burned with fire unto the heart of heaven" (Deut. 4:11). Why did Mount Sinai burn with a great fire? Why did God want to demonstrate that the Torah was given, the Law was given, through the flame? It symbolizes the eternal dedication and consecration, the emotional outburst, the emotional upheaval, the great love – "For love is strong as death, jealousy is cruel as the grave; the flashes thereof are flashes of fire, a very flame of the Lord" (Song 8:6), a great love burning like a flame which keeps on burning and spreading warmth and heat. You not only know it, you feel it.

Talmud Torah embraces both the intellectual engagement and the commitment to comply with the norm, a decision to make oneself ready to carry this particular burden. But for the decision to be dynamic and powerful, for it to actually become a reality, a volitional act does not suffice; one must get entangled in it emotionally. God's Word becomes a precious treasure, something which lends meaning and purposefulness to one's existence, a great vision which captivates the imagination, that stirs the soul, that gives a feeling of happiness and pleasure, and actually fills me with ecstasy when I think that I will realize the great goal. One not only abides by the Word and the norm but loves it; he is not only committed to it but also devoted and passionately affected. In a word, the kerygma becomes the central value around which one's axiological system revolves, the focus of all emotions and sentiments, that highest good after which one feels a deep yearning and a great longing. It is an ecstatic involvement in God's Word. (*Blessings and Thanksgiving*, pp. 59–60)

וַיֵּרֶד יהוה עַל־הַר סִינַי *And the Lord descended on Mount Sinai.* Infinity contracts itself; eternity concentrates itself in the fleeting and transient, the Divine Presence in dimensions and the glory of God in measurements. It is Judaism

יח וַיִּֽתְיַצְּבוּ בְּתַחְתִּית הָהָר׃ וְהַר סִינַי עָשַׁן כֻּלּוֹ מִפְּנֵי אֲשֶׁר יָרַד
עָלָיו יהוה בָּאֵשׁ וַיַּעַל עֲשָׁנוֹ כְּעֶשֶׁן הַכִּבְשָׁן וַיֶּחֱרַד כָּל־הָהָר
יט מְאֹד׃ וַיְהִי קוֹל הַשֹּׁפָר הוֹלֵךְ וְחָזֵק מְאֹד מֹשֶׁה יְדַבֵּר וְהָאֱלֹהִים
כ יַעֲנֶנּוּ בְקוֹל׃ *וַיֵּרֶד יהוה עַל־הַר סִינַי אֶל־רֹאשׁ הָהָר וַיִּקְרָא רביעי

Jacob. It was an intimate affair, a private wedding binding a single nation with the Holy One the way a covenant binds husband and wife. But *mattan Torah* was also an event of cosmic proportions, one that included not only six hundred thousand ex-slaves, but all of humanity, present and future. "The whole world trembled before You" (Musaf of Rosh Hashanah). There was not a single spot in the cosmos that was not aware that something unique and singular was transpiring. Not only human beings, but the beasts in the field – indeed, all living creatures – were involved in *mattan Torah*. With the arrival of the Messiah and the beginning of the eschatological era, nature – which appears to us not only indifferent but hostile to our dreams, aspirations, and hopes – will also be redeemed. At present, there is no element of *ḥesed* in nature; it is complete *din*. When the world is redeemed by Torah, the element of *ḥesed* will be injected not only in the law guiding society, but in the cosmic behavior of nature. Moral law and the law of nature will merge. Isaiah prophesies, "The wolf shall dwell with the lamb" (Isa. 11:6).

When Moses first ascended to Mount Sinai, the giving of the Torah was accompanied by thunder. The Holy One had to appear to His people in a way that would be audible to all humanity, resounding throughout the entire cosmos. It was necessary because all the peoples of the world had to know that this event would, in the end, have great significance for them and for the whole world. But when the second set of tablets was given, God told Moses, "And no man shall come up with you, neither let any man be seen throughout the entire mountain; neither let the flocks nor herds feed before the mountain" (Ex. 34:3). There was to be complete secrecy. Rashi (Ex. 34:3, s.v. *ve'ish*) explains: "Because the first tablets were given amidst great noises and alarms and a vast assembly, the evil eye had power over them; there is no finer quality than modesty." God told Moses: The world already knows, so I do not need any publicity this second time. Go up quietly. (*Vision and Leadership*, pp. 101–102)

וְהַר סִינַי עָשַׁן כֻּלּוֹ מִפְּנֵי אֲשֶׁר יָרַד עָלָיו יהוה בָּאֵשׁ *Mount Sinai was enveloped in*

21 and called Moses to the mountaintop, and Moses ascended. The
LORD told Moses, "Go back down – warn the people not to force
22 their way through to look at the LORD, or many will die. Even
priests who come near to the LORD must first consecrate them-
23 selves, or the LORD will break out against them." Moses replied to
the LORD, "The people cannot climb Mount Sinai. You Yourself
warned us to set a boundary around the mountain and consecrate
24 it." The LORD said to him, "Go down, and come back together
with Aaron. But do not let the priests or people force their way
through to come up to the LORD, or He will break out against them."
20 25 1 So Moses went down to the people and told them. Then

---

one must build a fence, a simple partition that can physically prevent it from walking into another person's field. A simple marker or sign will not help. A person needs neither partitions nor fences. It is enough to warn him that the territory does not belong to him. His boundary is an abstraction, an intangible separation.

Apparently, God did not want the people to refrain from ascending the mountain because a physical barrier blocked them. Thus He commanded Moses to descend and warn the people so they would restrain themselves because of Moses' command, and not because of a physical constraint.

This idea is a major motif in the Torah. For Jews, there are neither fences nor partitions. The prohibition and the warning alone are enough to prevent a Jew from transgression and wrongdoing. God had to emphasize to Moses that the whole Torah is contained in the words, "*Al yehersu*, do not let them force their way through" (verse 24) – do not break down any abstract boundaries or partitions. Judaism contends that the slave does not understand the concept of a division between sacred and profane, of "do not let them force their way through." The Gemara states, "A slave prefers a dissolute life" (*Gittin* 13a; *Ketubot* 11a). He takes as much as he can. Only physical power can stop him – a task master or a policeman. The most amazing thing about the Exodus, far greater than the signs and wonders, is the transformation of a nation of slaves who lived in a boundless state, who "preferred a dissolute life," who did not understand the meaning of laws and strictures and obeying laws when no taskmaster threatens. (*Festival of Freedom*, pp. 71–72)

כא יהוה לְמֹשֶׁה אֶל־רֹאשׁ הָהָר וַיַּעַל מֹשֶׁה: וַיֹּאמֶר יהוה אֶל־
מֹשֶׁה רֵד הָעֵד בָּעָם פֶּן־יֶהֶרְסוּ אֶל־יהוה לִרְאוֹת וְנָפַל מִמֶּנּוּ
כב רָב: וְגַם הַכֹּהֲנִים הַנִּגָּשִׁים אֶל־יהוה יִתְקַדָּשׁוּ פֶּן־יִפְרֹץ בָּהֶם
כג יהוה: וַיֹּאמֶר מֹשֶׁה אֶל־יהוה לֹא־יוּכַל הָעָם לַעֲלֹת אֶל־הַר
סִינָי כִּי־אַתָּה הַעֵדֹתָה בָּנוּ לֵאמֹר הַגְבֵּל אֶת־הָהָר וְקִדַּשְׁתּוֹ:
כד וַיֹּאמֶר אֵלָיו יהוה לֶךְ־רֵד וְעָלִיתָ אַתָּה וְאַהֲרֹן עִמָּךְ וְהַכֹּהֲנִים
כה וְהָעָם אַל־יֶהֶרְסוּ לַעֲלֹת אֶל־יהוה פֶּן־יִפְרָץ־בָּם: וַיֵּרֶד מֹשֶׁה אֶל־
כ א הָעָם וַיֹּאמֶר אֲלֵהֶם: וַיְדַבֵּר אֱלֹהִים אֵת כָּל־הַדְּבָרִים

---

that has given the world the secret of *tzimtzum*, of "contraction," contraction of the infinite within the finite, the transcendent within the concrete, the supernal within the empirical, and the divine within the realm of reality. When the Holy One, blessed be He, descended on Mount Sinai, He set an eternally binding precedent that it is God who descends to man, not man who ascends to God. When He said to Moses, "And let them make Me a sanctuary, that I may dwell among them" (Ex. 25:8), He thereby revealed the awesome mystery that God contracts His divine presence in this world. (*Halakhic Man*, p. 48)

רֵד הָעֵד בָּעָם פֶּן־יֶהֶרְסוּ אֶל־יהוה לִרְאוֹת וְנָפַל מִמֶּנּוּ רָב *Go back down – warn the people not to force their way through to look at the Lord, or many will die.* Why did the Creator again tell Moses to go down and warn the people and the priests that they were not to overstep the bounds he had marked off? Just a few days earlier, He had already given the command, "Set a boundary for the people around the mountain; tell them to take care not to ascend it, not even touch its edge" (verse 12). Moses had, in fact, carried out this mission. Why, on the day the Torah was given, after He had already called Moses to Him – "And the Lord… called Moses to the mountaintop" (verse 20) – did God once again warn the Jews? Moses himself asked (verse 23), but God ignored his question and told him once again to warn the Jews: "Go down" (verse 24).

There is a difference between the boundary that holds back a human, a rational being, and the boundary that holds back an animal. For an animal,

2 God spoke all these words: "I am the LORD your God
who brought you out of the land of Egypt, out of the house of
3 4 slaves. Have no other gods than Me. Do not make for your-
self any carved image or likeness of any creature in the heavens
above or the earth beneath or the water beneath the earth.
5 Do not bow down to them or worship them, for I the LORD
your God demand absolute loyalty. For those who hate Me, I
hold the descendants to account for the sins of the fathers to
6 the third and fourth generation, but to those who love Me and
keep My commands – I shall act with faithful love for thou-
7 sands. Do not speak the name of the LORD your God in
vain, for the LORD will not hold guiltless those who speak His name
in vain.

(s.v. *al panai*) comments: "that is, as long as I exist; so that you should not say that only that generation [that left Egypt] was enjoined against idolatry." This is a commandment for all generations. (*Vision and Leadership*, pp. 138–139)

לֹא תִשָּׂא אֶת־שֵׁם־יהוה אֱלֹהֶיךָ לַשָּׁוְא כִּי לֹא יְנַקֶּה יהוה אֵת אֲשֶׁר־יִשָּׂא אֶת־שְׁמוֹ לַשָּׁוְא *Do not speak the name of the Lord your God in vain, for the Lord will not hold guiltless those who speak His name in vain.* Onkelos translates the first instance of the word לַשָּׁוְא as לְמַגָּנָא ("in vain") and the second as לְשִׁקְרָא ("falsely"). Rashi says: "for no reason, idly." There are really two different offenses: *sheker* and *shav. Sheker* involves deceit. It is a statement which is not true, but which could be true. *Shav*, on the other hand, involves an obvious lie, such as swearing that a black book is red. It exposes one to humiliation and ridicule and degrades and corrupts the human personality. A man does not own himself; he belongs to God, and consequently, actions such as this involving self-degradation are forbidden.

But there is another aspect of *shav*, namely, to swear to an obvious truth. A man should not talk in stereotypes and cliches. A teacher should not teach if he cannot add anything to human knowledge. If you have nothing to say, do not repeat what everyone knows. It is a violation of human dignity. Modern man is increasingly losing his individuality; he repeats what the news media tell him. The Torah wants one to preserve his individuality. A person should be sure that what he says is meaningful. (*Shiurei Harav*, pp. 118–119)

הָאֵ֥לֶּה לֵאמֹֽר׃ אָֽנֹכִ֖י יְהוָ֣ה אֱלֹהֶ֑יךָ אֲשֶׁ֧ר הוֹצֵאתִ֛יךָ
מֵאֶ֥רֶץ מִצְרַ֖יִם מִבֵּ֣ית עֲבָדִ֑ים׃ לֹֽא־יִהְיֶ֥ה לְךָ֛ אֱלֹהִ֥ים אֲחֵרִ֖ים עַל־
פָּנָֽי לֹ֣א תַעֲשֶׂה־לְךָ֣ פֶ֣סֶל ׀ וְכָל־תְּמוּנָ֗ה אֲשֶׁ֤ר בַּשָּׁמַ֙יִם ׀ מִמַּ֙עַל
וַאֲשֶׁר֙ בָּאָ֣רֶץ מִתָּ֔חַת וַאֲשֶׁ֥ר בַּמַּ֖יִם ׀ מִתַּ֣חַת לָאָ֑רֶץ לֹֽא־תִשְׁתַּחֲוֶ֥ה
לָהֶם֮ וְלֹ֣א תָעָבְדֵ֒ם֒ כִּ֣י אָֽנֹכִ֞י יְהוָ֤ה אֱלֹהֶ֙יךָ֙ אֵ֣ל קַנָּ֔א פֹּ֠קֵד עֲוֺ֨ן
אָבֹ֧ת עַל־בָּנִ֛ים עַל־שִׁלֵּשִׁ֥ים וְעַל־רִבֵּעִ֖ים לְשֹׂנְאָ֑י וְעֹ֤שֶׂה חֶ֙סֶד֙
לַאֲלָפִ֔ים לְאֹהֲבַ֖י וּלְשֹׁמְרֵ֥י מִצְוֺתָֽי׃ לֹ֣א תִשָּׂ֛א אֶת־שֵֽׁם־
יְהוָ֥ה אֱלֹהֶ֖יךָ לַשָּׁ֑וְא כִּ֣י לֹ֤א יְנַקֶּה֙ יְהוָ֔ה אֵ֛ת אֲשֶׁר־יִשָּׂ֥א אֶת־שְׁמ֖וֹ
לַשָּֽׁוְא׃

אֲשֶׁר הוֹצֵאתִיךָ מֵאֶרֶץ מִצְרַיִם *Who brought you out of the land of Egypt.* Interestingly, the word הוֹצֵאתִיךָ, "who brought you out," is formulated in the singular in both Exodus and Deuteronomy. This is because God makes a separate covenant with every Jew individually. When six hundred thousand Jews stood at the foot of the mountain and shouted נַעֲשֶׂה וְנִשְׁמָע (Ex. 24:7), God made a covenant not with the community, not with the crowd, but with each of those Jews separately, just as He had with Abraham centuries before. The Ten Commandments are a confrontation not with six hundred thousand Jews collectively but with each one of them individually. Each of them has his own problems, each of them suffers, each is in despair. God deals with them individually. He likes the individual very much; He likes the lonely person. (*Abraham's Journey*, pp. 145–146)

לֹא־יִהְיֶה לְךָ אֱלֹהִים אֲחֵרִים עַל־פָּנָי *Have no other gods than Me.* Man does not belong to himself. All my aptitudes, capacities, talents, and capabilities are not mine; they were graciously given to me. If man understands this philosophy, then he may become truly great and stand before the Lord. If he tries to usurp power, to embezzle material goods and spiritual riches from God, then he forfeits his greatness, shrinks in personal stature, and becomes a mocking, destructive mephisto-idol. There are many injunctions in the Bible against idol worship. But there is no injunction against atheism, because there is, in truth, no atheism. There are only two choices – the true God or an idol. When a man revolts against God, he thinks he is being flexible and free, but soon he builds himself his own idol and worships himself. Rashi

8 9 Remember the Sabbath to keep it holy. Six days you shall work,
10 and carry out all your labors, but the seventh is a Sabbath to
the LORD your God. On it, do no work – neither you, nor your
son or daughter, your male or female servant, your livestock, or
11 the migrant within your gates. For in six days the LORD made
heaven and earth, the sea, and all that they contain, and He rested
on the seventh day. And so the LORD blessed the Sabbath day

וְיוֹם הַשְּׁבִיעִי שַׁבָּת לַיהוה אֱלֹהֶיךָ *But the seventh is a Sabbath to the LORD your God.* The charisma of *yamim kedoshim* expresses itself in human introspection or withdrawal. The Torah tells us, "Six days you shall work, and carry out all your labors, but the seventh is a Sabbath to the Lord your God." What idea lies behind the strange and enigmatic words "unto the Lord your God"? It would have been sufficient to say that for six days we are allowed to work, but on the seventh day we have to cease working.

I believe that these enigmatic words express an exalted idea in Judaism: *sod hatzimtzum,* the mystery of self-contraction or self-limitation, the mystery of self-restriction, withdrawal, and retreat. *Tzimtzum* means that the creation of the world is a sacrificial act on the part of the Almighty; He gave something up when He said, "Let there be light" (Gen. 1:3). Before the universe came into existence, God was one and His Name was one. By creating a world in general, and man in particular, God surrendered His aloneness and allowed a physical universe to share in His infinite being. He allowed something else to share with Him what had been exclusively His own. God had to withdraw and contract Himself in order to permit a world to be born out of nothingness. Creation means an act of self-restriction on the part of Infinity, permitting finitude to exist beside Infinity. The whole existence of the world is an absurdity, for how can finitude exist beside Infinity? But this absurdity is responsible for our existence. This is the great mystery of *tzimtzum.*

On the Sabbath and every *yom gadol vekadosh,* man is called upon to cease playing the role of master and lord, to acknowledge that he possesses nothing, owns nothing, masters nothing; he is nothing; he is not in control, neither of the work nor of himself, of his own talents and skills. A *yom kadosh* is not so much a day of rest as it is a day of cessation, of stopping, discontinuing, and giving up work. Abstention from work was chosen as the means of man's

זָכוֹר אֶת־יוֹם הַשַּׁבָּת לְקַדְּשׁוֹ שֵׁשֶׁת יָמִים תַּעֲבֹד וְעָשִׂיתָ כׇל־
מְלַאכְתֶּךָ וְיוֹם הַשְּׁבִיעִי שַׁבָּת ׀ לַיהוָה אֱלֹהֶיךָ לֹא תַעֲשֶׂה כׇל־
מְלָאכָה אַתָּה וּבִנְךָ וּבִתֶּךָ עַבְדְּךָ וַאֲמָתְךָ וּבְהֶמְתֶּךָ וְגֵרְךָ אֲשֶׁר
בִּשְׁעָרֶיךָ כִּי שֵׁשֶׁת־יָמִים עָשָׂה יהוה אֶת־הַשָּׁמַיִם וְאֶת־הָאָרֶץ
אֶת־הַיָּם וְאֶת־כׇּל־אֲשֶׁר־בָּם וַיָּנַח בַּיּוֹם הַשְּׁבִיעִי עַל־כֵּן בֵּרַךְ

זָכוֹר אֶת־יוֹם הַשַּׁבָּת לְקַדְּשׁוֹ *Remember the Sabbath to keep it holy.* When we shift our attention from halakhic thinking to halakhic feeling, from halakhic topics to axiological themata, we suddenly find ourselves in a new dimension, namely that of *kedushah,* holiness. Suddenly the Sabbath is transmuted or transformed from an abstract norm, from a formal concept, into a "reality," a living essence, a living entity: from a discipline in accordance with which one acts compulsorily into a great experience which one acts out spontaneously.

Of course, we have many passages in the Bible dealing with the Sabbath, but the basic biblical text containing the Sabbath idea within the topical frame of formal-systematic reference is the passage in the Decalogue dealing with the normative aspect of the Sabbath: "Remember the Sabbath to keep it holy, *lekaddesho.* Six days you shall work, and carry out all your labors, but the seventh is a Sabbath to the Lord your God. On it, do no work – neither you, nor your son..."

The verb *lekaddesho,* to keep it holy, if analyzed in the light of positive topical Halakhah, means only abstention from the daily routine or separation from work. In the topical context, the term *lekaddesho* does not refer to or imply a charismatic quality inherent in the seventh day. It is just set aside as a day in the week on which one must abstain from work; that is all. This is a formal approach to the Sabbath idea.

In contrast to the topical Halakhah, the text which forms the main motto of the thematic Halakhah with regard Shabbat would be, I believe, the mysterious passage in Genesis which concludes the story of creation: "And God blessed the seventh day and hallowed it, *va-yekaddesh oto*" (Gen. 2:3). A twenty-four-hour period was sanctified and hallowed. It has suddenly become a metaphysical entity upon which the Almighty has bestowed a unique endowment, a very strange endowment, namely, that of blessedness and sanctity. (*Out of the Whirlwind*, p. 90)

12 and made it holy. Honor your father and mother.
Then you will live long in the land that the LORD your God is
13 giving you. Do not murder. Do not
commit adultery. Do not steal. Do not
14 bear false witness against your neighbor. Do not

---

acted differently, but, alas, it is no longer possible to undo the damage. (*On Repentance*, pp. 257–258)

If it is correct to speak of our relationship to God in terms of general human relations, it is certainly proper to visualize our approach to the Almighty in terms of the child-parent community. "It is said, 'Honor your father and mother' (Ex. 20:12) and it is also said, '*Kabbed et Hashem mehonekha,* Honor the Lord with your substance' (Prov. 3:9). Thus Scripture compares the honor due to parents to that due to the Omnipresent" *(Kiddushin* 30b). The Baraita does not merely parallel the honor and fear that one is obligated to display towards one's parents with the honor and fear due to the Almighty. The Baraita rather identifies the two acts. When one honors or reveres his natural parent, father or mother, he, *ipso facto*, honors or reveres God. (*Family Redeemed*, pp. 167–168)

לֹא תִּרְצָח. לֹא תִּנְאָף. לֹא תִּגְנֹב *Do not murder. Do not commit adultery. Do not steal.* There is a consistent parallelism between the first commandments and the last ones. The Rabbis noticed that the latter five commandments correspond to the first five. *Anokhi,* the first commandment, corresponds to *lo tirtzaḥ* ("do not murder"), for the murderer reduces the divine image in the world; "do not steal" corresponds to do not take the name of God in vain, for the thief inevitably swear falsely in court, and so on. (See Song of Songs Rabbah 4:5.) Apparently God does not claim any privileges or unique rights. The same measure of honesty, loyalty, devotion which one owes to Him is due to one's fellow man as well, because covenant morality applies to both God and man. Therefore it is hardly possible to speak of ritual and cult in Judaism or of the traditional division of laws into *bein adam leḥavero,* between man and his fellow man, and *bein adam lamakom,* between man and God. One and the same ethos regulates social interrelationships. Man's contact with God should be seen against the backdrop of human-divine society. Even His kingdom should be understood as a political reality located within society. (*The Emergence of Ethical Man*, p. 198)

יְהוָ֖ה אֶת־י֥וֹם הַשַּׁבָּ֖ת וַֽיְקַדְּשֵֽׁהוּ׃ כַּבֵּ֥ד אֶת־אָבִ֖יךָ
וְאֶת־אִמֶּ֑ךָ לְמַ֙עַן֙ יַאֲרִכ֣וּן יָמֶ֔יךָ עַ֚ל הָאֲדָמָ֔ה אֲשֶׁר־יְהוָ֥ה אֱלֹהֶ֖יךָ
נֹתֵ֥ן לָֽךְ׃ לֹ֥א תִּרְצָֽח׃ לֹ֥א
תִּנְאָֽף׃ לֹ֥א תִּגְנֹֽב׃ לֹֽא־
יד תַעֲנֶ֥ה בְרֵעֲךָ֖ עֵ֥ד שָֽׁקֶר׃ לֹ֥א

---

humbling himself and pleading guilty of arrogance, of false pretenses, of an exaggerated notion of himself. Work was chosen by the Torah as the symbol of that basic change in man that ought to take place on a *yom kadosh*. (*Days of Deliverance*, pp. 109–110)

כַּבֵּד אֶת־אָבִיךָ וְאֶת־אִמֶּךָ *Honor your father and mother.* There seems to be a tragic flaw inherent in the nature of man from which no one can escape. The people and things that we love and cherish most are not fully appreciated as long as they are alive and present with us. We realize what they meant to us only after they are gone and their image has become faded and unreal. They seem to twinkle from afar as the stars in the night; we admire them but cannot touch them.

How many near and dear ones did we have whom we did not succeed in appreciating fully, as long as they were with us: mother, father, teacher, wife or husband? I am not speaking of those people who failed to properly observe the precept of honoring their father and mother or of those who neglected to show due respect to their teachers or love to their marital partner. I am speaking, specifically, of those who showed the utmost honor to their parents and who esteemed their teachers and were dedicated to their husband or wife. Even these people must suffer the burden of feelings of guilt for not having done what they could while their loved ones were still alive. Whoever fails to be tormented by such remorse does not know the real meaning of grief for a dearly loved one who is gone forever.

The practices relating to *shiva* (the initial seven-day period of mourning) and *shloshim* (the first thirty days after death) and the year of mourning are all practices of mourning which the sages have instituted in accordance with the nature of man. But the essence of mourning consists not only of grief for one who has gone but also in the pain of "would that I could" – if I only could, I would make amends now for what I didn't do when I could have

crave your neighbor's house. Do not
crave your neighbor's wife, his male or female servant, his ox, his
donkey, or anything else that is your neighbor's."

15 Every one of the people witnessed the thunder and lightning HAMISHI
and the sound of the ram's horn and the smoke-covered
mountain; they saw and they shook – and they stood at a dis-
16 tance, and said to Moses, "Speak to us yourself and we will listen,
17 but let not God say any more to us, or we will die." "Do not be
afraid," said Moses to the people, "God has come to lift you up,
so that the awe of Him will be with you always, keeping you
18 from sin." But the people remained at a distance while Moses
19 approached the thick darkness where God was. Then
the Lord said to Moses, "This is what you shall tell the Israelites:

---

from the Lord God" (Gen. 3:8); "...they saw and they shook – and they stood at a distance, and said to Moses, 'Speak to us yourself and we will listen, but let not God say any more to us, or we will die'"; "...the men who were with me did not see the vision, yet they were seized with great terror and fled into hiding" (Dan. 10:7). At times man fears God and runs away from Him, but God overtakes him. He hides, and God seeks him. God overtakes man when he is in distress, when man tries to elude Him; when the captive strives to loosen the bonds of the Absolute and remove its yoke, he falls wallowing in his failure. Jonah tried to escape but did not succeed. The revelation of the *Shekhinah* reveals the tension between finitude and infinity. The creature is weighed down by the burden of eternity, and when he rebels, his rebellion is in vain. When God reveals Himself to man, He does so not in order to realize an intellectual, scientific goal – to tell him about the cosmic drama – but to command him and to give him the responsibility for keeping laws and statutes, positive and negative commandments. The God of Sinai is the God of the Will, the Inscrutable One who commands us to follow a unique way of life without explaining why or for what purpose. This Will reveals itself to man, but instead of telling him the secrets of creation, it demands unlimited discipline absolute surrender. There is no refuge from God. (*And From There You Shall Seek*, pp. 34–35)

תַחְמֹד בֵּית רֵעֶךָ לֹא־
תַחְמֹד אֵשֶׁת רֵעֶךָ וְעַבְדּוֹ וַאֲמָתוֹ וְשׁוֹרוֹ וַחֲמֹרוֹ וְכֹל אֲשֶׁר
לְרֵעֶךָ׃
טו וְכָל־הָעָם רֹאִים אֶת־הַקּוֹלֹת וְאֶת־הַלַּפִּידִם וְאֵת קוֹל הַשֹּׁפָר חמישי
טז וְאֶת־הָהָר עָשֵׁן וַיַּרְא הָעָם וַיָּנֻעוּ וַיַּעַמְדוּ מֵרָחֹק׃ וַיֹּאמְרוּ אֶל־
מֹשֶׁה דַּבֵּר־אַתָּה עִמָּנוּ וְנִשְׁמָעָה וְאַל־יְדַבֵּר עִמָּנוּ אֱלֹהִים פֶּן־
יז נָמוּת׃ וַיֹּאמֶר מֹשֶׁה אֶל־הָעָם אַל־תִּירָאוּ כִּי לְבַעֲבוּר נַסּוֹת
אֶתְכֶם בָּא הָאֱלֹהִים וּבַעֲבוּר תִּהְיֶה יִרְאָתוֹ עַל־פְּנֵיכֶם לְבִלְתִּי
יח תֶחֱטָאוּ׃ וַיַּעֲמֹד הָעָם מֵרָחֹק וּמֹשֶׁה נִגַּשׁ אֶל־הָעֲרָפֶל אֲשֶׁר־
יט שָׁם הָאֱלֹהִים׃ וַיֹּאמֶר יהוה אֶל־מֹשֶׁה כֹּה תֹאמַר

לֹא־תַחְמֹד *Do not crave.* I was very envious as a child. I was envious of my friends, because they did not consider me a bright child. This impression was created because I was intellectually honest. I would declare that I did not comprehend a topic when I did not truly understand it. I was very envious of another child in *ḥeder,* who was reputed to know one hundred pages of the Talmud by heart. I remember my father called me in once and told me that envy is a *middah megunah,* a deplorable trait, a bad habit, an emotional enemy. These emotions have been forbidden by the Torah: לֹא תַחְמֹד, "Do not crave," וְלֹא תִתְאַוֶּה, "and do not desire" (Deut. 5:18). I began to train myself to overcome my envy, and I succeeded. Now there is no envy in my heart. On the contrary, I rejoice in the success of my fellow man. The Torah demanded of man to integrate into his personality constructive, cathartic emotions such as sympathy, love, and gratitude. One has freedom not only to control his physical acts but also to control his emotional life. (*Vision and Leadership,* pp. 64–65)

וְאַל־יְדַבֵּר עִמָּנוּ אֱלֹהִים פֶּן־נָמוּת *But let not God say any more to us, or we will die.* When man wants to avoid God's revelation, God seizes him; God closes in on him and there is no escape. If the creature attempts to run away and escape from the great, awesome God, God pursues him. "Adam and his wife hid

You yourselves have seen that I, from the heavens, have spoken to
20 you. Have no others alongside Me; make yourselves no silver gods,
21 no golden gods. Make for Me an altar of earth and on that sacrifice

---

design. Any object or any form which is considered as a representation of deity, or as endowed with a transcendental divine quality, is included in this injunction. The second prohibition applies to the making of images even if it be not for cultic but artistic purposes. This law includes three kinds of figured subjects: 1) the human form, 2) any representation of transcendental separate intelligences such as angels, seraphim, the four figures of the "Holy Chariot," etc., 3) images of the astral world such as stars and planets which in antiquity were conceived as deities. Besides these three classes of figures, it is also prohibited to create or possess any design which is usually associated with a cultic or religious motif, though the objective meaning of this work is purely artistic.

As to the prohibition against the human form, a controversy developed in the Middle Ages. One school of thought maintained that it applies to both sculpture and painting, while another school has adopted a more liberal attitude and restricted the law only to protruding three-dimensional works of art. At this same time another question came to the fore – whether the prohibition against the aforementioned three categories of artistic figures applied to possession as to manufacture. The religious practice has accepted the more liberal viewpoint in both cases. In the most traditional Jewish homes, paintings and photographs are to be found. Many do not object even to the display of sculptures if their esthetic character and universal meaning are so obvious that they exclude the possibility of association with a cultic motif.

In regard to the synagogue, we do not find in the halakhic literature (with the exception of a single passage in the *Mekhilta* quoted by Rashi, Ex. 20:20) a specific prohibition against paintings or any other design representing the human figure. On the contrary, our sages were more tolerant toward the display of human images in the synagogue than in the home. In the tractates *Rosh Hashanah* (24) and *Avodah Zarah* (43) we find that a statue of the king was displayed in a Babylonian synagogue and nevertheless, Rav, Samuel and Levi did not refrain from worshipping there, though they would have objected to the exhibition of the effigy in a private home. The reason for the distinction

אֶל־בְּנֵי יִשְׂרָאֵל אַתֶּם רְאִיתֶם כִּי מִן־הַשָּׁמַיִם דִּבַּרְתִּי עִמָּכֶם׃
כ כא לֹא תַעֲשׂוּן אִתִּי אֱלֹהֵי כֶסֶף וֵאלֹהֵי זָהָב לֹא תַעֲשׂוּ לָכֶם׃ מִזְבַּח

אַתֶּם רְאִיתֶם כִּי מִן־הַשָּׁמַיִם דִּבַּרְתִּי עִמָּכֶם *You yourselves have seen that I, from the heavens, have spoken to You.* When halakhic man pines for God, he does not venture to rise up to Him but rather strives to bring down His divine presence into the midst of our concrete world. "One verse says: 'I, from the heavens, have spoken to You,' and another verse says: 'And the Lord descended on Mount Sinai' (Ex. 19:20). How can both these verses be maintained? … R. Akiba says: Scripture teaches that the Holy One, blessed be He, bent down the heavens, lowering them to the top of the mountain. Rabbi says: Scripture thus teaches that the Holy One, blessed be He, bent down the lower heavens and the upper heaven of heavens, lowering them to the top of the mountain" [see *Mekhilta* on Ex. 20:19 and Ex. 19:20].

Homo religiosus, who thirsts for the living God, demolishes the bounds of this-worldliness, transforms himself into pure spirit, breaks through all barriers, and ascends on high. For him the approach to God consists in a leap from the empirical and concrete into the transcendent and the mysterious. Not so for halakhic man! When his soul yearns for God, he immerses himself in reality, plunges, with his entire being, into the very midst of concrete existence, and petitions God to descend upon the mountain and to dwell within our reality, with all its laws and principles. *Homo religiosus* ascends to God; God, however, descends to halakhic man. The latter desires not to transform finitude into infinity but rather infinity into finitude. He brings down the divine presence into a sanctuary bounded by twenty boards, holiness into a world situated within the realms of concrete reality, the Absolute into the relative and conditional. Transcendence becomes embodied in man's deeds, deeds that are shaped by the lawful physical order of which man is a part. The idea of holiness according to the halakhic world view does not signify a transcendent realm completely separate and removed from reality. (*Halakhic Man*, pp. 44–45)

לֹא תַעֲשׂוּן אִתִּי אֱלֹהֵי כֶסֶף וֵאלֹהֵי זָהָב לֹא תַעֲשׂוּ לָכֶם *Have no others alongside Me; make yourselves no silver gods, no golden gods.* There are two fundamental prohibitions against the making of images. One deals with the making or possessing of idols – objects of worship – and is not limited to a specific

your burnt offerings and peace offerings, your sheep and your cattle.
Wherever I cause My name to be invoked, I will come to you and
22 I will bless you. If you make Me an altar of stones, do not build it
23 of hewn stone, for in wielding a sword upon it, you profane it. Do
not ascend to My altar with steps, for your nakedness must not be
exposed on it.

HALF KADDISH

Before Maftir is read, the second Sefer Torah is placed on the bima and the Reader says Half Kaddish:

Reader: יִתְגַּדַּל Magnified and sanctified
may His great name be,
in the world He created by His will.
May He establish His kingdom
in your lifetime and in your days,
and in the lifetime of all the house of Israel,
swiftly and soon –
and say: Amen.

All: May His great name be blessed
for ever and all time.

---

congregation to remove from the synagogue a carpet which had animal designs woven in it. Likewise, we know of a controversy concerning the display of the lion of Judah above the ark that raged in the sixteenth century and in which Rabbi Moses of Trani, Rabbi Meir of Padua and Rabbi Joseph Karo were involved. There were many synagogues that did not tolerate panels representing animals. Yet again the practice was more liberal and all figures with the exception of the human form were introduced as architectural designs in the synagogue. As to the anthropomorphic symbols, there is almost unanimity of disapproval. (The fact that some excavations disclose such motives is irrelevant to us. The tradition as such has rejected them.) (*Community, Covenant, and Commitment*, pp. 4–6)

אֲדָמָה תַּעֲשֶׂה־לִּי וְזָבַחְתָּ עָלָיו אֶת־עֹלֹתֶיךָ וְאֶת־שְׁלָמֶיךָ אֶת־
צֹאנְךָ וְאֶת־בְּקָרֶךָ בְּכָל־הַמָּקוֹם אֲשֶׁר אַזְכִּיר אֶת־שְׁמִי אָבוֹא
כב אֵלֶיךָ וּבֵרַכְתִּיךָ׃ וְאִם־מִזְבַּח אֲבָנִים תַּעֲשֶׂה־לִּי לֹא־תִבְנֶה אֶתְהֶן
כג גָּזִית כִּי חַרְבְּךָ הֵנַפְתָּ עָלֶיהָ וַתְּחַלְלֶהָ׃ וְלֹא־תַעֲלֶה בְמַעֲלֹת
עַל־מִזְבְּחִי אֲשֶׁר לֹא־תִגָּלֶה עֶרְוָתְךָ עָלָיו׃

חצי קדיש

Before מפטיר *is read, the second* ספר תורה *is placed on the* שולחן *and the* קורא *says* חצי קדיש*:*

קורא: יִתְגַּדַּל וְיִתְקַדַּשׁ שְׁמֵהּ רַבָּא (קהל: אָמֵן)
בְּעָלְמָא דִּי בְרָא כִרְעוּתֵהּ
וְיַמְלִיךְ מַלְכוּתֵהּ
בְּחַיֵּיכוֹן וּבְיוֹמֵיכוֹן וּבְחַיֵּי דְכָל בֵּית יִשְׂרָאֵל
בַּעֲגָלָא וּבִזְמַן קָרִיב
וְאִמְרוּ אָמֵן. (קהל: אָמֵן)

קהל וקורא: יְהֵא שְׁמֵהּ רַבָּא מְבָרַךְ לְעָלַם וּלְעָלְמֵי עָלְמַיָּא.

---

between synagogue and home is that while in the synagogue no one would suspect the community of having the statute for a religious purpose, such suspicion would be warranted concerning a private home. In the course of time, however, tradition has reversed its attitude. While pictures were not banned from Jewish homes, the synagogue has excluded any image of man from its decorative motives. Moreover, many halakhic scholars insisted upon utmost simplicity of the synagogue, and disapproved of elaborate ornaments in general. Maimonides, for instance, objected to murals and mosaics which would confront the worshipper during his devotional meditation because they might serve as a distraction. An even stronger dislike was shown towards figured subjects such as animals. Rabbi Eliakim of Cologne ordered his

Reader: Blessed and praised, glorified and exalted,
raised and honored, uplifted and lauded
be the name of the Holy One, blessed be He,
beyond any blessing,
song, praise and consolation
uttered in the world –
and say: Amen.

HAGBAHA AND GELILA

The first Torah scroll is lifted and the congregation says:

וְזֹאת הַתּוֹרָה This is the Torah *Deut. 4*
that Moses placed before the children of Israel,
at the Lord's commandment, by the hand of Moses. *Num. 9*

Some add: It is a tree of life to those who grasp it, *Prov. 3*
and those who uphold it are happy.
Its ways are ways of pleasantness, and all its paths are peace.
Long life is in its right hand; in its left, riches and honor.
It pleased the Lord for the sake of [Israel's] righteousness, *Is. 42*
to make the Torah great and glorious.

The first Torah scroll is bound and covered and the oleh for Maftir is called to the second Torah scroll.

MAFTIR

.8 26 The day of first produce, when you bring an offering of new grain to *Numbers*
the Lord on your Festival of Weeks, shall be a sacred assembly for
27 you. On it you shall perform no laborious work. You shall present
a burnt offering as a pleasing aroma to the Lord: two young bulls,
28 one ram, and seven yearling lambs. Their grain offering shall be
fine flour mixed with oil: three-tenths of a measure for each bull,
29 two-tenths for the one ram, and one-tenth for each of the seven
30 lambs. Offer one male goat to atone for you. These you shall offer
31 in addition to the regular burnt offering, its grain offering and liba-
tions. They shall be without blemish.

קורא: יִתְבָּרַךְ וְיִשְׁתַּבַּח וְיִתְפָּאַר וְיִתְרוֹמַם וְיִתְנַשֵּׂא
וְיִתְהַדָּר וְיִתְעַלֶּה וְיִתְהַלָּל
שְׁמֵהּ דְּקֻדְשָׁא בְּרִיךְ הוּא (קהל: בְּרִיךְ הוּא)
לְעֵֽלָּא מִן כָּל בִּרְכָתָא וְשִׁירָתָא
תֻּשְׁבְּחָתָא וְנֶחֱמָתָא, דַּאֲמִירָן בְּעָלְמָא
וְאִמְרוּ אָמֵן. (קהל: אָמֵן)

הגבהה וגלילה

The first ספר תורה *is lifted and the* קהל *says:*

וְזֹאת הַתּוֹרָה אֲשֶׁר־שָׂם מֹשֶׁה לִפְנֵי בְּנֵי יִשְׂרָאֵל׃ דברים ד
עַל־פִּי יהוה בְּיַד מֹשֶׁה׃ במדבר ט

Some add עֵץ־חַיִּים הִיא לַמַּחֲזִיקִים בָּהּ וְתֹמְכֶיהָ מְאֻשָּׁר׃ משלי ג
דְּרָכֶיהָ דַרְכֵי־נֹעַם וְכָל־נְתִיבֹתֶיהָ שָׁלוֹם׃
אֹרֶךְ יָמִים בִּימִינָהּ, בִּשְׂמֹאולָהּ עֹשֶׁר וְכָבוֹד׃
יהוה חָפֵץ לְמַעַן צִדְקוֹ יַגְדִּיל תּוֹרָה וְיַאְדִּיר׃ ישעיה מב

The first ספר תורה *is bound and covered and the* עולה
for מפטיר *is called to the second* ספר תורה*.*

מפטיר

כח כו וּבְיוֹם הַבִּכּוּרִים בְּהַקְרִיבְכֶם מִנְחָה חֲדָשָׁה לַיהוָה בְּשָׁבֻעֹתֵיכֶם במדבר
מִקְרָא־קֹדֶשׁ יִהְיֶה לָכֶם כָּל־מְלֶאכֶת עֲבֹדָה לֹא תַעֲשׂוּ׃
כז וְהִקְרַבְתֶּם עוֹלָה לְרֵיחַ נִיחֹחַ לַיהוָה פָּרִים בְּנֵי־בָקָר שְׁנַיִם אַיִל
כח אֶחָד שִׁבְעָה כְבָשִׂים בְּנֵי שָׁנָה׃ וּמִנְחָתָם סֹלֶת בְּלוּלָה בַשָּׁמֶן
כט שְׁלֹשָׁה עֶשְׂרֹנִים לַפָּר הָאֶחָד שְׁנֵי עֶשְׂרֹנִים לָאַיִל הָאֶחָד׃ עִשָּׂרוֹן
ל עִשָּׂרוֹן לַכֶּבֶשׂ הָאֶחָד לְשִׁבְעַת הַכְּבָשִׂים׃ שְׂעִיר עִזִּים אֶחָד
לא לְכַפֵּר עֲלֵיכֶם׃ מִלְּבַד עֹלַת הַתָּמִיד וּמִנְחָתוֹ תַּעֲשׂוּ תְּמִימִם
יִהְיוּ־לָכֶם וְנִסְכֵּיהֶם׃

HAGBAHA AND GELILA

The second Torah scroll is lifted and the congregation says:

וְזֹאת הַתּוֹרָה This is the Torah *Deut. 4*
that Moses placed before the children of Israel,
at the LORD's commandment, by the hand of Moses. *Num. 9*

Some add: It is a tree of life to those who grasp it, *Prov. 3*
and those who uphold it are happy.
Its ways are ways of pleasantness, and all its paths are peace.
Long life is in its right hand; in its left, riches and honor.
It pleased the LORD for the sake of [Israel's] righteousness, *Is. 42*
to make the Torah great and glorious.

The second Torah scroll is bound and covered and the oleh for Maftir reads the Haftarah.

BLESSING BEFORE READING THE HAFTARAH

Before reading the Haftarah, the person called up for Maftir says:

בָּרוּךְ Blessed are You, LORD our God, King of the Universe, who chose good prophets and was pleased with their words, spoken in truth. Blessed are You, LORD, who chose the Torah, His servant Moses, His people Israel, and the prophets of truth and righteousness.

HAFTARAH FOR FIRST DAY OF SHAVUOT

1 1 It was in the thirtieth year in the fourth month on the fifth day of *Ezekiel*
the month. I was in the exile, by the Kevar River; the heavens
2 opened up, and I saw Godly visions. On the fifth day of the month,
3 the fifth year of the exile of King Jehoiachin, so it was: the word
of the LORD came to Ezekiel son of Buzi the priest, in the land of
the Chaldeans by the Kevar River; there the hand of the LORD
4 was upon him. And I looked: Behold, a storm wind came from
the north, a great cloud and a flaring fire with a radiance around it,

---

flaring fire with a radiance around it." God revealed Himself out of the storm wind, the destructive hurricane that left in its wake ruins and debris in the hills and plain of Judea and uprooted an entire people from its native soil, converting free, proud men into slaves and prisoners. Out of this cataclysmic whirlwind that wiped out Judea, the sanctuary, the glory and pride of Israel, out of the fire that caused havoc, out of the cloud of a dark, gloomy, lonely

הגבהה וגלילה

The second ספר תורה *is lifted and the* קהל *says:*

וְזֹאת הַתּוֹרָה אֲשֶׁר־שָׂם מֹשֶׁה לִפְנֵי בְּנֵי יִשְׂרָאֵל: דברים ד

עַל־פִּי יהוה בְּיַד מֹשֶׁה: במדבר ט

Some add עֵץ־חַיִּים הִיא לַמַּחֲזִיקִים בָּהּ וְתֹמְכֶיהָ מְאֻשָּׁר: משלי ג

דְּרָכֶיהָ דַרְכֵי־נֹעַם וְכָל־נְתִיבוֹתֶיהָ שָׁלוֹם:

אֹרֶךְ יָמִים בִּימִינָהּ, בִּשְׂמֹאולָהּ עֹשֶׁר וְכָבוֹד:

יהוה חָפֵץ לְמַעַן צִדְקוֹ יַגְדִּיל תּוֹרָה וְיַאְדִּיר: ישעיה מב

The second ספר תורה *is bound and covered and the* עולה *for* מפטיר *reads the* הפטרה.

ברכה קודם ההפטרה

Before reading the הפטרה*, the person called up for* מפטיר *says:*

בָּרוּךְ אַתָּה יהוה אֱלֹהֵינוּ מֶלֶךְ הָעוֹלָם אֲשֶׁר בָּחַר בִּנְבִיאִים טוֹבִים, וְרָצָה בְדִבְרֵיהֶם הַנֶּאֱמָרִים בֶּאֱמֶת. בָּרוּךְ אַתָּה יהוה, הַבּוֹחֵר בַּתּוֹרָה וּבְמֹשֶׁה עַבְדּוֹ וּבְיִשְׂרָאֵל עַמּוֹ וּבִנְבִיאֵי הָאֱמֶת וָצֶדֶק.

הפטרה ליום טוב ראשון של שבועות

א א וַיְהִי ׀ בִּשְׁלֹשִׁים שָׁנָה בָּרְבִיעִי בַּחֲמִשָּׁה לַחֹדֶשׁ וַאֲנִי בְתוֹךְ־ יחזקאל
הַגּוֹלָה עַל־נְהַר־כְּבָר נִפְתְּחוּ הַשָּׁמַיִם וָאֶרְאֶה מַרְאוֹת אֱלֹהִים:
ב בַּחֲמִשָּׁה לַחֹדֶשׁ הִיא הַשָּׁנָה הַחֲמִישִׁית לְגָלוּת הַמֶּלֶךְ יוֹיָכִין:
ג הָיֹה הָיָה דְבַר־יְהֹוָה אֶל־יְחֶזְקֵאל בֶּן־בּוּזִי הַכֹּהֵן בְּאֶרֶץ כַּשְׂדִּים
ד עַל־נְהַר־כְּבָר וַתְּהִי עָלָיו שָׁם יַד־יהוה: וָאֵרֶא וְהִנֵּה רוּחַ סְעָרָה
בָּאָה מִן־הַצָּפוֹן עָנָן גָּדוֹל וְאֵשׁ מִתְלַקַּחַת וְנֹגַהּ לוֹ סָבִיב וּמִתּוֹכָהּ

HAFTARAH FOR THE FIRST DAY

וָאֵרֶא וְהִנֵּה רוּחַ סְעָרָה בָּאָה מִן־הַצָּפוֹן *And I looked: Behold, a storm wind came from the north.* Ezekiel was the first prophet who encountered God in the whirlwind. He experienced the catastrophic revelation: God addressed Himself to Ezekiel through the fire of disaster and the hurricane of the north. "And I looked: Behold, a storm wind came from the north, a great cloud and a

5 and inside it, within the fire, the look of something luminous, and
within that was the form of four living beings. This was their appear-
6 ance: they had the form of a man; each one had four faces, and

---

private world leaving wreckage behind – he first hears the tumult of the *ḥayot* and *ofanim*, the noise of mechanical, nonsensical forces ruling the universe. Beyond this insensate, unalterable, causal nexus he sees the cold indifference of empty, bleak heavens. Satan's laughter can be heard out of the roar of the whirlwind. Yet Ezekiel suddenly perceived something new, a strange sound coming from afar, from a remote corner of Being, from above the icy firmament, penetrating this terrible icy spread which shut everything out of sight. This voice was not drowned out by the tumult of the wheels, the noise of the living creatures, the host of the great waters. It prevailed in spite of the roar of the tempest.

"A voice came from upon the expanse which was over their heads – standing still, they lowered their wings" (1:25). Everything suddenly came to a standstill. Ezekiel saw a new vision, reminiscent of Isaiah's encounter:

> Above the film which was over their heads, with the appearance of sapphire, was the form of a throne; and upon the form of the throne – upon it, above – was a form with the appearance of a man… It was like the appearance of a rainbow in the clouds on a rainy day; the radiance around it had that appearance. This was the appearance of the form of the glory of the Lord (1:26, 28).

God disclosed Himself suddenly to Ezekiel. After an allegedly futile search for God in the heavens, after vainly exploring creation for Him, at least for a trace of His glory and might, wisdom and beauty, after encountering living creatures, wheels, automatic senseless movement, a tumult and noise,after confronting a cold, indifferent heaven, after resigning himself to an absurd existence in a prison camp, after plunging into the abyss of black despair, the scenery changed suddenly. He heard a voice of one that spoke, a meaningful voice and not an absurd noise, not the tumult of mighty waters. He saw God in the likeness of man; the questing I met a lonely Thou, not in the temple, but in the camp of downtrodden, homeless prisoners. The words were addressed out of the whirlwind, and the likeness of the glory of the Lord emerged out of the frightening fire. God spoke out of the catastrophic event, out of the distressing encounter with nihility, out of the seeming void and emptiness, from above the icy firmament, from nowhere. It took Ezekiel a long time to make the great leap from an insane existence to the throne of God that stands above the ice crystal firmament, from the absurdity of a historical

ה כְּעֵין הַחַשְׁמַל מִתּוֹךְ הָאֵשׁ׃ וּמִתּוֹכָהּ דְּמוּת אַרְבַּע חַיּוֹת וְזֶה
ו מַרְאֵיהֶן דְּמוּת אָדָם לָהֵנָּה׃ וְאַרְבָּעָה פָנִים לְאֶחָת וְאַרְבַּע

---

night, God addressed Himself to Ezekiel. Where did the prophet behold the great apocalyptic vision? In the temple, in the courtyard, surrounded by the pomp and glory of an independent people like his predecessor Isaiah? No! He met God in a prison camp, in the land of the Chaldeans by the river Kevar. And the vision he saw lacked the simplicity of the Isaiah encounter, the direct apprehension of God's glory and the majesty of God's skirt filling the temple. He sees first not God but holy creatures whose visage is like burning coal, and like the appearance of torches; he notices wheels which went with the creatures – a strange apocalypse, filling the viewer with grisly fear. The whole vision is weird and frightening.

At the outset, Ezekiel missed God; he was confronted by mechanical forces in action. He perceived the tremendous energy potential entailed in this heavenly mechanism which is engaged in perpetual motion. "It passed among the living beings; the fire had a radiance, lightning flashed out from the fire" (1:13). Yet he did not see God in these heavens which were wide open to his searching glance and exploring mind. The creatures ruled; they set the wheels in motion, "for the spirit of the living being was also in the wheels" (1:20). And yet there was no vision of God. He heard the noise of the wings, like the noise of the great waters, as the noise of a host – but was there something behind all this activity, drive and movement, or was there nothing in the background? The creatures, the wheels, the fire, the lightning, the torches, the roar and tumult originate and end in a great void. They are born out of nothingness and move on to their own doom.

For the fraction of a second, Ezekiel beheld a weird vision: "Above the head of the living being was the form of an expanse with a look of ice, its overawing glare, suspended over their heads from above" (1:22). It seemed for a short moment that the terrifying vision beheld by Ezekiel was projected against an icy, cruel, insensitive and insensate reality. All prayers bounced back, all petitions echoed through the empty black spaces. The warm human voice which rose out of the depths of a yearning soul questing for God was chilled upon reaching the icy heavens. Man, with his aspirations, dreams, petitions and supplications, seemed a nonsensical, displaced being drifting along bleak uncharted lands, lonely and abandoned. Above his head spread forth an icy heaven, indifferent and irresponsive.

When catastrophe strikes man, when the whirlwind sweeps across his

7 each one of them had four wings; their legs were straight-stand-
ing, and their feet were like a calf's hoof, gleaming with a look of
8 burnished bronze; they had man's hands beneath their wings on
9 their four sides, and the four of them had faces and wings. Their
wings were joined to each other; they did not turn when they
10 moved but moved in the direction of one of the faces. Their faces
were in the form of the face of a man with the face of a lion on
the right of the four, the face of an ox on the left of the four, and
11 the face of an eagle on all four of them. Their faces and their wings
were separated above: each one had two joining it to the others
12 and two covering its body; each moved in the direction of one of
the faces – wherever the spirit would move, they moved – they did
13 not turn when they moved. The form of the living beings, their
appearance, was like coals burning, like the appearance of torch
flames; it passed among the living beings; the fire had a radiance,
14 lightning flashed out from the fire, and the living beings ran for-
15 ward and back with the appearance of darting flames. I looked
at the living beings, and there, a wheel was on the ground beside
16 each of the living beings with the four faces. The appearance of
the wheels and their design had the look of an aquamarine gem,
all four of them with the same form; their appearance and their
17 design were as though one wheel were inside the other. When they
moved, they moved on any of their four sides; they did not turn as
18 they moved. Their rims, towering, inspired fear; and the rims of all
19 four of them were covered, all around, with eyes. When the living
beings moved, the wheels moved beside them, and when the liv-
20 ing beings rose above the ground, the wheels also rose; wherever
the spirit would move, they moved; there where the spirit moved,
the wheels rose with them, for the spirit of the living being was

---

be the Lord who speaks to man out of the whirlwind and horrible fire. In our *Kedushah* we profess our faith in the cosmic and also in the catastrophic revelation of God. We are always confronted through our ontic and nihilitic experiences. (*Out of the Whirlwind*, pp. 144–147)

ז כְּנָפַיִם לְאַחַת לָהֶם: וְרַגְלֵיהֶם רֶגֶל יְשָׁרָה וְכַף רַגְלֵיהֶם כְּכַף
ח רֶגֶל עֵגֶל וְנֹצְצִים כְּעֵין נְחֹשֶׁת קָלָל: וידו אָדָם מִתַּחַת כַּנְפֵיהֶם וִידֵי
ט עַל אַרְבַּעַת רִבְעֵיהֶם וּפְנֵיהֶם וְכַנְפֵיהֶם לְאַרְבַּעְתָּם: חֹבְרֹת
אִשָּׁה אֶל־אֲחוֹתָהּ כַּנְפֵיהֶם לֹא־יִסַּבּוּ בְלֶכְתָּן אִישׁ אֶל־עֵבֶר פָּנָיו
י יֵלֵכוּ: וּדְמוּת פְּנֵיהֶם פְּנֵי אָדָם וּפְנֵי אַרְיֵה אֶל־הַיָּמִין לְאַרְבַּעְתָּם
יא וּפְנֵי־שׁוֹר מֵהַשְּׂמֹאול לְאַרְבַּעְתָּן וּפְנֵי־נֶשֶׁר לְאַרְבַּעְתָּן: וּפְנֵיהֶם
וְכַנְפֵיהֶם פְּרֻדוֹת מִלְמָעְלָה לְאִישׁ שְׁתַּיִם חֹבְרוֹת אִישׁ וּשְׁתַּיִם
יב מְכַסּוֹת אֵת גְּוִיֹּתֵיהֶנָה: וְאִישׁ אֶל־עֵבֶר פָּנָיו יֵלֵכוּ אֶל אֲשֶׁר
יג יִהְיֶה־שָּׁמָּה הָרוּחַ לָלֶכֶת יֵלֵכוּ לֹא יִסַּבּוּ בְּלֶכְתָּן: וּדְמוּת הַחַיּוֹת
מַרְאֵיהֶם כְּגַחֲלֵי־אֵשׁ בֹּעֲרוֹת כְּמַרְאֵה הַלַּפִּדִים הִיא מִתְהַלֶּכֶת
יד בֵּין הַחַיּוֹת וְנֹגַהּ לָאֵשׁ וּמִן־הָאֵשׁ יוֹצֵא בָרָק: וְהַחַיּוֹת רָצוֹא
טו וָשׁוֹב כְּמַרְאֵה הַבָּזָק: וָאֵרֶא הַחַיּוֹת וְהִנֵּה אוֹפַן אֶחָד בָּאָרֶץ
טז אֵצֶל הַחַיּוֹת לְאַרְבַּעַת פָּנָיו: מַרְאֵה הָאוֹפַנִּים וּמַעֲשֵׂיהֶם כְּעֵין
תַּרְשִׁישׁ וּדְמוּת אֶחָד לְאַרְבַּעְתָּן וּמַרְאֵיהֶם וּמַעֲשֵׂיהֶם כַּאֲשֶׁר
יז יִהְיֶה הָאוֹפַן בְּתוֹךְ הָאוֹפָן: עַל־אַרְבַּעַת רִבְעֵיהֶן בְּלֶכְתָּם
יח יֵלֵכוּ לֹא יִסַּבּוּ בְּלֶכְתָּן: וְגַבֵּיהֶן וְגֹבַהּ לָהֶם וְיִרְאָה לָהֶם וְגַבֹּתָם
יט מְלֵאֹת עֵינַיִם סָבִיב לְאַרְבַּעְתָּן: וּבְלֶכֶת הַחַיּוֹת יֵלְכוּ הָאוֹפַנִּים
כ אֶצְלָם וּבְהִנָּשֵׂא הַחַיּוֹת מֵעַל הָאָרֶץ יִנָּשְׂאוּ הָאוֹפַנִּים: עַל אֲשֶׁר
יִהְיֶה־שָּׁם הָרוּחַ לָלֶכֶת יֵלֵכוּ שָׁמָּה הָרוּחַ לָלֶכֶת וְהָאוֹפַנִּים

cataclysm to the great dialogue with the hidden, numinous, mysterious God, abiding behind the heavens. Suddenly a new light was shed over everything he beheld before. The weird creatures, the wheels, the great noise, the host, the mighty waters – these did not fill him with grisly fear any more; a spirit lifted him and he heard the voice (not the noise) of a great rushing, "Blessed is the Lord's glory from its place" (3:12), from His transcendence. Blessed

21 also in the wheels: when they moved, they too moved, and when
they stood still, they too stood still, and when they rose from the
ground, the wheels too rose with them because the spirit of the
22 living being was in the wheels. Above the head of the living being
was the form of an expanse with a look of ice, its overawing glare,
23 suspended over their heads from above, and beneath the expanse,
their wings reached out toward each other. Each had a pair cover-
24 ing them; each had a pair covering their bodies. I heard the sound
of their wings when they moved; it was like the sound of great
rushing waters, like the voice of Shaddai, a clamor like the noise of
25 a gathered army. Standing still, they lowered their wings; a voice
came from upon the expanse which was over their heads – stand-
26 ing still, they lowered their wings. Above the film which was over
their heads, with the appearance of a sapphire, was the form of a
throne; and upon the form of the throne – upon it, above – was
27 a form with the appearance of a man. And I saw: something that
looked luminous, the appearance of fire encasing it from what
appeared to be his waist and above; and from what appeared to be
his waist and below, I saw an appearance like fire with a radiance
28 around it; it was like the appearance of a rainbow in the clouds on
a rainy day; the radiance around it had that appearance. This was
the appearance of the form of the glory of the LORD. I saw it and I
fell upon my face, and I heard a voice speak.

3 12 A spirit then lifted me up, and I heard a great, thunderous noise *Ezekiel*
behind me: "Blessed is the LORD's glory from its place!"

---

thence you shall seek the Lord your God" (Deut. 4:29). You will search and quest for God out of existential narrowness, in exile and captivity, surrounded by human vulgarity and brutality, in a world that knows nothing besides hard matter and mechanical laws. You will crave for Him in spite of His silence, regardless of the absence of a response, notwithstanding that not a single word of solace will be forthcoming, that not a single hint from heaven will be noticeable. You will search for God when the heavens look the way Ezekiel described them – cold and awesome in their indifference and

כא יִנָּשְׂאוּ לְעֻמָּתָם כִּי רוּחַ הַחַיָּה בָּאוֹפַנִּים: בְּלֶכְתָּם יֵלֵכוּ וּבְעָמְדָם
יַעֲמֹדוּ וּבְהִנָּשְׂאָם מֵעַל הָאָרֶץ יִנָּשְׂאוּ הָאוֹפַנִּים לְעֻמָּתָם כִּי
כב רוּחַ הַחַיָּה בָּאוֹפַנִּים: וּדְמוּת עַל־רָאשֵׁי הַחַיָּה רָקִיעַ כְּעֵין
כג הַקֶּרַח הַנּוֹרָא נָטוּי עַל־רָאשֵׁיהֶם מִלְמָעְלָה: וְתַחַת הָרָקִיעַ
כַּנְפֵיהֶם יְשָׁרוֹת אִשָּׁה אֶל־אֲחוֹתָהּ לְאִישׁ שְׁתַּיִם מְכַסּוֹת לָהֵנָּה
כד וּלְאִישׁ שְׁתַּיִם מְכַסּוֹת לָהֵנָּה אֵת גְּוִיֹּתֵיהֶם: וָאֶשְׁמַע אֶת־קוֹל
כַּנְפֵיהֶם כְּקוֹל מַיִם רַבִּים כְּקוֹל־שַׁדַּי בְּלֶכְתָּם קוֹל הֲמֻלָּה כְּקוֹל
כה מַחֲנֶה בְּעָמְדָם תְּרַפֶּינָה כַנְפֵיהֶן: וַיְהִי־קוֹל מֵעַל לָרָקִיעַ אֲשֶׁר
כו עַל־רֹאשָׁם בְּעָמְדָם תְּרַפֶּינָה כַנְפֵיהֶן: וּמִמַּעַל לָרָקִיעַ אֲשֶׁר
עַל־רֹאשָׁם כְּמַרְאֵה אֶבֶן־סַפִּיר דְּמוּת כִּסֵּא וְעַל דְּמוּת הַכִּסֵּא
כז דְּמוּת כְּמַרְאֵה אָדָם עָלָיו מִלְמָעְלָה: וָאֵרֶא ׀ כְּעֵין חַשְׁמַל
כְּמַרְאֵה־אֵשׁ בֵּית־לָהּ סָבִיב מִמַּרְאֵה מָתְנָיו וּלְמָעְלָה וּמִמַּרְאֵה
כח מָתְנָיו וּלְמַטָּה רָאִיתִי כְּמַרְאֵה־אֵשׁ וְנֹגַהּ לוֹ סָבִיב: כְּמַרְאֵה
הַקֶּשֶׁת אֲשֶׁר יִהְיֶה בֶעָנָן בְּיוֹם הַגֶּשֶׁם כֵּן מַרְאֵה הַנֹּגַהּ סָבִיב
הוּא מַרְאֵה דְּמוּת כְּבוֹד־יְהוָה וָאֶרְאֶה וָאֶפֹּל עַל־פָּנַי וָאֶשְׁמַע
קוֹל מְדַבֵּר:

יחזקאל ג יב וַתִּשָּׂאֵנִי רוּחַ וָאֶשְׁמַע אַחֲרַי קוֹל רַעַשׁ גָּדוֹל בָּרוּךְ כְּבוֹד־יְהוָה
מִמְּקוֹמוֹ:

מַרְאֵה דְּמוּת כְּבוֹד־יהוה *The appearance of the form of the glory of the Lord.* Our historical destiny finds its fulfillment in the faith experience. The latter was described in the Torah as the search for God at a time when to seek God requires a superhuman effort. At a time of *hester panim,* when God is hidden in the transcendental recesses, at a time when the human search becomes a very frustrating and fatiguing experience, God wills man to search for Him and evoke Him while historical reality scoffs at the God-searcher. "When you are in distress and all these things come upon you" (Deut. 4:30); "From

BLESSINGS AFTER THE HAFTARAH

After the Haftarah, the person called up for Maftir says the following blessings:

בָּרוּךְ Blessed are You, LORD our God, King of the Universe, Rock of all worlds, righteous for all generations, the faithful God who says and does, speaks and fulfills, all of whose words are truth and righteousness. You are faithful, LORD our God, and faithful are Your words, not one of which returns unfulfilled, for You, God, are a faithful (and compassionate) King. Blessed are You, LORD, faithful in all His words.

רַחֵם Have compassion on Zion for it is the source of our life, and save the one grieved in spirit swiftly in our days. Blessed are You, LORD, who makes Zion rejoice in her children.

שַׂמְּחֵנוּ Grant us joy, LORD our God, through Elijah the prophet Your servant, and through the kingdom of the house of David Your anointed – may he soon come and make our hearts glad. May no stranger sit on his throne, and may others not continue to inherit his glory, for You promised him by Your holy name that his light would never be extinguished. Blessed are You, LORD, Shield of David.

עַל הַתּוֹרָה For the Torah, for divine worship, for the prophets, and for this day of the festival of Shavuot which You, LORD our God, have given us for gladness and joy, for honor and glory – for all these we thank and bless You, LORD our God, and may Your name be blessed by the mouth of all that lives, continually, for ever and all time. Blessed are You, LORD, who sanctifies Israel and the festive seasons.

The service continues on page 128.

Him, if you search with all your heart and with all your soul" (Deut. 4:29). Defying history itself, its causal sequence and dynamism, which contradict our expectations and aspirations, man will discover, like Ezekiel, that beyond the awesome spread of ice there is a seat of judgment. "Above the film which was over their heads, with the appearance of sapphire, was the form of a throne; and upon the form of the throne – upon it, above – was a form with the appearance of a man... This was the appearance of the form of the glory of the Lord" (1:26, 28). (*Days of Deliverance*, pp. 174–175)

ברכות לאחר ההפטרה

After the הפטרה*, the person called up for* מפטיר *says the following blessings:*

בָּרוּךְ אַתָּה יהוה אֱלֹהֵינוּ מֶלֶךְ הָעוֹלָם, צוּר כָּל הָעוֹלָמִים, צַדִּיק בְּכָל הַדּוֹרוֹת, הָאֵל הַנֶּאֱמָן, הָאוֹמֵר וְעוֹשֶׂה, הַמְדַבֵּר וּמְקַיֵּם, שֶׁכָּל דְּבָרָיו אֱמֶת וָצֶדֶק. נֶאֱמָן אַתָּה הוּא יהוה אֱלֹהֵינוּ וְנֶאֱמָנִים דְּבָרֶיךָ, וְדָבָר אֶחָד מִדְּבָרֶיךָ אָחוֹר לֹא יָשׁוּב רֵיקָם, כִּי אֵל מֶלֶךְ נֶאֱמָן (וְרַחֲמָן) אָתָּה. בָּרוּךְ אַתָּה יהוה, הָאֵל הַנֶּאֱמָן בְּכָל דְּבָרָיו.

רַחֵם עַל צִיּוֹן כִּי הִיא בֵּית חַיֵּינוּ, וְלַעֲלוּבַת נֶפֶשׁ תּוֹשִׁיעַ בִּמְהֵרָה בְיָמֵינוּ. בָּרוּךְ אַתָּה יהוה, מְשַׂמֵּחַ צִיּוֹן בְּבָנֶיהָ.

שַׂמְּחֵנוּ יהוה אֱלֹהֵינוּ בְּאֵלִיָּהוּ הַנָּבִיא עַבְדֶּךָ, וּבְמַלְכוּת בֵּית דָּוִד מְשִׁיחֶךָ, בִּמְהֵרָה יָבוֹא וְיָגֵל לִבֵּנוּ. עַל כִּסְאוֹ לֹא יֵשֶׁב זָר, וְלֹא יִנְחֲלוּ עוֹד אֲחֵרִים אֶת כְּבוֹדוֹ, כִּי בְשֵׁם קָדְשְׁךָ נִשְׁבַּעְתָּ לּוֹ שֶׁלֹּא יִכְבֶּה נֵרוֹ לְעוֹלָם וָעֶד. בָּרוּךְ אַתָּה יהוה, מָגֵן דָּוִד.

עַל הַתּוֹרָה וְעַל הָעֲבוֹדָה וְעַל הַנְּבִיאִים, וְעַל יוֹם חַג הַשָּׁבוּעוֹת הַזֶּה שֶׁנָּתַתָּ לָּנוּ, יהוה אֱלֹהֵינוּ לְשָׂשׂוֹן וּלְשִׂמְחָה, לְכָבוֹד וּלְתִפְאָרֶת. עַל הַכֹּל יהוה אֱלֹהֵינוּ אֲנַחְנוּ מוֹדִים לָךְ וּמְבָרְכִים אוֹתָךְ. יִתְבָּרַךְ שִׁמְךָ בְּפִי כָּל חַי תָּמִיד לְעוֹלָם וָעֶד. בָּרוּךְ אַתָּה יהוה, מְקַדֵּשׁ יִשְׂרָאֵל וְהַזְּמַנִּים.

The service continues on page 129.

---

muteness: "Above the head of the living being was the form of an expanse with a look of ice, its overawing glare, suspended over their heads from above" (1:22).

In spite of everything, man does not lose his faith; he searches for God with his whole heart and soul. This is the great act of faith. "You shall find

TORAH READING FOR THE SECOND DAY OF SHAVUOT

If the second day of Shavuot falls on Shabbat, start here. If it falls on a weekday, start with "Every firstborn male" on page 108.

4 22 Do not boil a kid in the milk of its mother. Each year, set aside a Deut.
23 tenth of the yield of all you have sown in the field. You shall eat
the tithe of your grain, wine, and oil, as well as the firstborn of
your herds and flocks in the presence of the LORD your God in
the place that He will choose as a dwelling for His name, so that
24 you may learn to hold the LORD your God in awe always. But if
the distance is too great for you to carry them, because the place
where the LORD your God chooses to set His name is far from you
25 and because the LORD your God has blessed you, then you may
exchange the tithe for money. Wrap up the money in your hand, go
26 to the place that the LORD your God will choose, and spend the
money on whatever you choose: cattle, sheep, wine, strong drink,
or whatever else you like. There you shall eat it in the presence of
27 the LORD your God, and rejoice together with your household. As
for the Levites living in your towns, do not neglect them, because
28 they have no share or inheritance as you do. At the end
of every third year, bring out the full tithe of your produce for that
29 year, and leave it within your towns, so that the Levites, who have
no share or inheritance as you have, together with the migrants,
orphans, and widows in your towns, may come and eat and be sat-
isfied, so that the LORD your God will grant you blessing in all the
15 1 work of your hands. At the end of every seventh year, you LEVI
2 shall grant a remission of debts. This is how the remission is carried
out: every creditor shall relinquish any debt owed by his fellow. He
shall not exact it from his brother, his fellow, because the LORD's
3 remission has been proclaimed. You may require payment from a
foreigner, but you must remit any debt owed to you by a brother.
4 There should be no poor among you, because the LORD will bless
you in the land that the LORD your God is giving you to possess
5 as your inheritance, if only you obey the LORD your God, staying

קריאת התורה ליום שני של שבועות

If the second day of שבועות *falls on* שבת*, start here.*
If it falls on a weekday, start with כָּל־הַבְּכוֹר *on page 109.*

יד כב עַשֵּׂר תְּעַשֵּׂר אֵת כָּל־תְּבוּאַת זַרְעֶךָ הַיֹּצֵא הַשָּׂדֶה שָׁנָה שָׁנָה׃ דברים
כג וְאָכַלְתָּ לִפְנֵי ׀ יְהוָה אֱלֹהֶיךָ בַּמָּקוֹם אֲשֶׁר־יִבְחַר לְשַׁכֵּן שְׁמוֹ
שָׁם מַעְשַׂר דְּגָנְךָ תִּירֹשְׁךָ וְיִצְהָרֶךָ וּבְכֹרֹת בְּקָרְךָ וְצֹאנֶךָ לְמַעַן
כד תִּלְמַד לְיִרְאָה אֶת־יְהוָה אֱלֹהֶיךָ כָּל־הַיָּמִים׃ וְכִי־יִרְבֶּה מִמְּךָ
הַדֶּרֶךְ כִּי לֹא תוּכַל שְׂאֵתוֹ כִּי־יִרְחַק מִמְּךָ הַמָּקוֹם אֲשֶׁר יִבְחַר
כה יְהוָה אֱלֹהֶיךָ לָשׂוּם שְׁמוֹ שָׁם כִּי יְבָרֶכְךָ יְהוָה אֱלֹהֶיךָ׃ וְנָתַתָּה
בַּכָּסֶף וְצַרְתָּ הַכֶּסֶף בְּיָדְךָ וְהָלַכְתָּ אֶל־הַמָּקוֹם אֲשֶׁר יִבְחַר יְהוָה
כו אֱלֹהֶיךָ בּוֹ׃ וְנָתַתָּה הַכֶּסֶף בְּכֹל אֲשֶׁר־תְּאַוֶּה נַפְשְׁךָ בַּבָּקָר
וּבַצֹּאן וּבַיַּיִן וּבַשֵּׁכָר וּבְכֹל אֲשֶׁר תִּשְׁאָלְךָ נַפְשֶׁךָ וְאָכַלְתָּ שָּׁם
כז לִפְנֵי יְהוָה אֱלֹהֶיךָ וְשָׂמַחְתָּ אַתָּה וּבֵיתֶךָ׃ וְהַלֵּוִי אֲשֶׁר־בִּשְׁעָרֶיךָ
כח לֹא תַעַזְבֶנּוּ כִּי אֵין לוֹ חֵלֶק וְנַחֲלָה עִמָּךְ׃ מִקְצֵה ׀
שָׁלֹשׁ שָׁנִים תּוֹצִיא אֶת־כָּל־מַעְשַׂר תְּבוּאָתְךָ בַּשָּׁנָה הַהִוא
כט וְהִנַּחְתָּ בִּשְׁעָרֶיךָ׃ וּבָא הַלֵּוִי כִּי אֵין־לוֹ חֵלֶק וְנַחֲלָה עִמָּךְ וְהַגֵּר
וְהַיָּתוֹם וְהָאַלְמָנָה אֲשֶׁר בִּשְׁעָרֶיךָ וְאָכְלוּ וְשָׂבֵעוּ לְמַעַן יְבָרֶכְךָ
טו א יְהוָה אֱלֹהֶיךָ בְּכָל־מַעֲשֵׂה יָדְךָ אֲשֶׁר תַּעֲשֶׂה׃ מִקֵּץ לוי
ב שֶׁבַע־שָׁנִים תַּעֲשֶׂה שְׁמִטָּה׃ וְזֶה דְּבַר הַשְּׁמִטָּה שָׁמוֹט כָּל־בַּעַל
מַשֵּׁה יָדוֹ אֲשֶׁר יַשֶּׁה בְּרֵעֵהוּ לֹא־יִגֹּשׂ אֶת־רֵעֵהוּ וְאֶת־אָחִיו
ג כִּי־קָרָא שְׁמִטָּה לַיהוָה׃ אֶת־הַנָּכְרִי תִּגֹּשׂ וַאֲשֶׁר יִהְיֶה לְךָ אֶת־
ד אָחִיךָ תַּשְׁמֵט יָדֶךָ׃ אֶפֶס כִּי לֹא יִהְיֶה־בְּךָ אֶבְיוֹן כִּי־בָרֵךְ יְבָרֶכְךָ
ה יְהוָה בָּאָרֶץ אֲשֶׁר יְהוָה אֱלֹהֶיךָ נֹתֵן־לְךָ נַחֲלָה לְרִשְׁתָּהּ׃ רַק

vigilant to keep all the command with which I am charging you
6 this day. For the LORD your God will bless you as He has promised
you. You will lend to many nations, but will not borrow. You will
7 rule over many nations, and they will not rule over you. If
there be a poor person among your brothers in any of your towns
in the land that the LORD your God is giving you, do not harden
8 your heart or close your hand toward your brother in need. Open
your hand generously and freely lend him enough to answer all his
9 needs. Be vigilant: let your heart not whisper a base thought: 'The
seventh year, the year of remission, is close,' making you miserly
toward your brother in need, giving him nothing. He will cry out to

---

of *re'a* is too weak. You need a stronger bond – that of *aḥ*, a brother! (*Vision and Leadership*, p. 155)

הִשָּׁמֶר לְךָ פֶּן־יִהְיֶה דָבָר עִם־לְבָבְךָ בְלִיַּעַל *Be vigilant: let your heart not whisper a base thought.* It appears that one who gives *tzedakah* to the poor and cheers the heart of the impoverished has not only performed the mechanical, technical act of giving; he actually fulfills the commandment to act mercifully. Although its complete fulfillment is something of which only a select few are capable, the Torah rewards even the hard-hearted who give as if they had performed the commandment out of genuine compassion. The personality is elevated to ethical heights through the external act. However, when the miserly or cruel person does not overcome his inner inclinations and fails to respond to the cry of the poor, or shames him while giving *tzedakah,* the Halakhah demands from him a good heart, not merely pleasant words and appearances. He is called to account not only for his harsh conduct but also for the profound wickedness of a soul lacking in good qualities, unable to respond to the unfortunate person quaking before him. Of course, there is no comparison between a sin limited to externalities and a sin that is existential, a distinction that determines whether a person is eligible for divine mercy or subject to everlasting abhorrence.

Maimonides expresses the idea as follows:

He who has compassion for others will be awarded compassion for himself, as it is said, "That the Lord may ... show you mercy, and have compassion

אִם־שָׁמוֹעַ תִּשְׁמַע בְּקוֹל יהוה אֱלֹהֶיךָ לִשְׁמֹר לַעֲשׂוֹת אֶת־
ו כָּל־הַמִּצְוָה הַזֹּאת אֲשֶׁר אָנֹכִי מְצַוְּךָ הַיּוֹם׃ כִּי־יהוה אֱלֹהֶיךָ
בֵּרַכְךָ כַּאֲשֶׁר דִּבֶּר־לָךְ וְהַעֲבַטְתָּ גּוֹיִם רַבִּים וְאַתָּה לֹא תַעֲבֹט
ז וּמָשַׁלְתָּ בְּגוֹיִם רַבִּים וּבְךָ לֹא יִמְשֹׁלוּ׃ כִּי־יִהְיֶה
בְךָ אֶבְיוֹן מֵאַחַד אַחֶיךָ בְּאַחַד שְׁעָרֶיךָ בְּאַרְצְךָ אֲשֶׁר־יהוה
אֱלֹהֶיךָ נֹתֵן לָךְ לֹא תְאַמֵּץ אֶת־לְבָבְךָ וְלֹא תִקְפֹּץ אֶת־יָדְךָ
ח מֵאָחִיךָ הָאֶבְיוֹן׃ כִּי־פָתֹחַ תִּפְתַּח אֶת־יָדְךָ לוֹ וְהַעֲבֵט תַּעֲבִיטֶנּוּ
ט דֵּי מַחְסֹרוֹ אֲשֶׁר יֶחְסַר לוֹ׃ הִשָּׁמֶר לְךָ פֶּן־יִהְיֶה דָבָר עִם־
לְבָבְךָ בְלִיַּעַל לֵאמֹר קָרְבָה שְׁנַת־הַשֶּׁבַע שְׁנַת הַשְּׁמִטָּה וְרָעָה

TORAH READING FOR THE SECOND DAY

כִּי־יִהְיֶה בְךָ אֶבְיוֹן מֵאַחַד אַחֶיךָ *If there be a poor person among your brothers.* As long as one is cognizant of the existence of others, one is categorized as a *re'a,* an acquaintance or neighbor. But the very instant that one begins to perceive another – not just to know him but to feel his existence, experience his joys and frustrations, agonies and hopes – one turns from a *re'a* into an *aḥ,* a brother. This is a higher degree of co-existence, of interrelatedness and companionship.

Brothers are united by existential bonds – one destiny, one memory. The precepts of *tzedakah* and *gemilut ḥasadim* are nurtured by the doctrine of the sympathetic, brotherly, open existence. In speaking of *tzedakah,* the Torah constantly employs the term *aḥ,* not *re'a*: "If your brother becomes impoverished" (Lev. 25:25, 35, 39); "If there be a poor person among your brothers."

On the other hand, when the Torah speaks about civil law not to inflict harm on someone – it employs the term *re'a.* "Do not covet the house of *re'ekha*" (Ex. 20:14). "Do not move the landmark of *re'akha*" (Deut. 19:14). The fact that he is my neighbor imposes a duty and an obligation upon me. I should respect his property and his rights; I must not inflict any harm or damage on him. But this does not entitle the *re'a* to my support – that I should share his troubles and be helpful to him in times of need. For that, the bond

10 the LORD about you, and you will be held guilty. Give to him gener-
ously, and do not let your heart begrudge it, for by merit of this the
LORD your God will grant you blessing in all your work and all your
11 hands' endeavors. There will never cease to be poor people in the
land. And so I command you: open your hand generously to your
12 kinsmen, your poor and needy, who share your land. If a
fellow Hebrew, man or woman, is sold to you, he or she shall work for
you for six years; in the seventh year you shall send him or her forth
13 free. And when you send one forth free, do not send him empty-
14 handed. Provide for him liberally from your flock, your threshing
floor, and your winepress, giving him a share in the things with which
15 the LORD your God has blessed you. Remember: you were a slave in
Egypt and the LORD your God redeemed you; and so I give you this
16 command today. But if he says to you, 'I do not want to leave you' –
because he loves you and your household and he fares well with you,
17 then take an awl and put it through his ear into the door, and he will
be your slave for all time; you shall do the same with a female slave.
18 Do not consider it a hardship when you set him free, because for six
years he has given you twice the service of a hired laborer; and the
LORD your God will bless you in all your work.

---

awareness and ethical drive, who is devoid of conscience and is deaf to the call of justice and law. *Tzedakah* is not an act of discretionary kindness. It is an act that is imposed; it is imperative behavior. The ethico-legal yoke compels a person to submit to this normative demand. Accordingly, one who fails to carry out this commandment is considered as one who has rebelled against the kingdom of heaven, as he attempts to cast off the yoke of norms and becomes a non-normative (amoral and non-legal) creature. He thereby defaces his godly likeness and impairs the divine image in man, which is expressed through man's moral nature. The Sages said that wherever the Torah uses the term *beliya'al*, it refers to loss of one's reward in the World to Come (*Sanhedrin* 111b); in other words, the spiritual personality is lost. (*Halakhic Morality*, pp. 156–158)

עֵינְךָ בְּאָחִיךָ הָאֶבְיוֹן וְלֹא תִתֵּן לוֹ וְקָרָא עָלֶיךָ אֶל־יהוה
י וְהָיָה בְךָ חֵטְא: נָתוֹן תִּתֵּן לוֹ וְלֹא־יֵרַע לְבָבְךָ בְּתִתְּךָ לוֹ כִּי
בִּגְלַל ׀ הַדָּבָר הַזֶּה יְבָרֶכְךָ יהוה אֱלֹהֶיךָ בְּכָל־מַעֲשֶׂךָ וּבְכֹל
יא מִשְׁלַח יָדֶךָ: כִּי לֹא־יֶחְדַּל אֶבְיוֹן מִקֶּרֶב הָאָרֶץ עַל־כֵּן אָנֹכִי
מְצַוְּךָ לֵאמֹר פָּתֹחַ תִּפְתַּח אֶת־יָדְךָ לְאָחִיךָ לַעֲנִיֶּךָ וּלְאֶבְיֹנְךָ
יב בְּאַרְצֶךָ: כִּי־יִמָּכֵר לְךָ אָחִיךָ הָעִבְרִי אוֹ הָעִבְרִיָּה
וַעֲבָדְךָ שֵׁשׁ שָׁנִים וּבַשָּׁנָה הַשְּׁבִיעִת תְּשַׁלְּחֶנּוּ חָפְשִׁי מֵעִמָּךְ:
יג יד וְכִי־תְשַׁלְּחֶנּוּ חָפְשִׁי מֵעִמָּךְ לֹא תְשַׁלְּחֶנּוּ רֵיקָם: הַעֲנֵיק תַּעֲנִיק
לוֹ מִצֹּאנְךָ וּמִגָּרְנְךָ וּמִיִּקְבֶךָ אֲשֶׁר בֵּרַכְךָ יהוה אֱלֹהֶיךָ תִּתֶּן־לוֹ:
טו וְזָכַרְתָּ כִּי עֶבֶד הָיִיתָ בְּאֶרֶץ מִצְרַיִם וַיִּפְדְּךָ יהוה אֱלֹהֶיךָ עַל־כֵּן
טז אָנֹכִי מְצַוְּךָ אֶת־הַדָּבָר הַזֶּה הַיּוֹם: וְהָיָה כִּי־יֹאמַר אֵלֶיךָ לֹא
יז אֵצֵא מֵעִמָּךְ כִּי אֲהֵבְךָ וְאֶת־בֵּיתֶךָ כִּי־טוֹב לוֹ עִמָּךְ: וְלָקַחְתָּ
אֶת־הַמַּרְצֵעַ וְנָתַתָּה בְאָזְנוֹ וּבַדֶּלֶת וְהָיָה לְךָ עֶבֶד עוֹלָם וְאַף
יח לַאֲמָתְךָ תַּעֲשֶׂה־כֵּן: לֹא־יִקְשֶׁה בְעֵינֶךָ בְּשַׁלֵּחֲךָ אֹתוֹ חָפְשִׁי
מֵעִמָּךְ כִּי מִשְׁנֶה שְׂכַר שָׂכִיר עֲבָדְךָ שֵׁשׁ שָׁנִים וּבֵרַכְךָ יהוה
אֱלֹהֶיךָ בְּכֹל אֲשֶׁר תַּעֲשֶׂה:

---

upon you" (Deut. 13:18). He who turns his eyes away from *tzedakah* is called a base fellow (*beliya'al*), just as is he who worships idols. Concerning worship of idols Scripture says, "Certain base fellows (*benei beliya'al*) are gone out" (Deut. 13:14), and concerning him who turns his eyes away from *tzedakah* it says, "Be vigilant: let your heart not whisper a base (*beliya'al*) thought" (Deut. 15:9)… (*Hilkhot Matenot Aniyim* 10:2–3).

"Base" (*beliya'al*) is interpreted by our Sages as a compound word meaning "without a yoke" (*beli ol*), that is, a person who has thrown off the yoke of heaven (*Sanhedrin* 111b). It refers to an individual who lacks normative

If the second day of Shavuot falls on a weekday, start here:

19 Every firstborn male among your herd and flock you shall con- (*Shabbat:* SHELISHI)
secrate to the LORD your God. Do not work your firstborn ox or
20 shear your firstborn sheep. You and your household shall eat them
year by year in the presence of the LORD your God in the place
21 that the LORD will choose. If the animal has a blemish, a serious
blemish such as lameness or blindness, you shall not sacrifice it to
22 the LORD your God. The impure as well as the pure among you
23 shall eat it within your towns, as you would a gazelle or a deer. Its
blood, however, you must not eat. You must pour it out onto the
ground like water.

16 1 Observe the month of Aviv by offering a Passover sacrifice to the LEVI (*Shabbat:* REVI'I)
LORD your God; for in the month of Aviv the LORD your God
2 brought you out of Egypt by night. You shall offer up the Passover
sacrifice to the LORD your God, from the flock and the herd, at
the place that the LORD will choose as a dwelling for His name.
3 You must not eat anything leavened with it. For seven days, eat

---

Religious inspiration awakens a vision of God as the frame and space of the world. "I live in God; I think, feel, and exist through Him; He permeates my life and gives it meaning and content." The dualism that is prevalent in other religions, namely the division of the profane and sacred domain, is transcended. The entire universe is converted into one monistic realm, the domain of God. Street and home, the synagogue and shop, merge. The whole of man's life becomes dedicated to God.

Thus, the Jews gave God the remarkable attribute of *makom*, place. The Lord is envisaged as the *Mekomo shel olam*, the repository of the universe. What is this attribute of "place" for a God Who is infinite and omnipresent? By intuiting the attribute of *makom*, the Halakhah revealed to the world a revolutionary concept of God. He is not transcendent, mysterious, and inapproachable, but our immediate Companion. We live in God and experience Him in His full immediacy. As the settler experiences his home, as man intuits space, so does the Jew intuit God. He does not arrive at Him through philosophical speculation or metaphysical inference, but he meets Him through experience and intuition. God is the repository of the universe. All is

If the second day of שבועות *falls on a weekday, start here:*

יט כָּל־הַבְּכוֹר אֲשֶׁר יִוָּלֵד בִּבְקָרְךָ וּבְצֹאנְךָ הַזָּכָר תַּקְדִּישׁ לַיהוָה (בשבת שלישי)
כ אֱלֹהֶיךָ לֹא תַעֲבֹד בִּבְכֹר שׁוֹרֶךָ וְלֹא תָגֹז בְּכוֹר צֹאנֶךָ: לִפְנֵי
יְהוָה אֱלֹהֶיךָ תֹאכְלֶנּוּ שָׁנָה בְשָׁנָה בַּמָּקוֹם אֲשֶׁר־יִבְחַר יְהוָה
כא אַתָּה וּבֵיתֶךָ: וְכִי־יִהְיֶה בוֹ מוּם פִּסֵּחַ אוֹ עִוֵּר כֹּל מוּם רָע לֹא
כב תִזְבָּחֶנּוּ לַיהוָה אֱלֹהֶיךָ: בִּשְׁעָרֶיךָ תֹּאכְלֶנּוּ הַטָּמֵא וְהַטָּהוֹר
כג יַחְדָּו כַּצְּבִי וְכָאַיָּל: רַק אֶת־דָּמוֹ לֹא תֹאכֵל עַל־הָאָרֶץ תִּשְׁפְּכֶנּוּ
כַּמָּיִם:
טז א שָׁמוֹר אֶת־חֹדֶשׁ הָאָבִיב וְעָשִׂיתָ פֶּסַח לַיהוָה אֱלֹהֶיךָ כִּי בְּחֹדֶשׁ לוי (בשבת רביעי)
ב הָאָבִיב הוֹצִיאֲךָ יְהוָה אֱלֹהֶיךָ מִמִּצְרָיִם לָיְלָה: וְזָבַחְתָּ פֶּסַח
לַיהוָה אֱלֹהֶיךָ צֹאן וּבָקָר בַּמָּקוֹם אֲשֶׁר יִבְחַר יְהוָה לְשַׁכֵּן שְׁמוֹ
ג שָׁם: לֹא־תֹאכַל עָלָיו חָמֵץ שִׁבְעַת יָמִים תֹּאכַל־עָלָיו מַצּוֹת

כָּל־הַבְּכוֹר *Every firstborn.* The fact that the first budding of life must be consecrated to Him is a logical consequence of the idea that God is the rightful owner of all life. Every living creature owes its very existence to Him (in the simplest juridic meaning), and it is in the firstling that God's life-giving breath is most clearly manifest. The daybreak of life belongs to God, but is leased to man. As a result, Judaism proclaimed the idea of *bekhor,* the firstborn. "Sanctify to Me all the firstborn, whatever opens the womb among the children of Israel, both of man and of beast, it is Mine" (Ex. 13:2). The firstborn shall be consecrated to God. The *bekhor* – man or animal – is claimed by the master. In the case of a clean animal, the firstborn is surrendered to God in the form of a sacrifice; in reference to humans and unclean animals, the Torah recommends redemption, a symbolic performance that still retains its aboriginal meaning in the formula which was composed by the Geonim: "*ma ba'it tefei*?" – "which do you prefer: to give away your firstborn son…or to redeem him…?" (*The Emergence of Ethical Man,* p. 45)

בַּמָּקוֹם אֲשֶׁר־יִבְחַר יהוה *In the place that the Lord will choose.* The religious telos finds its full realization in the passionate religious life, permeated with enthusiasm and rapture, which opens to man new vistas and enchanted horizons.

unleavened bread – the bread of affliction – because you left Egypt
in haste. This is for you to remember the day you left Egypt all the
4 days of your life. *For seven days no leaven shall be found with you SHELISHI (*Shabbat:* ḤAMISHI)
in all your land. And do not let any of the meat that you sacrificed
5 on the evening of the first day remain until morning. You may not
slaughter the Passover sacrifice in any of the towns that the LORD
6 your God is giving you. Only at the place that the LORD your God
chooses as a dwelling for His name, there shall you slaughter the
Passover sacrifice in the evening; at sunset, at the time appointed
7 to leave Egypt, you shall cook and eat it at the place that the LORD
your God will choose, and on the following morning you may set
8 out to your tents. For six days you shall eat unleavened bread and,
on the seventh day, you shall hold an assembly for the LORD your
9 God and perform no work. You shall count seven weeks. REVI'I (*Shabbat:* SHISHI)

Sensitivity and compassion are the central axis of our moral experience. To hurt the feelings of a person by uttering some innocuous remark is a severe transgression.

Without the experience of Egypt, we would have remained emotionally coarse and tough. That is the reason for the frequent mention of the Exodus whenever the Torah speaks of our duty to respect the feelings of others, particularly the feelings of the defenseless, helpless, and lonely people. (*Days of Deliverance*, pp. 22–23)

שִׁבְעָה שָׁבֻעֹת תִּסְפָּר־לָךְ *You shall count seven weeks.* The Jew is aware experientially of the past and committed to the future, which is a reality to him. To exist as a Jew means to be at the juncture of past and future, of that which is no longer real and that which is not yet real. Our mission is to live in both dimensions.

This experiential merger of past and future, of recollection and anticipation, is symbolized by the process of counting. When one counts, one ushers in a mathematical series, a continuum. Kant remarked that at any position in which you find yourself while counting, you have to be aware of two things: the preceding positions and those that follow (*Critique of Pure Reason* [1781], Introduction, sec. V). For instance, when we count the thirty-third day of the *omer*, we *ipso facto* state that this position was preceded by thirty-two

לֶחֶם עֹנִי כִּי בְחִפָּזוֹן יָצָאתָ מֵאֶרֶץ מִצְרַיִם לְמַעַן תִּזְכֹּר אֶת־יוֹם
ד צֵאתְךָ מֵאֶרֶץ מִצְרַיִם כֹּל יְמֵי חַיֶּיךָ: *וְלֹא־יֵרָאֶה לְךָ שְׂאֹר בְּכָל־ שלישי (בשבת חמישי)
גְּבֻלְךָ שִׁבְעַת יָמִים וְלֹא־יָלִין מִן־הַבָּשָׂר אֲשֶׁר תִּזְבַּח בָּעֶרֶב בַּיּוֹם
ה הָרִאשׁוֹן לַבֹּקֶר: לֹא תוּכַל לִזְבֹּחַ אֶת־הַפָּסַח בְּאַחַד שְׁעָרֶיךָ
ו אֲשֶׁר־יהוה אֱלֹהֶיךָ נֹתֵן לָךְ: כִּי אִם־אֶל־הַמָּקוֹם אֲשֶׁר־יִבְחַר
יהוה אֱלֹהֶיךָ לְשַׁכֵּן שְׁמוֹ שָׁם תִּזְבַּח אֶת־הַפֶּסַח בָּעָרֶב כְּבוֹא
ז הַשֶּׁמֶשׁ מוֹעֵד צֵאתְךָ מִמִּצְרָיִם: וּבִשַּׁלְתָּ וְאָכַלְתָּ בַּמָּקוֹם אֲשֶׁר
ח יִבְחַר יהוה אֱלֹהֶיךָ בּוֹ וּפָנִיתָ בַבֹּקֶר וְהָלַכְתָּ לְאֹהָלֶיךָ: שֵׁשֶׁת
יָמִים תֹּאכַל מַצּוֹת וּבַיּוֹם הַשְּׁבִיעִי עֲצֶרֶת לַיהוה אֱלֹהֶיךָ לֹא
ט תַעֲשֶׂה מְלָאכָה: שִׁבְעָה שָׁבֻעֹת תִּסְפָּר־לָךְ מֵהָחֵל רביעי (בשבת ששי)

---

contained in Him. He does not repose in me; He is not just one phase of my world perspective; He envelops all. If the universe is unthinkable without a space frame (and this is, indeed, the crux of Kant's a priori concept), so much more so is the Jewish world incomprehensible without an all-embracing God.

It is these two elements, cognition and integration, that make for a world perspective and, for the Jew, a *kedushat makom*. Without the idea of place-consciousness, the state of *kedushah*, sanctity, can never be acquired or held. For the approach to God is only through the application of place-consciousness. When one implants himself in the cultural sphere of the Torah and merges with its intrinsic trends, he may claim that he has found God. Without the all-enveloping and all-inclusive space intuition, the ideation of divinity is almost impossible. Even the atheist experiences, at times, the mysterious feeling of the pantheist, of being enveloped by God. (*Shiurei Harav*, pp. 13–14)

לְמַעַן תִּזְכֹּר אֶת־יוֹם צֵאתְךָ מֵאֶרֶץ מִצְרַיִם כֹּל יְמֵי חַיֶּיךָ *This is for you to remember the day when you left Egypt all the days of your life.* Egypt is a central experience that underlies the very morality of the Jew. The unique morality of the Jew is rooted in a very sensitive, exceptionally tender, and warm approach to man. The Torah is concerned with *kevod haberiyot*, human dignity. The latter must not be abused. It must not be denied to the weak and the helpless.

At the time when you first put sickle to standing grain, begin
10 your count of seven weeks. And then celebrate the Festival of
Weeks to the LORD your God, bringing a freewill offering, accord-
11 ing to the blessing the LORD your God has granted you. And
rejoice before the LORD your God – you and your sons and daugh-
ters, your male and female slaves, and the Levites living in your

---

Reb Yoshe Ber told the woman to step aside. He took her place and began to announce aloud how beautiful the flowers were, how tender and green the twigs and leaves. People suddenly encountered a strange scene. Their world-renowned rabbi in his festival garments was zealously selling flowers – and charging exorbitant prices. Of course, all the flowers were sold quickly despite the prohibitive prices.

Whether the story is true or untrue, the fact that such a folk-story is told is indicative of the demands the Jew makes upon his own conscience as regards *kedushah*. In other words, to help someone in distress, you must sacrifice not only your money but your very dignity and pride. This conception is the product not of the idea of *tzedakah*, but of *kedushah*. To help others is not only an ethical act but also a great experience through which you come one or two steps closer to the Almighty. Serving one's fellow man is *eo ipso* the most sublime service to God. (*Abraham's Journey*, pp. 107–108)

כַּאֲשֶׁר יְבָרֶכְךָ יהוה אֱלֹהֶיךָ *According to the blessing the Lord your God has granted you.* The Torah has tied the norm of charity to the feeling of happiness, security and pride in one's accomplishments. "According to the blessing the Lord your God has granted you" is the motif which is conjoined with the commandment of charity. Compassion is the socialized expression of joy. A person is summoned to serve God by serving his fellow man when he is least inclined to place himself at the disposal of others, when he is preoccupied with himself and the only service to which he attributes any value is self-service. He is contented with himself; he has been successful, he rejoices at his own great achievements, and he is ready to shut out the whole world in his exultation over his marvelous self. Exactly then, the call to service sounds. Man suddenly realizes that there is another side to life which he overlooked in his excessive joy; there are frustrated hopes, suffering and failure, and as long as destitution, poverty and pain prevail, no one can consider himself happy and successful. Out of the dialectical experience, the feeling of sympathy emerges. (*Out of the Whirlwind*, p. 206)

י חֶרְמֵשׁ בַּקָּמָה תָּחֵל לִסְפֹּר שִׁבְעָה שָׁבֻעוֹת׃ וְעָשִׂיתָ חַג שָׁבֻעוֹת
לַיהוָה אֱלֹהֶיךָ מִסַּת נִדְבַת יָדְךָ אֲשֶׁר תִּתֵּן כַּאֲשֶׁר יְבָרֶכְךָ יְהוָה
יא אֱלֹהֶיךָ׃ וְשָׂמַחְתָּ לִפְנֵי ׀ יְהוָה אֱלֹהֶיךָ אַתָּה וּבִנְךָ וּבִתֶּךָ וְעַבְדְּךָ

---

previous positions. At the same time, we know that thirty-three is not the last station; from here we will move on to additional positions. In other words, any act of counting embraces retrospection as well as anticipation. I look backward and I am aware of what I did last night, and I look forward and I know that the counting tonight is not the final one. The Jew who approaches Mount Sinai to receive the Torah is rooted in the ancient past and at the same time committed to a future pre-experienced as a reality. (*Festival of Freedom*, pp. 177–181)

תָּחֵל לִסְפֹּר שִׁבְעָה שָׁבֻעוֹת *Begin your count of seven weeks.* When the Jews were delivered from the Egyptian oppression and Moses rose to undertake the almost impossible task of metamorphosing a tribe of slaves into a "nation of priests" (Ex. 19:16), he was told by God that the path leading from the holiday of Pesaḥ to Shavuot, from initial liberation to consummate freedom (*Gilui Shekhinah*, Revelation), leads through the medium of time. The commandment of *sefirah* was entrusted the Jew; the wondrous test of counting forty-nine successive days was put to him. These forty-nine days must be whole. If one day be missed, the act of numeration is invalidated.

A slave who is capable of appreciating each day, of grasping its meaning and worth, of weaving every thread of time into a glorious fabric, quantitatively stretching over the period of seven weeks but qualitatively forming the warp and woof of centuries of change, is eligible for Torah. He has achieved freedom. (*Shiurei Harav*, pp. 17–18)

וְעָשִׂיתָ חַג שָׁבֻעוֹת *And then celebrate the Festival of Weeks.* A story is told about Reb Yoshe Ber of Brisk that one *erev Shavuot,* late in the afternoon on his way to the synagogue, he noticed a flower stand that was still open. He went over to the woman and said: "My dear, it is late. We will usher in the *Yom Tov* pretty soon. Why don't you go home to your family?" "Yes, Rabbi," the woman answered, "but I haven't sold any flowers. The count sent in a wagon loaded with flowers, and everyone brought greenery from the count. In fact, his flowers and branches were much better than mine. What shall I do, Rabbi? There is nothing in the house, no food, no wine, no candles! I have nothing to look forward to."

towns, together with the migrants, orphans, and widows among
you – at the place that the LORD your God will choose as a dwell-
12 ing for His name. Remember that you were a slave in Egypt, and
so take care to fulfill these decrees.

13 You shall keep the Festival of Tabernacles for seven days, after you HAMISHI (*Shabbat:* SHEVI'I)
have gathered the produce from your threshing floor and winepress.
14 Rejoice in your festival, you and your sons and daughters; your
male and female servants; the Levites; and the migrants, orphans,
15 and widows living in your towns. For seven days, celebrate before
the LORD your God at the place that the LORD will choose, for
the LORD your God will grant you blessing in all your harvest
and in all the work of your hands, and you shall be wholly joyful.
16 Three times a year, all the males among you shall appear before the
LORD your God in the place that He will choose: on the Festival

---

שָׁלוֹשׁ פְּעָמִים בַּשָּׁנָה יֵרָאֶה כָל־זְכוּרְךָ אֶת־פְּנֵי יהוה אֱלֹהֶיךָ *Three times a year, all the males among you shall appear before the Lord your God.* Time is sanctified if man, who has a temporal existence, joins with eternity, with God. Making an appearance in the Temple courtyard is the first of the commandments of the three pilgrimage holidays. And what is the essence of this commandment? Appearing before God, as it is written, "Three times a year, all the males among you shall appear before the Lord your God." The holiday joy is revealed in man's joining with God, in standing before Him: "and you shall rejoice before the Lord your God seven days" (Lev. 23:40). When a quorum of ten Jews recite the sacred prayers, they bring the *Deus Absconditus*, the hidden God, whom the entire heavens cannot contain, into their confines. "And I will be sanctified among the children of Israel" (Lev. 22:32) – "in every group of ten the *Shekhinah* abides" (*Sanhedrin* 39a). When a group of ten Jews sit and study Torah together and complete their study, one of them stands up and proclaims aloud the vision of the *Shekhinah*'s redemption and man's cleaving to his Creator: "*Yitgaddel ve-yitkadesh* (May His name be magnified and sanctified)... in the world that will be unified in the future." But even when a single individual studies the Torah, the *Shekhinah* is with him, for whenever a Jew studies the Torah he brings about the gradual realization of the vision of the End of Days. The state of cleaving to God, whose essence is in the eschatological vision found in the prophecies of the End of Days, has begun to

וַאֲמָתֶךָ וְהַלֵּוִי אֲשֶׁר בִּשְׁעָרֶיךָ וְהַגֵּר וְהַיָּתוֹם וְהָאַלְמָנָה אֲשֶׁר
בְּקִרְבֶּךָ בַּמָּקוֹם אֲשֶׁר יִבְחַר יְהוָה אֱלֹהֶיךָ לְשַׁכֵּן שְׁמוֹ שָׁם׃
יב וְזָכַרְתָּ כִּי־עֶבֶד הָיִיתָ בְּמִצְרָיִם וְשָׁמַרְתָּ וְעָשִׂיתָ אֶת־הַחֻקִּים
הָאֵלֶּה׃
יג חַג הַסֻּכֹּת תַּעֲשֶׂה לְךָ שִׁבְעַת יָמִים בְּאָסְפְּךָ מִגָּרְנְךָ וּמִיִּקְבֶךָ׃ חמישי (בשבת שביעי)
יד וְשָׂמַחְתָּ בְּחַגֶּךָ אַתָּה וּבִנְךָ וּבִתֶּךָ וְעַבְדְּךָ וַאֲמָתֶךָ וְהַלֵּוִי וְהַגֵּר
טו וְהַיָּתוֹם וְהָאַלְמָנָה אֲשֶׁר בִּשְׁעָרֶיךָ׃ שִׁבְעַת יָמִים תָּחֹג לַיהוָה
אֱלֹהֶיךָ בַּמָּקוֹם אֲשֶׁר־יִבְחַר יְהוָה כִּי יְבָרֶכְךָ יְהוָה אֱלֹהֶיךָ בְּכֹל־
טז תְּבוּאָתְךָ וּבְכֹל מַעֲשֵׂה יָדֶיךָ וְהָיִיתָ אַךְ שָׂמֵחַ׃ שָׁלוֹשׁ פְּעָמִים ׀
בַּשָּׁנָה יֵרָאֶה כָל־זְכוּרְךָ אֶת־פְּנֵי ׀ יְהוָה אֱלֹהֶיךָ בַּמָּקוֹם אֲשֶׁר

וְהַגֵּר וְהַיָּתוֹם וְהָאַלְמָנָה אֲשֶׁר בְּקִרְבֶּךָ *Together with the migrants, orphans, and widows among you.* When man is engaged in a carnal pursuit such as eating, and his own need presses the most, insisting upon immediate remedial action that is insanely centered about himself, the Torah expects of him attentiveness to the need of the other self. The norm of charity comes to the fore. Invite not the rich, the one upon whom God has showered His blessings in abundance, but the poor, the destitute, the lonely and abandoned who crave food and companionship. While answering the call of the *physis,* man must obey the summons of the *ethos.* Eat not your food alone, share with others, form a community of "haves" and "have-nots," since the bread of which you partake is not yours but God's; it is out of His hand that you eat. When you are hungry, even though you have garnered in your storehouses enough grain to last you for many years, a new reality is laid bare before you, the one of pain and discomfort. A new challenge rises out of this reality, one to which you must respond quickly and unhesitatingly. Your own travail summons you to sympathetic action with regard to the other self; you must share your meal with him. You and he must join a new community, where the small and the great meet and the servant is equal to his master. If the flavor of a delicious dish has excited your appetite, you must hallow this excitement by letting the other self sit at your table and form a fellowship with you. Every physical excitement contains a challenge, a demand, which you must meet courageously. Thus, the meal is transposed into a sacrificial institution, into an act of *caritas.* (*Festival of Freedom,* pp. 24–25)

of Unleavened Bread, the Festival of Weeks, and the Festival of
Tabernacles. They shall not appear before the LORD empty-handed;
17 each shall bring a gift, in keeping with the blessing that the LORD
your God has given you.

HALF KADDISH

Before Maftir is read, the second Sefer Torah is placed on the bima and the Reader says Half Kaddish:

Reader: יִתְגַּדַּל Magnified and sanctified may His great name be,
in the world He created by His will.
May He establish His kingdom
in your lifetime and in your days,
and in the lifetime of all the house of Israel,
swiftly and soon – and say: Amen.

---

in business. But how can Halakhah demand that I deny my grief? How can Halakhah expect me to recite *Hallel* while my soul is cloaked in heavy mourning? But this is what Halakhah demands. This is how we must behave. The Master of the World is "long-suffering," and we too must, to the degree possible, espouse this trait.

This can be illustrated with an actual event. It was the first night of Shavuot in Volozhin. The entire yeshiva was filled with light. Hundreds of students were sitting and learning Torah. Suddenly, the fatherly figure of the Netziv, Rabbi Naftali Tzvi Yehuda Berlin, appeared, and he called out: "*Rabbotai*, let us go dance in honor of the giving of the Torah." The entire yeshiva, with the Netziv at the head, went out to dance in a sacred circle, with fiery passion. While they were dancing, an agent from the telegraph office ran over and handed the Netziv an open telegraph. He gave it a quick glance and then placed it in his pocket, saying, as an afterthought, "It's nothing; let's keep dancing." Thus, the entire holiday of Shavuot passed in Volozhin amid dancing, rejoicing, and celebration through Torah study. At the end of the festival, the Netziv made *Havdala*, concluding with the *berakhah*, "Blessed are You... who separates the sacred from the profane." Suddenly, as the sanctity of the holiday vanished in that moment, the Netziv fainted. The telegraph that arrived on the first night of Shavuot had informed him of the death of his little sister.

This is a story of patience and forbearance. This is the greatest ransom that a Jew must pay to the Almighty. (*Blessings and Thanksgiving*, pp. 144–145)

יִבְחָר בְּחַג הַמַּצּוֹת וּבְחַג הַשָּׁבֻעוֹת וּבְחַג הַסֻּכּוֹת וְלֹא יֵרָאֶה
יז אֶת־פְּנֵי יְהוָה רֵיקָם׃ אִישׁ כְּמַתְּנַת יָדוֹ כְּבִרְכַּת יְהוָה אֱלֹהֶיךָ
אֲשֶׁר נָתַן־לָךְ׃

חצי קדיש

Before מפטיר *is read, the second* ספר תורה *is placed on the* שולחן *and the* קורא *says* חצי קדיש:

קורא: יִתְגַּדַּל וְיִתְקַדַּשׁ שְׁמֵהּ רַבָּא (קהל: אָמֵן)
בְּעָלְמָא דִּי בְרָא כִרְעוּתֵהּ
וְיַמְלִיךְ מַלְכוּתֵהּ
בְּחַיֵּיכוֹן וּבְיוֹמֵיכוֹן וּבְחַיֵּי דְכָל בֵּית יִשְׂרָאֵל
בַּעֲגָלָא וּבִזְמַן קָרִיב, וְאִמְרוּ אָמֵן. (קהל: אָמֵן)

---

be realized even in this divided world, in the actual life of man with his flawed, sterile existence. Judaism has always known about the continuity between temporal and eternal existence, between the world that struggles to exist and the world that is redeemed, between the world that is polluted and the world that is all purity and goodness. (*And From There You Shall Seek*, pp. 84–85)

וּבְחַג הַשָּׁבֻעוֹת *The Festival of Weeks.* Judaism demands a level of emotional discipline and psychological fortitude to an extent which can transcend human capabilities. One loses a parent, sibling, or spouse, God forbid, on the day before Passover, and the burial takes place that day. The grieving Jew returns home in the late afternoon, removes his shoes, and begins sitting *shiva*. His home is gloomy and desolate, attesting to the fresh loss of a loved one. The entire household wails with heartbreak.

Then the sun sets and the festival of Passover begins. Halakhah suddenly commands the end of the mourning period: A festival cancels mourning. Light candles in honor of the holiday! Recite the *berakhah* of *Sheheḥeyanu*, blessing God "who has given us life, sustained us, and brought us to this time"! Go to the synagogue, and upon your return, recline at the Seder like princes. Rejoice because God delivered our ancestors and delivers us. "This is the day that the Lord has made-let us exult and rejoice on it" (Ps. 118:24).

How can Halakhah demand such behavior? I accept many obligations that Halakhah imposes: Shabbat, *kashrut*, family purity, *tefillin*, and honesty

All: May His great name be blessed for ever and all time.

Reader: Blessed and praised, glorified and exalted,
raised and honored, uplifted and lauded
be the name of the Holy One,
blessed be He,
beyond any blessing,
song, praise and consolation
uttered in the world – and say: Amen.

HAGBAHA AND GELILA

The first Torah scroll is lifted and the congregation says:

וְזֹאת הַתּוֹרָה This is the Torah *Deut. 4*
that Moses placed before the children of Israel,
at the Lord's commandment, by the hand of Moses. *Num. 9*

Some add: It is a tree of life to those who grasp it, *Prov. 3*
and those who uphold it are happy.
Its ways are ways of pleasantness, and all its paths are peace.
Long life is in its right hand; in its left, riches and honor.
It pleased the Lord for the sake of [Israel's] righteousness, *Is. 42*
to make the Torah great and glorious.

The first Torah scroll is bound and covered and the oleh for Maftir is called to the second Torah scroll.

MAFTIR

28 26 The day of first produce, when you bring an offering of new grain to *Numbers*
the Lord on your Festival of Weeks, shall be a sacred assembly for
27 you. On it you shall perform no laborious work. You shall present
a burnt offering as a pleasing aroma to the Lord: two young bulls,
28 one ram, and seven yearling lambs. Their grain offering shall be
fine flour mixed with oil: three-tenths of a measure for each bull,
29 two-tenths for the one ram, and one-tenth for each of the seven
30 lambs. Offer one male goat to atone for you. These you shall offer
31 in addition to the regular burnt offering, its grain offering and liba-
tions. They shall be without blemish.

קהל וקורא: יְהֵא שְׁמֵהּ רַבָּא מְבָרַךְ לְעָלַם וּלְעָלְמֵי עָלְמַיָּא.

קורא: יִתְבָּרַךְ וְיִשְׁתַּבַּח וְיִתְפָּאַר וְיִתְרוֹמַם וְיִתְנַשֵּׂא
וְיִתְהַדָּר וְיִתְעַלֶּה וְיִתְהַלָּל
שְׁמֵהּ דְּקֻדְשָׁא בְּרִיךְ הוּא (קהל: בְּרִיךְ הוּא)
לְעֵלָּא מִן כָּל בִּרְכָתָא וְשִׁירָתָא
תֻּשְׁבְּחָתָא וְנֶחֱמָתָא, דַּאֲמִירָן בְּעָלְמָא
וְאִמְרוּ אָמֵן. (קהל: אָמֵן)

הגבהה וגלילה

The first ספר תורה *is lifted and the* קהל *says:*

וְזֹאת הַתּוֹרָה אֲשֶׁר־שָׂם מֹשֶׁה לִפְנֵי בְּנֵי יִשְׂרָאֵל: דברים ד
עַל־פִּי יהוה בְּיַד מֹשֶׁה: במדבר ט

Some add עֵץ־חַיִּים הִיא לַמַּחֲזִיקִים בָּהּ וְתֹמְכֶיהָ מְאֻשָּׁר: משלי ג
דְּרָכֶיהָ דַרְכֵי־נֹעַם וְכָל־נְתִיבוֹתֶיהָ שָׁלוֹם:
אֹרֶךְ יָמִים בִּימִינָהּ, בִּשְׂמֹאולָהּ עֹשֶׁר וְכָבוֹד:
יהוה חָפֵץ לְמַעַן צִדְקוֹ יַגְדִּיל תּוֹרָה וְיַאְדִּיר: ישעיה מב

The first ספר תורה *is bound and covered and the* עולה
for מפטיר *is called to the second* ספר תורה.

מפטיר

כח כו וּבְיוֹם הַבִּכּוּרִים בְּהַקְרִיבְכֶם מִנְחָה חֲדָשָׁה לַיהוה בְּשָׁבֻעֹתֵיכֶם במדבר
מִקְרָא־קֹדֶשׁ יִהְיֶה לָכֶם כָּל־מְלֶאכֶת עֲבֹדָה לֹא תַעֲשׂוּ:
כז וְהִקְרַבְתֶּם עוֹלָה לְרֵיחַ נִיחֹחַ לַיהוה פָּרִים בְּנֵי־בָקָר שְׁנַיִם אַיִל
כח אֶחָד שִׁבְעָה כְבָשִׂים בְּנֵי שָׁנָה: וּמִנְחָתָם סֹלֶת בְּלוּלָה בַשָּׁמֶן
כט שְׁלֹשָׁה עֶשְׂרֹנִים לַפָּר הָאֶחָד שְׁנֵי עֶשְׂרֹנִים לָאַיִל הָאֶחָד: עִשָּׂרוֹן
ל עִשָּׂרוֹן לַכֶּבֶשׂ הָאֶחָד לְשִׁבְעַת הַכְּבָשִׂים: שְׂעִיר עִזִּים אֶחָד
לא לְכַפֵּר עֲלֵיכֶם: מִלְּבַד עֹלַת הַתָּמִיד וּמִנְחָתוֹ תַּעֲשׂוּ תְּמִימִם
יִהְיוּ־לָכֶם וְנִסְכֵּיהֶם:

HAGBAHA AND GELILA

The second Torah scroll is lifted and the congregation says:

וְזֹאת הַתּוֹרָה This is the Torah Deut. 4
that Moses placed before the children of Israel,
at the Lord's commandment, by the hand of Moses. Num. 9

Some add: It is a tree of life to those who grasp it, and those who uphold it are happy. *Prov. 3*
Its ways are ways of pleasantness, and all its paths are peace.
Long life is in its right hand; in its left, riches and honor.
It pleased the Lord for the sake of [Israel's] righteousness, *Is. 42*
to make the Torah great and glorious.

The second Torah scroll is bound and covered and the oleh for Maftir reads the Haftarah.

HAFTARAH FOR THE SECOND DAY OF SHAVUOT

2 22 But the Lord is in His heavenly dwelling. All the earth, be silent *Hab.*
3 1 before Him. A prayer Habakkuk the prophet sung with
shiggayon:

Many say the following in the Haftarah.

יַצִּיב פִּתְגָם May this praise be desired, for God, Sign and Witness, alone among myriad myriad angels. / Where is it that He dwells, among that company of angels who dismissed the four great mountains [and chose Sinai]. / Out before Him springs and flows, into His wells, a river of fire. / In a mountain of snow bright light shines out, and sparks and brands of fire, / and He creates and sees all that lies in darkness, for present with Him is all light. / He oversees all distances, judging without hastiness, and to Him are revealed all the world's secrets. / From Him will I ask permission to read; and afterwards also from the people before me, / who know the Law the Mishna, Tosefta, Sifra and Sifrei. / The King who lives for evermore will destroy the people that subjugates them. / For they have been told that they will be like sand, too many to be counted, like dust of the earth. / Make their valleys white today, with produce, their vats flowing over with wine. / Bring what they wish for, make their faces shine – let them shine out like morning light. / Grant me strength, and lift Your eyes to see Your enemies, those who deny You, / and make them like straw within the bricks; like stones, silent and ashamed. / As I stand here, translating the words of the most superior of books, / the Lord has given [Torah] through the humble [Moses], and so to Him – our gracious thanks.

הגבהה וגלילה

The second ספר תורה *is lifted and the* קהל *says:*

וְזֹאת הַתּוֹרָה אֲשֶׁר־שָׂם מֹשֶׁה לִפְנֵי בְּנֵי יִשְׂרָאֵל: דברים ד
עַל־פִּי יהוה בְּיַד מֹשֶׁה: במדבר ט

Some add
עֵץ־חַיִּים הִיא לַמַּחֲזִיקִים בָּהּ וְתֹמְכֶיהָ מְאֻשָּׁר: משלי ג
דְּרָכֶיהָ דַרְכֵי־נֹעַם וְכָל־נְתִיבֹתֶיהָ שָׁלוֹם:
אֹרֶךְ יָמִים בִּימִינָהּ, בִּשְׂמֹאולָהּ עֹשֶׁר וְכָבוֹד:
יהוה חָפֵץ לְמַעַן צִדְקוֹ יַגְדִּיל תּוֹרָה וְיַאְדִּיר: ישעיה מב

The second ספר תורה *is bound and covered and the* עולה *for* מפטיר *reads the* הפטרה.

הפטרה ליום טוב השני של שבועות

ב כ וַיהוָה בְּהֵיכַל קָדְשׁוֹ הַס מִפָּנָיו כָּל־הָאָרֶץ: ג א תְּפִלָּה חבקוק
לַחֲבַקּוּק הַנָּבִיא עַל שִׁגְיֹנוֹת:

Many say the following in the הפטרה.

יַצִּיב פִּתְגָם, לְאָת וּדְגַם, בְּרִבּוֹ רִבְבָן עִירִין.
עָנֵה אֲנָא, בְּמִנְיָנָא, דְּפָסְלִין אַרְבְּעָה טוּרִין.
קֳדָמוֹהִי, לְגוֹ מוֹהִי, נְגִיד וּנְפִיק נְהַר דִּי נוּרִין.
בְּטוּר תַּלְגָּא, נְהוֹר שְׁרָגָא, וְזִיקִין דִּי נוּר וּבָעוֹרִין.
בְּרָא וּסְכָא, מַה בַּחֲשׁוֹכָא, וְעִמֵּהּ שָׁרְיִין נְהוֹרִין.
רְחִיקִין צְפָא, בְּלָא שִׁטְפָּא, וּגְלַיִן לֵהּ דְּמִטַּמְרִין.
בְּעֵית מִנֵּהּ, יָת הַרְמָנֵהּ, וּבָתְרוֹהִי עֲדֵי גְבָרִין.
יָדְעֵי הִלְכְתָא, וּמַתְנִיתָא, וְתוֹסֶפְתָּא סִפְרָא וְסִפְרִין.
מֶלֶךְ חַיָּא, לְעָלְמַיָּא, יְמַגַּר עַם לְהוֹן מְשַׁחֲרִין.
אֲמִיר עֲלֵיהוֹן, כְּחָלָא יְהוֹן, וְלָא יִתְמְנוֹן הֵיךְ עַפְרִין.
יְחַוְּרוּן כְּעַן, לְהוֹן בִּקְעָן, יְטוּפוּן נַעֲוֵי חַמְרִין.
רְעוּתְהוֹן הַב, וְאַפֵּיהוֹן צְהַב, יְנַהֲרוּן כִּנְהוֹר צַפְרִין.
לִי הַב תְּקוֹף, וְעֵינָךְ זְקוֹף, חֲזִי עָדָךְ דְּבָךְ כָּפְרִין.
יְהוֹן כְּתִבְנָא, בְּגוֹ לִבְנָא, כְּאַבְנָא יִשְׁתְּקוּן חָפְרִין.
כְּקָאֱמְנָא, וְתַרְגְּמָנָא, בְּמִלּוֹי דִּבְחִיר סָפְרִין.
יְהוֹנָתָן, גְּבַר עִנְוְתָן, בְּכֵן נַמְטִין אַפְּרִין.

2 Lord, I have heard accounts of You and am afraid. O Lord, in the
coming years renew Your deeds; in the coming years, make Yourself
3 known; in wrath, remember mercy. God appears from Teiman,
the Holy One from Mount Paran. Selah His splendor covers the
4 heavens; the earth is filled with His glory. His radiance illuminates
like light; rays emanate from His every side; therein lies His hidden
5 6 strength. Before Him will come plague, fiery blight at His feet. He
stands and the earth shakes; He looks and nations tremble; age-old
mountains shatter; everlasting hills bow low; all the world's ways
7 are His. I saw Kushan's tents afflicted for sinning, the curtains in the
8 land of Midian quiver. Is the Lord angry at the rivers; is
it against the rivers that You rage? Is Your fury against the ocean
so that You ride upon Your horses of war, Your chariots of deliver-
9 ance? Your bow is unsheathed; You keep Your word, Your oath to
10 the tribes, Selah, and split the earth open with rivers. When the
mountains see You they shiver; streams of water flow through; the
11 deep sounds with thunder, lifting its hands up high. The sun, the
moon stand still in their spheres;by the light of Your bolts the world
12 will march, by the glow of Your flashing spear. In rage, You tread the
13 earth; in wrath, You trample nations. You emerge to liberate Your
people, to liberate Your king. You crush the head of the house of evil,
14 stripping it from the core up to its neck, Selah. You pierce
heads of cities with their own spears, they who come in a storm to
15 shatter me, rejoicing as though secretly devouring the needy. You
16 trample the ocean floor with Your steeds, stirring mighty seas. I hear
this, and my gut churns; my lips tremble at the sound. Rot eats at my
bones; I shudder in my place. Could I rest on the day of terror, the
17 day God rises up for His nation? Though the fig tree will not flower,
nor will fruit fill the vines, olives will grow gaunt and grain fields
yield no produce, sheep will be removed from their pens, and cattle
18 will not be found in the sheds, yet I will delight in the Lord; I will
19 rejoice in the God who will save me. God, my Lord, my strength,
He makes my legs like a deer's and guides me to stride to the
heights. This song is for the conductor; to Him I offer my melodies.

ב יהוה שָׁמַעְתִּי שִׁמְעֲךָ יָרֵאתִי יהוה פָּעָלְךָ בְּקֶרֶב שָׁנִים חַיֵּיהוּ
ג בְּקֶרֶב שָׁנִים תּוֹדִיעַ בְּרֹגֶז רַחֵם תִּזְכּוֹר: אֱלוֹהַּ מִתֵּימָן יָבוֹא
וְקָדוֹשׁ מֵהַר־פָּארָן סֶלָה כִּסָּה שָׁמַיִם הוֹדוֹ וּתְהִלָּתוֹ מָלְאָה
ד הָאָרֶץ: וְנֹגַהּ כָּאוֹר תִּהְיֶה קַרְנַיִם מִיָּדוֹ לוֹ וְשָׁם חֶבְיוֹן עֻזֹּה:
ה ו לְפָנָיו יֵלֶךְ דָּבֶר וְיֵצֵא רֶשֶׁף לְרַגְלָיו: עָמַד ׀ וַיְמֹדֶד אֶרֶץ רָאָה
וַיַּתֵּר גּוֹיִם וַיִּתְפֹּצְצוּ הַרְרֵי־עַד שַׁחוּ גִּבְעוֹת עוֹלָם הֲלִיכוֹת
ז עוֹלָם לוֹ: תַּחַת אָוֶן רָאִיתִי אָהֳלֵי כוּשָׁן יִרְגְּזוּן יְרִיעוֹת אֶרֶץ
ח מִדְיָן: הֲבִנְהָרִים חָרָה יהוה אִם בַּנְּהָרִים אַפֶּךָ אִם־
ט בַּיָּם עֶבְרָתֶךָ כִּי תִרְכַּב עַל־סוּסֶיךָ מַרְכְּבֹתֶיךָ יְשׁוּעָה: עֶרְיָה
תֵעוֹר קַשְׁתֶּךָ שְׁבֻעוֹת מַטּוֹת אֹמֶר סֶלָה נְהָרוֹת תְּבַקַּע־אָרֶץ:
י רָאוּךָ יָחִילוּ הָרִים זֶרֶם מַיִם עָבָר נָתַן תְּהוֹם קוֹלוֹ רוֹם יָדֵיהוּ
יא נָשָׂא: שֶׁמֶשׁ יָרֵחַ עָמַד זְבֻלָה לְאוֹר חִצֶּיךָ יְהַלֵּכוּ לְנֹגַהּ בְּרַק
יב יג חֲנִיתֶךָ: בְּזַעַם תִּצְעַד־אָרֶץ בְּאַף תָּדוּשׁ גּוֹיִם: יָצָאתָ לְיֵשַׁע
עַמֶּךָ לְיֵשַׁע אֶת־מְשִׁיחֶךָ מָחַצְתָּ רֹּאשׁ מִבֵּית רָשָׁע עָרוֹת יְסוֹד
יד עַד־צַוָּאר סֶלָה: נָקַבְתָּ בְמַטָּיו רֹאשׁ פְּרָזָו יִסְעֲרוּ
טו לַהֲפִיצֵנִי עֲלִיצֻתָם כְּמוֹ־לֶאֱכֹל עָנִי בַּמִּסְתָּר: דָּרַכְתָּ בַיָּם סוּסֶיךָ
טז חֹמֶר מַיִם רַבִּים: שָׁמַעְתִּי ׀ וַתִּרְגַּז בִּטְנִי לְקוֹל צָלְלוּ שְׂפָתַי יָבוֹא
רָקָב בַּעֲצָמַי וְתַחְתַּי אֶרְגָּז אֲשֶׁר אָנוּחַ לְיוֹם צָרָה לַעֲלוֹת לְעַם
יז יְגוּדֶנּוּ: כִּי־תְאֵנָה לֹא־תִפְרָח וְאֵין יְבוּל בַּגְּפָנִים כִּחֵשׁ מַעֲשֵׂה־זַיִת
וּשְׁדֵמוֹת לֹא־עָשָׂה אֹכֶל גָּזַר מִמִּכְלָה צֹאן וְאֵין בָּקָר בָּרְפָתִים:
יח יט וַאֲנִי בַּיהוָה אֶעְלוֹזָה אָגִילָה בֵּאלֹהֵי יִשְׁעִי: יֱהוִה אֲדֹנָי חֵילִי
וַיָּשֶׂם רַגְלַי כָּאַיָּלוֹת וְעַל־בָּמוֹתַי יַדְרִכֵנִי לַמְנַצֵּחַ בִּנְגִינוֹתָי:

BLESSINGS AFTER THE HAFTARAH

After the Haftarah, the person called up for Maftir says the following blessings:

בָּרוּךְ Blessed are You, Lord our God, King of the Universe, Rock of all worlds, righteous for all generations, the faithful God who says and does, speaks and fulfills, all of whose words are truth and righteousness. You are faithful, Lord our God, and faithful are Your words, not one of which returns unfulfilled, for You, God, are a faithful (and compassionate) King. Blessed are You, Lord, faithful in all His words.

רַחֵם Have compassion on Zion for it is the source of our life, and save the one grieved in spirit swiftly in our days. Blessed are You, Lord, who makes Zion rejoice in her children.

שַׂמְּחֵנוּ Grant us joy, Lord our God, through Elijah the prophet Your servant, and through the kingdom of the house of David Your anointed – may he soon come and make our hearts glad. May no stranger sit on his throne, and may others not continue to inherit his glory, for You promised him by Your holy name that his light would never be extinguished. Blessed are You, Lord, Shield of David.

On Shabbat add the words in parentheses:

עַל הַתּוֹרָה For the Torah, for divine worship, for the prophets, (for this Sabbath day) and for this day of the Festival of Shavuot which You, Lord our God, have given us (for holiness and rest), for joy and gladness, honor and glory – for all these we thank and bless You, Lord our God, and may Your name be blessed by the mouth of all that lives, continually, for ever and all time. Blessed are You, Lord, who sanctifies (the Sabbath and) Israel and the festivals.

The following three paragraphs are not said on a Yom Tov occurring on a weekday.
On a weekday the service continues on page 128.

יְקוּם פֻּרְקָן May deliverance arise from heaven, bringing grace, love and compassion, long life, ample sustenance and heavenly help, physical health and enlightenment of mind, living and thriving

ברכות לאחר ההפטרה

After the הפטרה*, the person called up for* מפטיר *says the following blessings:*

בָּרוּךְ אַתָּה יהוה אֱלֹהֵינוּ מֶלֶךְ הָעוֹלָם, צוּר כָּל הָעוֹלָמִים, צַדִּיק בְּכָל הַדּוֹרוֹת, הָאֵל הַנֶּאֱמָן, הָאוֹמֵר וְעוֹשֶׂה, הַמְדַבֵּר וּמְקַיֵּם, שֶׁכָּל דְּבָרָיו אֱמֶת וָצֶדֶק. נֶאֱמָן אַתָּה הוּא יהוה אֱלֹהֵינוּ וְנֶאֱמָנִים דְּבָרֶיךָ, וְדָבָר אֶחָד מִדְּבָרֶיךָ אָחוֹר לֹא יָשׁוּב רֵיקָם, כִּי אֵל מֶלֶךְ נֶאֱמָן (וְרַחֲמָן) אָתָּה. בָּרוּךְ אַתָּה יהוה, הָאֵל הַנֶּאֱמָן בְּכָל דְּבָרָיו.

רַחֵם עַל צִיּוֹן כִּי הִיא בֵּית חַיֵּינוּ, וְלַעֲלוּבַת נֶפֶשׁ תּוֹשִׁיעַ בִּמְהֵרָה בְיָמֵינוּ. בָּרוּךְ אַתָּה יהוה, מְשַׂמֵּחַ צִיּוֹן בְּבָנֶיהָ.

שַׂמְּחֵנוּ יהוה אֱלֹהֵינוּ בְּאֵלִיָּהוּ הַנָּבִיא עַבְדֶּךָ, וּבְמַלְכוּת בֵּית דָּוִד מְשִׁיחֶךָ, בִּמְהֵרָה יָבוֹא וְיָגֵל לִבֵּנוּ. עַל כִּסְאוֹ לֹא יֵשֶׁב זָר, וְלֹא יִנְחֲלוּ עוֹד אֲחֵרִים אֶת כְּבוֹדוֹ, כִּי בְשֵׁם קָדְשְׁךָ נִשְׁבַּעְתָּ לּוֹ שֶׁלֹּא יִכְבֶּה נֵרוֹ לְעוֹלָם וָעֶד. בָּרוּךְ אַתָּה יהוה, מָגֵן דָּוִד.

On שבת *add the words in parentheses:*

עַל הַתּוֹרָה וְעַל הָעֲבוֹדָה וְעַל הַנְּבִיאִים (וְעַל יוֹם הַשַּׁבָּת הַזֶּה), וְעַל יוֹם חַג הַשָּׁבוּעוֹת הַזֶּה שֶׁנָּתַתָּ לָּנוּ, יהוה אֱלֹהֵינוּ (לִקְדֻשָּׁה וְלִמְנוּחָה) לְשָׂשׂוֹן וּלְשִׂמְחָה, לְכָבוֹד וּלְתִפְאָרֶת. עַל הַכֹּל יהוה אֱלֹהֵינוּ אֲנַחְנוּ מוֹדִים לָךְ וּמְבָרְכִים אוֹתָךְ. יִתְבָּרַךְ שִׁמְךָ בְּפִי כָּל חַי תָּמִיד לְעוֹלָם וָעֶד. בָּרוּךְ אַתָּה יהוה, מְקַדֵּשׁ (הַשַּׁבָּת וְ)יִשְׂרָאֵל וְהַזְּמַנִּים.

The following three paragraphs are not said on a יום טוב *occurring on a weekday.*
On a weekday the service continues on page 129.

יְקוּם פֻּרְקָן מִן שְׁמַיָּא, חִנָּא וְחִסְדָּא וְרַחֲמֵי וְחַיֵּי אֲרִיכֵי וּמְזוֹנֵי רְוִיחֵי, וְסִיַּעְתָּא דִשְׁמַיָּא, וּבַרְיוּת גּוּפָא וּנְהוֹרָא מַעַלְיָא, זַרְעָא חַיָּא

children who will neither interrupt nor cease from the words of the Torah – to our masters and teachers of the holy communities in the land of Israel and Babylon; to the leaders of assemblies and the leaders of communities in exile; to the heads of academies and to the judges in the gates; to all their disciples and their disciples' disciples, and to all who occupy themselves in study of the Torah. May the King of the Universe bless them, prolonging their lives, increasing their days, and adding to their years. May they be redeemed and delivered from all distress and illness. May our Master in heaven be their help at all times and seasons; and let us say: Amen.

יְקוּם פֻּרְקָן May deliverance arise from heaven, bringing grace, love and compassion, long life, ample sustenance and heavenly help, physical health and enlightenment of mind, living and thriving children who will neither interrupt nor cease from the words of the Torah – to all this holy congregation, great and small, women and children. May the King of the Universe bless you, prolonging your lives, increasing your days, and adding to your years. May you be redeemed and delivered from all distress and illness. May our Master in heaven be your help at all times and seasons; and let us say: Amen.

מִי שֶׁבֵּרַךְ May He who blessed our fathers, Abraham, Isaac and Jacob, bless all this holy congregation, together with all other holy congregations: them, their wives, their sons and daughters, and all that is theirs. May He bless those who unite to form synagogues for prayer and those who come there to pray; those who provide lamps for light and wine for Kiddush and Havdala, food for visitors and charity for the poor, and all who faithfully occupy themselves with the needs of the community. May the Holy One, blessed be He, give them their reward; may He remove from them all illness, grant them complete healing, and forgive all their sins. May He send blessing and success to all the work of their hands, together with all Israel their brethren; and let us say: Amen.

וְקַיָּמָא, זַרְעָא דִּי לָא יִפְסֻק וְדִי לָא יִבְטֻל מִפִּתְגָּמֵי אוֹרַיְתָא, לְמָרָנָן וְרַבָּנָן חֲבוּרָתָא קַדִּישָׁתָא דִּי בְּאַרְעָא דְיִשְׂרָאֵל וְדִי בְּבָבֶל, לְרֵישֵׁי כַלָּה, וּלְרֵישֵׁי גַלְוָתָא, וּלְרֵישֵׁי מְתִיבָתָא, וּלְדַיָּנֵי דְבָבָא, לְכָל תַּלְמִידֵיהוֹן, וּלְכָל תַּלְמִידֵי תַלְמִידֵיהוֹן, וּלְכָל מָאן דְּעָסְקִין בְּאוֹרַיְתָא. מַלְכָּא דְעָלְמָא יְבָרֵךְ יָתְהוֹן, יַפֵּשׁ חַיֵּיהוֹן וְיַסְגֵּא יוֹמֵיהוֹן, וְיִתֵּן אַרְכָא לִשְׁנֵיהוֹן, וְיִתְפָּרְקוּן וְיִשְׁתֵּיזְבוּן מִן כָּל עָקָא וּמִן כָּל מַרְעִין בִּישִׁין. מָרַן דִּי בִשְׁמַיָּא יְהֵא בְסַעְדְּהוֹן כָּל זְמַן וְעִדָּן, וְנֹאמַר אָמֵן.

יְקוּם פֻּרְקָן מִן שְׁמַיָּא, חִנָּא וְחִסְדָּא וְרַחֲמֵי וְחַיֵּי אֲרִיכֵי וּמְזוֹנֵי רְוִיחֵי, וְסִיַּעְתָּא דִשְׁמַיָּא, וּבַרְיוּת גּוּפָא וּנְהוֹרָא מְעַלְּיָא, זַרְעָא חַיָּא וְקַיָּמָא, זַרְעָא דִּי לָא יִפְסֻק וְדִי לָא יִבְטֻל מִפִּתְגָּמֵי אוֹרַיְתָא, לְכָל קְהָלָא קַדִּישָׁא הָדֵין, רַבְרְבַיָּא עִם זְעֵרַיָּא, טַפְלָא וּנְשַׁיָּא. מַלְכָּא דְעָלְמָא יְבָרֵךְ יָתְכוֹן, יַפֵּשׁ חַיֵּיכוֹן וְיַסְגֵּא יוֹמֵיכוֹן, וְיִתֵּן אַרְכָא לִשְׁנֵיכוֹן, וְתִתְפָּרְקוּן וְתִשְׁתֵּיזְבוּן מִן כָּל עָקָא וּמִן כָּל מַרְעִין בִּישִׁין. מָרַן דִּי בִשְׁמַיָּא יְהֵא בְסַעְדְּכוֹן כָּל זְמַן וְעִדָּן, וְנֹאמַר אָמֵן.

מִי שֶׁבֵּרַךְ אֲבוֹתֵינוּ אַבְרָהָם יִצְחָק וְיַעֲקֹב, הוּא יְבָרֵךְ אֶת כָּל הַקָּהָל הַקָּדוֹשׁ הַזֶּה עִם כָּל קְהִלּוֹת הַקֹּדֶשׁ, הֵם וּנְשֵׁיהֶם וּבְנֵיהֶם וּבְנוֹתֵיהֶם וְכָל אֲשֶׁר לָהֶם, וּמִי שֶׁמְּיַחֲדִים בָּתֵּי כְנֵסִיּוֹת לִתְפִלָּה, וּמִי שֶׁבָּאִים בְּתוֹכָם לְהִתְפַּלֵּל, וּמִי שֶׁנּוֹתְנִים נֵר לַמָּאוֹר וְיַיִן לְקִדּוּשׁ וּלְהַבְדָּלָה וּפַת לָאוֹרְחִים וּצְדָקָה לַעֲנִיִּים, וְכָל מִי שֶׁעוֹסְקִים בְּצָרְכֵי צִבּוּר בֶּאֱמוּנָה. הַקָּדוֹשׁ בָּרוּךְ הוּא יְשַׁלֵּם שְׂכָרָם, וְיָסִיר מֵהֶם כָּל מַחֲלָה, וְיִרְפָּא לְכָל גּוּפָם, וְיִסְלַח לְכָל עֲוֹנָם, וְיִשְׁלַח בְּרָכָה וְהַצְלָחָה בְּכָל מַעֲשֵׂי יְדֵיהֶם עִם כָּל יִשְׂרָאֵל אֲחֵיהֶם, וְנֹאמַר אָמֵן.

PRAYER FOR THE WELFARE OF THE GOVERNMENT

The Leader says the following:

הַנּוֹתֵן תְּשׁוּעָה May He who gives salvation to kings and dominion to princes, whose kingdom is an everlasting kingdom, who delivers His servant David from the evil sword, who makes a way in the sea and a path through the mighty waters, bless and protect, guard and help, exalt, magnify and uplift the President, Vice President and all officials of this land. May the Supreme King of kings in His mercy put into their hearts and the hearts of all their counselors and officials, to deal kindly with us and all Israel. In their days and in ours, may Judah be saved and Israel dwell in safety, and may the Redeemer come to Zion. May this be His will, and let us say: Amen.

PRAYER FOR THE SAFETY OF THE AMERICAN MILITARY FORCES

The Leader says the following:

אַדִּיר בַּמָּרוֹם God on high who dwells in might, the King to whom peace belongs, look down from Your holy habitation and bless the soldiers of the American military forces who risk their lives for the sake of peace on earth. Be their shelter and stronghold, and let them not falter. Give them the strength and courage to thwart the plans of the enemy and end the rule of evil. May their enemies be scattered and their foes flee before them, and may they rejoice in Your salvation. Bring them back safely to their homes, as is
written: "The Lord will guard you from all harm, He will guard *Ps. 121*
your life. The Lord will guard your going and coming, now and
for evermore." And may there be fulfilled for us the verse: "Nation *Is. 2*
shall not lift up sword against nation, nor shall they learn war any more." Let all the inhabitants on earth know that sovereignty is Yours and Your name inspires awe over all You have created – and let us say: Amen.

תפילה לשלום המלכות

The שליח ציבור *says the following:*

**הַנּוֹתֵן תְּשׁוּעָה לַמְּלָכִים וּמֶמְשָׁלָה לַנְּסִיכִים, מַלְכוּתוֹ מַלְכוּת
כָּל עוֹלָמִים, הַפּוֹצֶה אֶת דָּוִד עַבְדּוֹ מֵחֶרֶב רָעָה, הַנּוֹתֵן בַּיָּם
דֶּרֶךְ וּבְמַיִם עַזִּים נְתִיבָה, הוּא יְבָרֵךְ וְיִשְׁמֹר וְיִנְצֹר וְיַעֲזֹר וִירוֹמֵם
וִיגַדֵּל וִינַשֵּׂא לְמַעְלָה אֶת הַנָּשִׂיא וְאֵת מִשְׁנֵהוּ וְאֶת כָּל שָׂרֵי
הָאָרֶץ הַזֹּאת. מֶלֶךְ מַלְכֵי הַמְּלָכִים, בְּרַחֲמָיו יִתֵּן בְּלִבָּם וּבְלֵב כָּל
יוֹעֲצֵיהֶם וְשָׂרֵיהֶם לַעֲשׂוֹת טוֹבָה עִמָּנוּ וְעִם כָּל יִשְׂרָאֵל. בִּימֵיהֶם
וּבְיָמֵינוּ תִּוָּשַׁע יְהוּדָה, וְיִשְׂרָאֵל יִשְׁכֹּן לָבֶטַח, וּבָא לְצִיּוֹן גּוֹאֵל.
וְכֵן יְהִי רָצוֹן, וְנֹאמַר אָמֵן.**

תפילה לשלום חיילי צבא ארצות הברית

The שליח ציבור *says the following:*

**אַדִּיר בַּמָּרוֹם שׁוֹכֵן בִּגְבוּרָה, מֶלֶךְ שֶׁהַשָּׁלוֹם שֶׁלּוֹ, הַשְׁקִיפָה
מִמְּעוֹן קָדְשְׁךָ, וּבָרֵךְ אֶת חַיָּלֵי צְבָא אַרְצוֹת הַבְּרִית, הַמְחָרְפִים
נַפְשָׁם בְּלֶכְתָּם לָשִׂים שָׁלוֹם בָּאָרֶץ. הֱיֵה נָא לָהֶם מַחֲסֶה וּמָעוֹז,
וְאַל תִּתֵּן לַמּוֹט רַגְלָם, חַזֵּק יְדֵיהֶם וְאַמֵּץ רוּחָם לְהָפֵר עֲצַת
אוֹיֵב וּלְהַעֲבִיר מֶמְשֶׁלֶת זָדוֹן, יָפוּצוּ אוֹיְבֵיהֶם וְיָנוּסוּ מְשַׂנְאֵיהֶם
מִפְּנֵיהֶם, וְיִשְׂמְחוּ בִּישׁוּעָתֶךָ. הֲשִׁיבֵם בְּשָׁלוֹם אֶל בֵּיתָם, כַּכָּתוּב
בְּדִבְרֵי קָדְשֶׁךָ: יהוה יִשְׁמָרְךָ מִכָּל־רָע, יִשְׁמֹר אֶת־נַפְשֶׁךָ: יהוה** תהלים קכא
**יִשְׁמָר־צֵאתְךָ וּבוֹאֶךָ, מֵעַתָּה וְעַד־עוֹלָם: וְקַיֵּם בָּנוּ מִקְרָא
שֶׁכָּתוּב: לֹא־יִשָּׂא גוֹי אֶל־גּוֹי חֶרֶב, וְלֹא־יִלְמְדוּ עוֹד מִלְחָמָה:** ישעיה ב
**וְיֵדְעוּ כָּל יוֹשְׁבֵי תֵבֵל כִּי לְךָ מְלוּכָה יָאֲתָה, וְשִׁמְךָ נוֹרָא עַל כָּל
מַה שֶּׁבָּרָאתָ. וְנֹאמַר אָמֵן.**

PRAYER FOR THE STATE OF ISRAEL

The Leader says the following prayer:

אָבִינוּ שֶׁבַּשָּׁמַיִם Heavenly Father, Israel's Rock and Redeemer, bless the State of Israel, the first flowering of our redemption. Shield it under the wings of Your loving-kindness and spread over it the Tabernacle of Your peace. Send Your light and truth to its leaders, ministers and counselors, and direct them with good counsel before You.

Strengthen the hands of the defenders of our Holy Land; grant them deliverance, our God, and crown them with the crown of victory. Grant peace in the land and everlasting joy to its inhabitants.

As for our brothers, the whole house of Israel, remember them in all the lands of our (*In Israel say:* their) dispersion, and swiftly lead us (*In Israel say:* them) upright to Zion Your city, and Jerusalem Your dwelling place, as is written in the Torah of Moses Your servant: "Even if you are scattered to the furthermost lands under the heavens, from there the LORD your God will gather you and take you back. The LORD your God will bring you to the land your ancestors possessed and you will possess it; and He will make you more prosperous and numerous than your ancestors. Then the LORD your God will open up your heart and the heart of your descendants, to love the LORD your God with all your heart and with all your soul, that you may live." *Deut. 30*

Unite our hearts to love and revere Your name and observe all the words of Your Torah, and swiftly send us Your righteous anointed one of the house of David, to redeem those who long for Your salvation.

Appear in Your glorious majesty over all the dwellers on earth, and let all who breathe declare: The LORD God of Israel is King and His kingship has dominion over all. Amen, Selah.

תפילה לשלום מדינת ישראל

The שליח ציבור *says the following prayer:*

אָבִינוּ שֶׁבַּשָּׁמַיִם, צוּר יִשְׂרָאֵל וְגוֹאֲלוֹ, בָּרֵךְ אֶת מְדִינַת יִשְׂרָאֵל, רֵאשִׁית צְמִיחַת גְּאֻלָּתֵנוּ. הָגֵן עָלֶיהָ בְּאֶבְרַת חַסְדֶּךָ וּפְרֹשׂ עָלֶיהָ סֻכַּת שְׁלוֹמֶךָ, וּשְׁלַח אוֹרְךָ וַאֲמִתְּךָ לְרָאשֶׁיהָ, שָׂרֶיהָ וְיוֹעֲצֶיהָ, וְתַקְּנֵם בְּעֵצָה טוֹבָה מִלְּפָנֶיךָ.

חַזֵּק אֶת יְדֵי מְגִנֵּי אֶרֶץ קָדְשֵׁנוּ, וְהַנְחִילֵם אֱלֹהֵינוּ יְשׁוּעָה וַעֲטֶרֶת נִצָּחוֹן תְּעַטְּרֵם, וְנָתַתָּ שָׁלוֹם בָּאָרֶץ וְשִׂמְחַת עוֹלָם לְיוֹשְׁבֶיהָ.

וְאֶת אַחֵינוּ כָּל בֵּית יִשְׂרָאֵל, פְּקָד נָא בְּכָל אַרְצוֹת פְּזוּרֵינוּ, וְתוֹלִיכֵנוּ / בארץ ישראל: פְּזוּרֵיהֶם, וְתוֹלִיכֵם/ מְהֵרָה קוֹמְמִיּוּת לְצִיּוֹן עִירֶךָ וְלִירוּשָׁלַיִם מִשְׁכַּן שְׁמֶךָ, כַּכָּתוּב בְּתוֹרַת מֹשֶׁה עַבְדֶּךָ: אִם־יִהְיֶה נִדַּחֲךָ בִּקְצֵה הַשָּׁמָיִם, מִשָּׁם יְקַבֶּצְךָ יהוה אֱלֹהֶיךָ דברים ל וּמִשָּׁם יִקָּחֶךָ: וֶהֱבִיאֲךָ יהוה אֱלֹהֶיךָ אֶל־הָאָרֶץ אֲשֶׁר־יָרְשׁוּ אֲבֹתֶיךָ וִירִשְׁתָּהּ, וְהֵיטִבְךָ וְהִרְבְּךָ מֵאֲבֹתֶיךָ: וּמָל יהוה אֱלֹהֶיךָ אֶת־לְבָבְךָ וְאֶת־לְבַב זַרְעֶךָ, לְאַהֲבָה אֶת־יהוה אֱלֹהֶיךָ בְּכָל־לְבָבְךָ וּבְכָל־נַפְשְׁךָ, לְמַעַן חַיֶּיךָ:

וְיַחֵד לְבָבֵנוּ לְאַהֲבָה וּלְיִרְאָה אֶת שְׁמֶךָ, וְלִשְׁמֹר אֶת כָּל דִּבְרֵי תוֹרָתֶךָ, וּשְׁלַח לָנוּ מְהֵרָה בֶּן דָּוִד מְשִׁיחַ צִדְקֶךָ, לִפְדּוֹת מְחַכֵּי קֵץ יְשׁוּעָתֶךָ.

וְהוֹפַע בַּהֲדַר גְּאוֹן עֻזֶּךָ עַל כָּל יוֹשְׁבֵי תֵּבֵל אַרְצֶךָ וְיֹאמַר כֹּל אֲשֶׁר נְשָׁמָה בְאַפּוֹ, יהוה אֱלֹהֵי יִשְׂרָאֵל מֶלֶךְ וּמַלְכוּתוֹ בַּכֹּל מָשָׁלָה, אָמֵן סֶלָה.

PRAYER FOR ISRAEL'S DEFENSE FORCES

The Leader says the following prayer:

מִי שֶׁבֵּרַךְ May He who blessed our ancestors, Abraham, Isaac and Jacob, bless the members of Israel's Defense Forces and its security services who stand guard over our land and the cities of our God from the Lebanese border to the Egyptian desert, from the Mediterranean sea to the approach of the Aravah, and wherever else they are, on land, in air and at sea. May the Lord make the enemies who rise against us be struck down before them. May the Holy One, blessed be He, protect and deliver them from all trouble and distress, affliction and illness, and send blessing and success to all the work of their hands. May He subdue our enemies under them and crown them with deliverance and victory. And may there be fulfilled in them the verse, "It is *Deut. 20*
the Lord your God who goes with you to fight for you against your enemies, to deliver you." And let us say: Amen.

PRAYER FOR THOSE BEING HELD IN CAPTIVITY

If Israeli soldiers or civilians are being held in captivity, the Leader says the following:

מִי שֶׁבֵּרַךְ May He who blessed our ancestors, Abraham, Isaac and Jacob, Joseph, Moses and Aaron, David and Solomon, bless, protect and guard the members of Israel's Defense Forces missing in action or held captive, and other captives among our brethren, the whole house of Israel, who are in distress or captivity, as we, the members of this holy congregation, pray on their behalf. May the Holy One, blessed be He, have compassion on them and bring them out from darkness and the shadow of death; may He break their bonds, deliver them from their distress, and bring them swiftly back to their families'
embrace. Give thanks to the Lord for His loving-kindness and for the *Ps. 107*
wonders He does for the children of men; and may there be fulfilled in
them the verse: "Those redeemed by the Lord will return; they will *Is. 35*
enter Zion with singing, and everlasting joy will crown their heads. Gladness and joy will overtake them, and sorrow and sighing will flee away." And let us say: Amen.

When Yizkor is not said, the service continues on page 142.

מי שברך לחיילי צה״ל

The שליח ציבור *says the following prayer:*

מִי שֶׁבֵּרַךְ אֲבוֹתֵינוּ אַבְרָהָם יִצְחָק וְיַעֲקֹב הוּא יְבָרֵךְ אֶת חַיָּלֵי צְבָא הַהֲגָנָה לְיִשְׂרָאֵל וְאַנְשֵׁי כֹּחוֹת הַבִּטָּחוֹן, הָעוֹמְדִים עַל מִשְׁמַר אַרְצֵנוּ וְעָרֵי אֱלֹהֵינוּ, מִגְּבוּל הַלְּבָנוֹן וְעַד מִדְבַּר מִצְרַיִם וּמִן הַיָּם הַגָּדוֹל עַד לְבוֹא הָעֲרָבָה וּבְכָל מָקוֹם שֶׁהֵם, בַּיַּבָּשָׁה, בָּאֲוִיר וּבַיָּם. יִתֵּן יהוה אֶת אוֹיְבֵינוּ הַקָּמִים עָלֵינוּ נִגָּפִים לִפְנֵיהֶם. הַקָּדוֹשׁ בָּרוּךְ הוּא יִשְׁמֹר וְיַצִּיל אֶת חַיָּלֵינוּ מִכָּל צָרָה וְצוּקָה וּמִכָּל נֶגַע וּמַחֲלָה, וְיִשְׁלַח בְּרָכָה וְהַצְלָחָה בְּכָל מַעֲשֵׂי יְדֵיהֶם. יַדְבֵּר שׂוֹנְאֵינוּ תַּחְתֵּיהֶם וִיעַטְּרֵם בְּכֶתֶר יְשׁוּעָה וּבַעֲטֶרֶת נִצָּחוֹן. וִיקֻיַּם בָּהֶם הַכָּתוּב: כִּי יהוה אֱלֹהֵיכֶם הַהֹלֵךְ עִמָּכֶם לְהִלָּחֵם דברים כ
לָכֶם עִם־אֹיְבֵיכֶם לְהוֹשִׁיעַ אֶתְכֶם: וְנֹאמַר אָמֵן.

מי שברך לשבויים

If Israeli soldiers or civilians are being held in captivity, the שליח ציבור *says the following:*

מִי שֶׁבֵּרַךְ אֲבוֹתֵינוּ אַבְרָהָם יִצְחָק וְיַעֲקֹב, יוֹסֵף מֹשֶׁה וְאַהֲרֹן, דָּוִד וּשְׁלֹמֹה, הוּא יְבָרֵךְ וְיִשְׁמֹר וְיִנְצֹר אֶת נֶעְדְּרֵי צְבָא הַהֲגָנָה לְיִשְׂרָאֵל וּשְׁבוּיָו, וְאֶת כָּל אַחֵינוּ הַנְּתוּנִים בְּצָרָה וּבְשִׁבְיָה, בַּעֲבוּר שֶׁכָּל הַקָּהָל הַקָּדוֹשׁ הַזֶּה מִתְפַּלֵּל בַּעֲבוּרָם. הַקָּדוֹשׁ בָּרוּךְ הוּא יִמָּלֵא רַחֲמִים עֲלֵיהֶם, וְיוֹצִיאֵם מֵחֹשֶׁךְ וְצַלְמָוֶת, וּמוֹסְרוֹתֵיהֶם יְנַתֵּק,
וּמִמְּצוּקוֹתֵיהֶם יוֹשִׁיעֵם, וִישִׁיבֵם מְהֵרָה לְחֵיק מִשְׁפְּחוֹתֵיהֶם. יוֹדוּ תהלים קז
לַיהוה חַסְדּוֹ וְנִפְלְאוֹתָיו לִבְנֵי אָדָם: וִיקֻיַּם בָּהֶם מִקְרָא שֶׁכָּתוּב:
וּפְדוּיֵי יהוה יְשֻׁבוּן, וּבָאוּ צִיּוֹן בְּרִנָּה, וְשִׂמְחַת עוֹלָם עַל־רֹאשָׁם, ישעיה לה
שָׂשׂוֹן וְשִׂמְחָה יַשִּׂיגוּ, וְנָסוּ יָגוֹן וַאֲנָחָה: וְנֹאמַר אָמֵן.

When יזכור *is not said, the service continues on page 143.*

YIZKOR

On the second day of Shavuot (in Israel on the first), the Yizkor (memorial) service is said. In some communities, those who have not been bereaved of a parent or close relative do not participate in the service, but leave the synagogue and return for "Father of compassion" on page 140.

יהוה LORD, what is man that You care for him, a mortal that You notice him? *Ps. 144*
Man is like a fleeting breath, his days like a passing shadow.
In the morning he flourishes and grows; *Ps. 90*
in the evening he withers and dries up.
Teach us to number our days, that we may get a heart of wisdom.
Mark the blameless, note the upright, for the end of such a person is peace. *Ps. 37*
God will redeem my soul from the grave, for He will receive me, Selah. *Ps. 49*
My flesh and my heart may fail, *Ps. 73*
but God is the strength of my heart and my portion for ever.
The dust returns to the earth as it was, *Eccl. 12*
but the spirit returns to God who gave it.

יֹשֵׁב He who lives in the shelter of the Most High dwells in the shadow of the Almighty. I say of the LORD, my Refuge and Stronghold, my God in whom I trust, that He will save you from the fowler's snare and the deadly pestilence. With His pinions He will cover you, and beneath His wings you will find shelter; His faithfulness is an encircling shield. You need not fear terror by night, nor the arrow that flies by day; not the pestilence that stalks in darkness, nor the plague that ravages at noon. A thousand may fall at your side, ten thousand at your right hand, but it will not come near you. You will only look with your eyes and see the punishment of the wicked. Because you said, "the LORD is my Refuge," taking the Most High as your shelter, no harm will befall you, no plague will come near your tent, for He will command His angels about you, to guard you in all your ways. They will lift you in their hands, lest your foot stumble on a stone. You will tread on lions and vipers; you will trample on young lions and snakes. [God says:] "Because he loves Me, I will rescue him; I will protect him, because he acknowledges My name. When he calls on Me, I will answer him; I will be with him in distress, I will deliver him and bring him honor. With long life I will satisfy him and show him My salvation. *Ps. 91*

With long life I will satisfy him and show him My salvation.

---

man and shares in his covenantal existence. Finitude and infinity, temporality and eternity, creature and Creator become involved in the same community.

סדר הזכרת נשמות

On the second day of שבועות *(in* ארץ ישראל *on the first), the* יזכור *(memorial) service is said.*
In some communities, those who have not been bereaved of a parent or
close relative do not participate in the service, but leave the
בית כנסת *and return for* אב הרחמים *on page 141.*

יהוה מָה־אָדָם וַתֵּדָעֵהוּ, בֶּן־אֱנוֹשׁ וַתְּחַשְּׁבֵהוּ: תהלים קמד
אָדָם לַהֶבֶל דָּמָה, יָמָיו כְּצֵל עוֹבֵר:
בַּבֹּקֶר יָצִיץ וְחָלָף, לָעֶרֶב יְמוֹלֵל וְיָבֵשׁ: תהלים צ
לִמְנוֹת יָמֵינוּ כֵּן הוֹדַע, וְנָבִא לְבַב חָכְמָה:
שְׁמָר־תָּם וּרְאֵה יָשָׁר, כִּי־אַחֲרִית לְאִישׁ שָׁלוֹם: תהלים לז
אַךְ־אֱלֹהִים יִפְדֶּה נַפְשִׁי מִיַּד שְׁאוֹל, כִּי יִקָּחֵנִי סֶלָה: תהלים מט
כָּלָה שְׁאֵרִי וּלְבָבִי, צוּר־לְבָבִי וְחֶלְקִי אֱלֹהִים לְעוֹלָם: תהלים עג
וְיָשֹׁב הֶעָפָר עַל־הָאָרֶץ כְּשֶׁהָיָה, וְהָרְוּחַ תָּשׁוּב אֶל־הָאֱלֹהִים אֲשֶׁר נְתָנָהּ: קהלת יב

יֹשֵׁב בְּסֵתֶר עֶלְיוֹן, בְּצֵל שַׁדַּי יִתְלוֹנָן: אֹמַר לַיהוה מַחְסִי וּמְצוּדָתִי, תהלים צא
אֱלֹהַי אֶבְטַח־בּוֹ: כִּי הוּא יַצִּילְךָ מִפַּח יָקוּשׁ, מִדֶּבֶר הַוּוֹת: בְּאֶבְרָתוֹ
יָסֶךְ לָךְ, וְתַחַת־כְּנָפָיו תֶּחְסֶה, צִנָּה וְסֹחֵרָה אֲמִתּוֹ: לֹא־תִירָא מִפַּחַד
לָיְלָה, מֵחֵץ יָעוּף יוֹמָם: מִדֶּבֶר בָּאֹפֶל יַהֲלֹךְ, מִקֶּטֶב יָשׁוּד צָהֳרָיִם:
יִפֹּל מִצִּדְּךָ אֶלֶף, וּרְבָבָה מִימִינֶךָ, אֵלֶיךָ לֹא יִגָּשׁ: רַק בְּעֵינֶיךָ תַבִּיט,
וְשִׁלֻּמַת רְשָׁעִים תִּרְאֶה: כִּי־אַתָּה יהוה מַחְסִי, עֶלְיוֹן שַׂמְתָּ מְעוֹנֶךָ:
לֹא־תְאֻנֶּה אֵלֶיךָ רָעָה, וְנֶגַע לֹא־יִקְרַב בְּאָהֳלֶךָ: כִּי מַלְאָכָיו יְצַוֶּה־לָּךְ,
לִשְׁמָרְךָ בְּכָל־דְּרָכֶיךָ: עַל־כַּפַּיִם יִשָּׂאוּנְךָ, פֶּן־תִּגֹּף בָּאֶבֶן רַגְלֶךָ: עַל־
שַׁחַל וָפֶתֶן תִּדְרֹךְ, תִּרְמֹס כְּפִיר וְתַנִּין: כִּי בִי חָשַׁק וַאֲפַלְּטֵהוּ, אֲשַׂגְּבֵהוּ
כִּי־יָדַע שְׁמִי: יִקְרָאֵנִי וְאֶעֱנֵהוּ, עִמּוֹ־אָנֹכִי בְצָרָה, אֲחַלְּצֵהוּ וַאֲכַבְּדֵהוּ:
אֹרֶךְ יָמִים אַשְׂבִּיעֵהוּ, וְאַרְאֵהוּ בִּישׁוּעָתִי:
אֹרֶךְ יָמִים אַשְׂבִּיעֵהוּ, וְאַרְאֵהוּ בִּישׁוּעָתִי:

YIZKOR

יִקְרָאֵנִי וְאֶעֱנֵהוּ, עִמּוֹ־אָנֹכִי בְצָרָה *When he calls on Me, I will answer him; I will be with him in distress.* God is never outside the covenantal community. He joins

For one's father:

יִזְכֹּר May God remember the soul of my father, my teacher (*name* son of *father's name*) who has gone to his eternal home, and to this I pledge (without formal vow) to give charity on his behalf, that his soul may be bound in the bond of everlasting life together with the souls of Abraham, Isaac and Jacob, Sarah, Rebecca, Rachel and Leah, and all the other righteous men and women in the Garden of Eden, and let us say: Amen.

For one's mother:

יִזְכֹּר May God remember the soul of my mother, my teacher (*name* daughter of *father's name*) who has gone to her eternal home, and to this I pledge (without formal vow) to give charity on her behalf, that her soul may be bound in the bond of everlasting life together with the souls of Abraham, Isaac and Jacob, Sarah, Rebecca, Rachel and Leah, and all the other righteous men and women in the Garden of Eden, and let us say: Amen.

---

significance of the past. When we are no longer at one with our values, we first begin to appreciate, evaluate, and even worship them. It is through this effect of contrast that we first arrive at qualitative time consciousness, a multidimensional continuum of past, present, and future. It Is through contrast that quantitative time must have a stop and qualitative time a renewed impetus. And so is it with persons or values. When they have disappeared from the stage of the present, they take on a new and profound significance in contrast with the changed scene. Then the hills become smaller and the mountains larger, as time and perspective recede.

What is it that breeds complacency in man to his vital values while he has them? Because these values form such an integral part of his physical and mental makeup, they become identical with his psyche, and he, therefore, loses the perspective that only an Archimedean point of distance and contrast may give him. Man is most shortsighted when he would view his own psyche. Man walking the circular Earth sees only a plain.

It is in this light that our Sages envisaged the great man's role. His inspiration may flourish on after his death for those with a qualitative appreciation of time and history. (*Shiurei Harav*, pp. 25–26)

For one's father:

יִזְכֹּר אֱלֹהִים נִשְׁמַת אָבִי מוֹרִי (פלוני בֶּן פלוני) שֶׁהָלַךְ לְעוֹלָמוֹ, בַּעֲבוּר שֶׁבְּלִי נֶדֶר אֶתֵּן צְדָקָה בַּעֲדוֹ. בִּשְׂכַר זֶה תְּהֵא נַפְשׁוֹ צְרוּרָה בִּצְרוֹר הַחַיִּים עִם נִשְׁמוֹת אַבְרָהָם יִצְחָק וְיַעֲקֹב, שָׂרָה רִבְקָה רָחֵל וְלֵאָה, וְעִם שְׁאָר צַדִּיקִים וְצִדְקָנִיּוֹת שֶׁבְּגַן עֵדֶן, וְנֹאמַר אָמֵן.

For one's mother:

יִזְכֹּר אֱלֹהִים נִשְׁמַת אִמִּי מוֹרָתִי (פלונית בַּת פלוני) שֶׁהָלְכָה לְעוֹלָמָהּ, בַּעֲבוּר שֶׁבְּלִי נֶדֶר אֶתֵּן צְדָקָה בַּעֲדָהּ. בִּשְׂכַר זֶה תְּהֵא נַפְשָׁהּ צְרוּרָה בִּצְרוֹר הַחַיִּים עִם נִשְׁמוֹת אַבְרָהָם יִצְחָק וְיַעֲקֹב, שָׂרָה רִבְקָה רָחֵל וְלֵאָה, וְעִם שְׁאָר צַדִּיקִים וְצִדְקָנִיּוֹת שֶׁבְּגַן עֵדֶן, וְנֹאמַר אָמֵן.

They bind themselves together and participate in a unitive existence. The whole concept of עִמּוֹ אָנֹכִי בְצָרָה, "I will be with him in distress," can only be understood within the perspective of the covenantal community which involves God in the destiny of His fellow members. (Vide *Sanhedrin* 46a; Yerushalmi, *Sukkah* 4:3.) (*Lonely Man of Faith*, pp. 31–32)

וְעִם שְׁאָר צַדִּיקִים וְצִדְקָנִיּוֹת *And all the other righteous men and women.* On the yahrzeit of my father, R. Moses Soloveitchik, it seems to me as if my father were yet alive, although four years have come and gone since his death. It is in a qualitative sense that I experience his nearness and spirit tonight. I cannot explain the דמות דיוקנו של אביו (*Sotah* 36b), the spiritual picture of father that hovers near me tonight as in a yesteryear of physical existence.

Our Sages have said, גדולים צדיקים במיתתן יותר מבחייהן – "The righteous are exalted in death more than in life" (*Ḥullin* 7b). If time be measured qualitatively, we may understand how their influence lingers on after their death and why the past is eternally bound with the present. Yet, how do their mortal lives acquire a new significance in death?

Qualitative time awareness reduces, in effect, to interspersing the text of chronology with values and creativity. These values appear in their true perspective when the stream of time undulates them away to the shores of yesterday. From the vantage point of the present, we first evaluate the

For martyrs:

יִזְכֹּר May God remember the soul of (*name*, son/daughter of *father's name*), and the souls of all my relatives, on my father's or mother's side, who were killed, murdered, slaughtered, burned, drowned or strangled for the sanctification of God's name, and to this I pledge (without formal vow) to give charity in their memory. May their souls be bound in the bond of everlasting life together with the souls of Abraham, Isaac and Jacob, Sarah, Rebecca, Rachel and Leah, and all the other righteous men and women in the Garden of Eden, and let us say: Amen.

For a male close relative:

אֵל מָלֵא רַחֲמִים God, full of mercy, who dwells on high, grant fitting rest on the wings of the Divine Presence, in the heights of the holy and the pure who shine like the radiance of heaven, to the soul of (*name* son of *father's name*) who has gone to his eternal home, and to this I pledge (without formal vow) to give charity in his memory, may his resting place be in the Garden of Eden. Therefore, Master of compassion, shelter him in the shadow of Your wings forever and bind his soul in the bond of everlasting life. The LORD is his heritage; may he rest in peace, and let us say: Amen.

For a female close relative:

אֵל מָלֵא רַחֲמִים God, full of mercy, who dwells on high, grant fitting rest on the wings of the Divine Presence, in the heights of the holy and the pure who shine like the radiance of heaven, to the soul of (*name* daughter of *father's name*) who has gone to her eternal home, and to this I pledge (without formal vow) to give charity in her memory, may her resting place be in the Garden of Eden. Therefore, Master of compassion, shelter her in the shadow of Your wings forever and bind her soul in the bond of everlasting life. The LORD is her heritage; may she rest in peace, and let us say: Amen.

For the Israeli soldiers:

אֵל מָלֵא רַחֲמִים God, full of mercy, who dwells on high, grant fitting rest on the wings of the Divine Presence, in the heights of the holy, the pure and the brave, who shine like the radiance of heaven, to the souls of the holy ones who fought in any of Israel's battles, in clandestine operations and in Israel's Defense Forces, who fell in battle and sacrificed their lives for the consecration of God's name, for the people and the land, and for this we pray for the ascent of their souls. Therefore, Master of compassion, shelter them in the shadow of Your wings forever, and bind their souls in the bond

For martyrs:

יִזְכֹּר אֱלֹהִים נִשְׁמַת (*male* פלוני בֶּן פלוני / *female* פלונית בַּת פלוני) וְנִשְׁמוֹת כָּל קְרוֹבַי וּקְרוֹבוֹתַי, הֵן מִצַּד אָבִי הֵן מִצַּד אִמִּי, שֶׁהוּמְתוּ וְשֶׁנֶּהֶרְגוּ וְשֶׁנִּשְׁחֲטוּ וְשֶׁנִּשְׂרְפוּ וְשֶׁנִּטְבְּעוּ וְשֶׁנֶּחְנְקוּ עַל קִדּוּשׁ הַשֵּׁם, בַּעֲבוּר שֶׁבְּלִי נֶדֶר אֶתֵּן צְדָקָה בְּעַד הַזְכָּרַת נִשְׁמוֹתֵיהֶם. בִּשְׂכַר זֶה תִּהְיֶינָה נַפְשׁוֹתֵיהֶם צְרוּרוֹת בִּצְרוֹר הַחַיִּים עִם נִשְׁמוֹת אַבְרָהָם יִצְחָק וְיַעֲקֹב, שָׂרָה רִבְקָה רָחֵל וְלֵאָה, וְעִם שְׁאָר צַדִּיקִים וְצִדְקָנִיּוֹת שֶׁבְּגַן עֵדֶן, וְנֹאמַר אָמֵן.

For a male close relative:

אֵל מָלֵא רַחֲמִים, שׁוֹכֵן בַּמְּרוֹמִים, הַמְצֵא מְנוּחָה נְכוֹנָה עַל כַּנְפֵי הַשְּׁכִינָה, בְּמַעֲלוֹת קְדוֹשִׁים וּטְהוֹרִים, כְּזֹהַר הָרָקִיעַ מַזְהִירִים, לְנִשְׁמַת (פלוני בֶּן פלוני) שֶׁהָלַךְ לְעוֹלָמוֹ, בַּעֲבוּר שֶׁבְּלִי נֶדֶר אֶתֵּן צְדָקָה בְּעַד הַזְכָּרַת נִשְׁמָתוֹ, בְּגַן עֵדֶן תְּהֵא מְנוּחָתוֹ. לָכֵן, בַּעַל הָרַחֲמִים יַסְתִּירֵהוּ בְּסֵתֶר כְּנָפָיו לְעוֹלָמִים, וְיִצְרֹר בִּצְרוֹר הַחַיִּים אֶת נִשְׁמָתוֹ, יהוה הוּא נַחֲלָתוֹ, וְיָנוּחַ בְּשָׁלוֹם עַל מִשְׁכָּבוֹ, וְנֹאמַר אָמֵן.

For a female close relative:

אֵל מָלֵא רַחֲמִים, שׁוֹכֵן בַּמְּרוֹמִים, הַמְצֵא מְנוּחָה נְכוֹנָה עַל כַּנְפֵי הַשְּׁכִינָה, בְּמַעֲלוֹת קְדוֹשִׁים וּטְהוֹרִים, כְּזֹהַר הָרָקִיעַ מַזְהִירִים, לְנִשְׁמַת (פלונית בַּת פלוני) שֶׁהָלְכָה לְעוֹלָמָהּ, בַּעֲבוּר שֶׁבְּלִי נֶדֶר אֶתֵּן צְדָקָה בְּעַד הַזְכָּרַת נִשְׁמָתָהּ, בְּגַן עֵדֶן תְּהֵא מְנוּחָתָהּ. לָכֵן, בַּעַל הָרַחֲמִים יַסְתִּירֶהָ בְּסֵתֶר כְּנָפָיו לְעוֹלָמִים, וְיִצְרֹר בִּצְרוֹר הַחַיִּים אֶת נִשְׁמָתָהּ, יהוה הוּא נַחֲלָתָהּ, וְתָנוּחַ בְּשָׁלוֹם עַל מִשְׁכָּבָהּ, וְנֹאמַר אָמֵן.

For the Israeli soldiers:

אֵל מָלֵא רַחֲמִים, שׁוֹכֵן בַּמְּרוֹמִים, הַמְצֵא מְנוּחָה נְכוֹנָה עַל כַּנְפֵי הַשְּׁכִינָה, בְּמַעֲלוֹת קְדוֹשִׁים טְהוֹרִים וְגִבּוֹרִים, כְּזֹהַר הָרָקִיעַ מַזְהִירִים, לְנִשְׁמוֹת הַקְּדוֹשִׁים שֶׁנִּלְחֲמוּ בְּכָל מַעַרְכוֹת יִשְׂרָאֵל, בַּמַּחְתֶּרֶת וּבִצְבָא הַהֲגָנָה לְיִשְׂרָאֵל, וְשֶׁנָּפְלוּ בְּמִלְחַמְתָּם וּמָסְרוּ נַפְשָׁם עַל קְדֻשַּׁת הַשֵּׁם, הָעָם וְהָאָרֶץ, בַּעֲבוּר שֶׁאָנוּ מִתְפַּלְּלִים לְעִלּוּי נִשְׁמוֹתֵיהֶם. לָכֵן, בַּעַל

of everlasting life. The LORD is their heritage; may the Garden of Eden be their resting place, may they rest in peace, may their merit stand for all Israel, and may they receive their reward at the End of Days, and let us say: Amen.

For the Holocaust victims:

אֵל מָלֵא רַחֲמִים God, full of mercy, Justice of widows and Father of orphans, please do not be silent and hold Your peace for the blood of Israel that was shed like water. Grant fitting rest on the wings of the Divine Presence, in the heights of the holy and the pure who shine and radiate light like the radiance of heaven, to the souls of the millions of Jews, men, women and children, who were murdered, slaughtered, burned, strangled, and buried alive, in the lands touched by the German enemy and its followers. They were all holy and pure; among them were great scholars and righteous individuals, cedars of Lebanon and noble masters of Torah, may the Garden of Eden be their resting place. Therefore, Master of compassion, shelter them in the shadow of Your wings forever, and bind their souls in the bond of everlasting life. The LORD is their heritage; may they rest in peace, and let us say: Amen.

Congregation and Leader:

אַב הָרַחֲמִים Father of compassion, who dwells on high: may He remember in His compassion the pious, the upright and the blameless – holy communities who sacrificed their lives for the sanctification of God's name. Lovely and pleasant in their lives, in death they were not parted. They were swifter than eagles and stronger than lions to do the will of their Maker and the desire of their Creator. O our God, remember them for good with the other righteous of the world, and may He exact retribution for the shed blood of His servants, as it is written in the Torah of Moses, the man of God: "O nations, acclaim *Deut. 32*
His people, for He will avenge the blood of His servants, wreak vengeance on His foes, and make clean His people's land." And by Your servants, the prophets, it is written: "I shall cleanse their blood which I have not yet *Joel 4*
cleansed, says the LORD who dwells in Zion." And in the holy Writings it says: "Why should the nations say: Where is their God? Before our eyes, may *Ps. 79*
those nations know that You avenge the shed blood of Your servants." And it also says: "For the Avenger of blood remembers them and does not forget the *Ps. 9*
cry of the afflicted." And it further says: "He will execute judgment among *Ps. 110*
the nations, filled with the dead, crushing rulers far and wide. From the brook by the wayside he will drink, then he will hold his head high."

הָרַחֲמִים יַסְתִּירֵם בְּסֵתֶר כְּנָפָיו לְעוֹלָמִים, וְיִצְרֹר בִּצְרוֹר הַחַיִּים אֶת נִשְׁמוֹתֵיהֶם, יהוה הוּא נַחֲלָתָם, בְּגַן עֵדֶן תְּהֵא מְנוּחָתָם, וְיָנוּחוּ בְּשָׁלוֹם עַל מִשְׁכְּבוֹתֵיהֶם וְתַעֲמֹד לְכָל יִשְׂרָאֵל זְכוּתָם, וְיַעַמְדוּ לְגוֹרָלָם לְקֵץ הַיָּמִין, וְנֹאמַר אָמֵן.

For the Holocaust victims:

אֵל מָלֵא רַחֲמִים, דַּיַּן אַלְמָנוֹת וַאֲבִי יְתוֹמִים, אַל נָא תֶחֱשֶׁה וְתִתְאַפַּק לְדַם יִשְׂרָאֵל שֶׁנִּשְׁפַּךְ כַּמַּיִם. הַמְצֵא מְנוּחָה נְכוֹנָה עַל כַּנְפֵי הַשְּׁכִינָה, בְּמַעֲלוֹת קְדוֹשִׁים וּטְהוֹרִים, כְּזֹהַר הָרָקִיעַ מְאִירִים וּמַזְהִירִים, לְנִשְׁמוֹתֵיהֶם שֶׁל רִבְבוֹת אַלְפֵי יִשְׂרָאֵל, אֲנָשִׁים וְנָשִׁים, יְלָדִים וִילָדוֹת, שֶׁנֶּהֶרְגוּ וְנִשְׁחֲטוּ וְנִשְׂרְפוּ וְנֶחְנְקוּ וְנִקְבְּרוּ חַיִּים, בָּאֲרָצוֹת אֲשֶׁר נָגְעָה בָהֶן יַד הַצּוֹרֵר הַגֶּרְמָנִי וּגְרוּרָיו. כֻּלָּם קְדוֹשִׁים וּטְהוֹרִים, וּבָהֶם גְּאוֹנִים וְצַדִּיקִים, אַרְזֵי הַלְּבָנוֹן אַדִּירֵי הַתּוֹרָה. בְּגַן עֵדֶן תְּהֵא מְנוּחָתָם. לָכֵן, בַּעַל הָרַחֲמִים יַסְתִּירֵם בְּסֵתֶר כְּנָפָיו לְעוֹלָמִים, וְיִצְרֹר בִּצְרוֹר הַחַיִּים אֶת נִשְׁמָתָם, יהוה הוּא נַחֲלָתָם, וְיָנוּחוּ בְּשָׁלוֹם עַל מִשְׁכָּבָם, וְנֹאמַר אָמֵן.

קהל ושליח ציבור:

אַב הָרַחֲמִים שׁוֹכֵן מְרוֹמִים, בְּרַחֲמָיו הָעֲצוּמִים הוּא יִפְקֹד בְּרַחֲמִים הַחֲסִידִים וְהַיְשָׁרִים וְהַתְּמִימִים, קְהִלּוֹת הַקֹּדֶשׁ שֶׁמָּסְרוּ נַפְשָׁם עַל קְדֻשַּׁת הַשֵּׁם, הַנֶּאֱהָבִים וְהַנְּעִימִים בְּחַיֵּיהֶם, וּבְמוֹתָם לֹא נִפְרָדוּ, מִנְּשָׁרִים קַלּוּ וּמֵאֲרָיוֹת גָּבֵרוּ לַעֲשׂוֹת רְצוֹן קוֹנָם וְחֵפֶץ צוּרָם. יִזְכְּרֵם אֱלֹהֵינוּ לְטוֹבָה עִם שְׁאָר צַדִּיקֵי עוֹלָם, וְיִנְקֹם לְעֵינֵינוּ נִקְמַת דַּם עֲבָדָיו
הַשָּׁפוּךְ, כַּכָּתוּב בְּתוֹרַת מֹשֶׁה אִישׁ הָאֱלֹהִים, הַרְנִינוּ גוֹיִם עַמּוֹ, כִּי דברים לב
דַם־עֲבָדָיו יִקּוֹם, וְנָקָם יָשִׁיב לְצָרָיו, וְכִפֶּר אַדְמָתוֹ עַמּוֹ: וְעַל יְדֵי עֲבָדֶיךָ
הַנְּבִיאִים כָּתוּב לֵאמֹר, וְנִקֵּיתִי, דָּמָם לֹא־נִקֵּיתִי, וַיהוה שֹׁכֵן בְּצִיּוֹן: יואל ד
וּבְכִתְבֵי הַקֹּדֶשׁ נֶאֱמַר, לָמָּה יֹאמְרוּ הַגּוֹיִם אַיֵּה אֱלֹהֵיהֶם, יִוָּדַע בַּגּוֹיִם תהלים עט
לְעֵינֵינוּ נִקְמַת דַּם־עֲבָדֶיךָ הַשָּׁפוּךְ: וְאוֹמֵר, כִּי־דֹרֵשׁ דָּמִים אוֹתָם זָכָר, תהלים ט
לֹא־שָׁכַח צַעֲקַת עֲנָוִים: וְאוֹמֵר, יָדִין בַּגּוֹיִם מָלֵא גְוִיּוֹת, מָחַץ רֹאשׁ תהלים קי
עַל־אֶרֶץ רַבָּה: מִנַּחַל בַּדֶּרֶךְ יִשְׁתֶּה, עַל־כֵּן יָרִים רֹאשׁ:

Most congregations omit the following on days that Yizkor is said.
Some also omit on Shabbat.

יָהּ אֵלִי Lord my God and Redeemer, I will stand to greet You,
[God] who was and will be, was and is,
the land of every nation is Yours.

The thanksgiving-offering, burnt-offering, meal-offering, sin-offering,
guilt-offering, peace-offering and inauguration-offering are all offerings to You.
Remember the weary nation that has borne much,
and bring it back to Your land.
I will always praise You with
"Happy are those who dwell in Your House."

Fine beyond fine, undecipherable, His understanding is
unfathomable, Awesome God who distinguishes between
good and evil with a single glance.

The thanksgiving-offering, burnt-offering, meal-offering, sin-offering,
guilt-offering, peace-offering and inauguration-offering are all offerings to You.
Remember the weary nation that has borne much,
and bring it back to Your land.
I will always praise You with
"Happy are those who dwell in Your House."

Lord of hosts, with many wonders, He joined all His tent,
making all blossom in the ways of the heart:
the Rock, perfect is His work.

The thanksgiving-offering, burnt-offering, meal-offering, sin-offering,
guilt-offering, peace-offering and inauguration-offering are all offerings to You.
Remember the weary nation that has borne much,
and bring it back to Your land.
I will always praise You with
"Happy are those who dwell in Your House."

Most congregations omit the following on days that יזכור *is said.*
Some also omit on שבת*.*

יָהּ אֵלִי וְגוֹאֲלִי, אֶתְיַצְּבָה לִקְרָאתֶךָ
הָיָה וְיִהְיֶה, הָיָה וְהֹוֶה, כָּל גּוֹי אַדְמָתֶךָ.

וְתוֹדָה וְלָעוֹלָה וְלַמִּנְחָה וְלַחַטָּאת וְלָאָשָׁם
וְלַשְּׁלָמִים וְלַמִּלּוּאִים כָּל קָרְבָּנֶךָ.
זְכֹר נִלְאָה אֲשֶׁר נָשְׂאָה וְהָשִׁיבָה לְאַדְמָתֶךָ
סֶלָה אֲהַלְלָךְ בְּאַשְׁרֵי יוֹשְׁבֵי בֵיתֶךָ.

דַּק עַל דַּק, עַד אֵין נִבְדָּק, וְלִתְבוּנָתוֹ אֵין חֵקֶר
הָאֵל נוֹרָא, בְּאַחַת סְקִירָה, בֵּין טוֹב לָרַע יְבַקֵּר.

וְתוֹדָה וְלָעוֹלָה וְלַמִּנְחָה וְלַחַטָּאת וְלָאָשָׁם
וְלַשְּׁלָמִים וְלַמִּלּוּאִים כָּל קָרְבָּנֶךָ.
זְכֹר נִלְאָה אֲשֶׁר נָשְׂאָה וְהָשִׁיבָה לְאַדְמָתֶךָ
סֶלָה אֲהַלְלָךְ בְּאַשְׁרֵי יוֹשְׁבֵי בֵיתֶךָ.

אֲדוֹן צְבָאוֹת, בְּרֹב פְּלָאוֹת, חִבֵּר כָּל אָהֳלוֹ
בִּנְתִיבוֹת לֵב לִבְלֵב, הַצּוּר תָּמִים פָּעֳלוֹ.

וְתוֹדָה וְלָעוֹלָה וְלַמִּנְחָה וְלַחַטָּאת וְלָאָשָׁם
וְלַשְּׁלָמִים וְלַמִּלּוּאִים כָּל קָרְבָּנֶךָ.
זְכֹר נִלְאָה אֲשֶׁר נָשְׂאָה וְהָשִׁיבָה לְאַדְמָתֶךָ
סֶלָה אֲהַלְלָךְ בְּאַשְׁרֵי יוֹשְׁבֵי בֵיתֶךָ.

אַשְׁרֵי Happy are those who dwell in Your House; Ps. 84
they shall continue to praise You, Selah!
Happy are the people for whom this is so; Ps. 144
happy are the people whose God is the LORD.

A song of praise by David. Ps. 145

I will exalt You, my God, the King, and bless Your name for ever and all time. Every day I will bless You, and praise Your name for ever and all time. Great is the LORD and greatly to be praised; His greatness is unfathomable. One generation will praise Your works to the next, and tell of Your mighty deeds. On the glorious splendor of Your majesty I will meditate, and on the acts of Your wonders. They shall talk of the power of Your awesome deeds, and I will tell of Your greatness. They shall recite the record of Your great goodness, and sing with joy of Your righteousness. The LORD is gracious and compassionate, slow to anger and great in loving-kindness. The LORD is good to all, and His compassion extends to all His works. All Your works shall thank You, LORD, and Your devoted ones shall bless You. They shall talk of the glory of Your kingship, and speak of Your might. To make known to mankind His mighty deeds and the glorious majesty of His kingship. Your kingdom is an everlasting kingdom, and Your reign is for all generations. The LORD supports all who fall, and raises all who are bowed down. All raise their eyes to You in hope, and You give them their food in due season. You open Your hand, and satisfy every living thing with favor. The LORD is righteous in all His ways, and kind in all He does. The LORD is close to all who call on Him, to all who call on Him in truth. He fulfills the will of those who revere Him; He hears their cry and saves them. The LORD guards all who love Him, but all the wicked He will destroy. ▸ My mouth shall speak the praise of the LORD, and all creatures shall bless His holy name for ever and all time.

We will bless the LORD now and for ever. Halleluya! Ps. 115

אַשְׁרֵי יוֹשְׁבֵי בֵיתֶךָ, עוֹד יְהַלְלוּךָ סֶּלָה: תהלים פד
אַשְׁרֵי הָעָם שֶׁכָּכָה לּוֹ, אַשְׁרֵי הָעָם שֶׁיהוה אֱלֹהָיו: תהלים קמד
תְּהִלָּה לְדָוִד תהלים קמה

אֲרוֹמִמְךָ אֱלוֹהַי הַמֶּלֶךְ, וַאֲבָרְכָה שִׁמְךָ לְעוֹלָם וָעֶד:
בְּכָל־יוֹם אֲבָרְכֶךָּ, וַאֲהַלְלָה שִׁמְךָ לְעוֹלָם וָעֶד:
גָּדוֹל יהוה וּמְהֻלָּל מְאֹד, וְלִגְדֻלָּתוֹ אֵין חֵקֶר:
דּוֹר לְדוֹר יְשַׁבַּח מַעֲשֶׂיךָ, וּגְבוּרֹתֶיךָ יַגִּידוּ:
הֲדַר כְּבוֹד הוֹדֶךָ, וְדִבְרֵי נִפְלְאֹתֶיךָ אָשִׂיחָה:
וֶעֱזוּז נוֹרְאֹתֶיךָ יֹאמֵרוּ, וּגְדוּלָּתְךָ אֲסַפְּרֶנָּה:
זֵכֶר רַב־טוּבְךָ יַבִּיעוּ, וְצִדְקָתְךָ יְרַנֵּנוּ:
חַנּוּן וְרַחוּם יהוה, אֶרֶךְ אַפַּיִם וּגְדָל־חָסֶד:
טוֹב־יהוה לַכֹּל, וְרַחֲמָיו עַל־כָּל־מַעֲשָׂיו:
יוֹדוּךָ יהוה כָּל־מַעֲשֶׂיךָ, וַחֲסִידֶיךָ יְבָרְכוּכָה:
כְּבוֹד מַלְכוּתְךָ יֹאמֵרוּ, וּגְבוּרָתְךָ יְדַבֵּרוּ:
לְהוֹדִיעַ לִבְנֵי הָאָדָם גְּבוּרֹתָיו, וּכְבוֹד הֲדַר מַלְכוּתוֹ:
מַלְכוּתְךָ מַלְכוּת כָּל־עֹלָמִים, וּמֶמְשַׁלְתְּךָ בְּכָל־דּוֹר וָדֹר:
סוֹמֵךְ יהוה לְכָל־הַנֹּפְלִים, וְזוֹקֵף לְכָל־הַכְּפוּפִים:
עֵינֵי־כֹל אֵלֶיךָ יְשַׂבֵּרוּ, וְאַתָּה נוֹתֵן־לָהֶם אֶת־אָכְלָם בְּעִתּוֹ:
פּוֹתֵחַ אֶת־יָדֶךָ, וּמַשְׂבִּיעַ לְכָל־חַי רָצוֹן:
צַדִּיק יהוה בְּכָל־דְּרָכָיו, וְחָסִיד בְּכָל־מַעֲשָׂיו:
קָרוֹב יהוה לְכָל־קֹרְאָיו, לְכֹל אֲשֶׁר יִקְרָאֻהוּ בֶאֱמֶת:
רְצוֹן־יְרֵאָיו יַעֲשֶׂה, וְאֶת־שַׁוְעָתָם יִשְׁמַע, וְיוֹשִׁיעֵם:
שׁוֹמֵר יהוה אֶת־כָּל־אֹהֲבָיו, וְאֵת כָּל־הָרְשָׁעִים יַשְׁמִיד:
› תְּהִלַּת יהוה יְדַבֶּר פִּי, וִיבָרֵךְ כָּל־בָּשָׂר שֵׁם קָדְשׁוֹ לְעוֹלָם וָעֶד:
וַאֲנַחְנוּ נְבָרֵךְ יָהּ מֵעַתָּה וְעַד־עוֹלָם, הַלְלוּיָהּ: תהלים קטו

RETURNING THE TORAH TO THE ARK

The Ark is opened. All stand. The Leader takes the Torah scroll and says:

יְהַלְלוּ Let them praise the name of the LORD, *Ps. 148*
for His name alone is sublime.

The congregation responds:

הוֹדוֹ His majesty is above earth and heaven.
He has raised the horn of His people,
for the glory of all His devoted ones,
the children of Israel, the people close to Him.
Halleluya!

On a Yom Tov occurring on a weekday say:

לְדָוִד מִזְמוֹר A psalm of David. The earth is the LORD's and all it *Ps. 24*
contains, the world and all who live in it. For He founded it on the seas and established it on the streams. Who may climb the mountain of the LORD? Who may stand in His holy place? He who has clean hands and a pure heart, who has not taken My name in vain, or sworn deceitfully. He shall receive blessing from the LORD, and just reward from God, his salvation. This is a generation of those who seek Him, the descendants of Jacob who seek Your presence, Selah! Lift up your heads, O gates; be uplifted, eternal doors, so that the King of glory may enter. Who is the King of glory? It is the LORD, strong and mighty, the LORD mighty in battle. Lift up your heads, O gates; lift them up, eternal doors, so that the King of glory may enter. ▸ Who is He, the King of glory? The LORD of hosts, He is the King of glory, Selah!

On a Yom Tov occurring on Shabbat say:

מִזְמוֹר לְדָוִד A psalm of David. Render to the LORD, you angelic *Ps. 29*
powers, render to the LORD glory and might. Render to the LORD the glory due to His name. Bow to the LORD in the beauty of holiness. The LORD's voice echoes over the waters; the God of glory thunders; the LORD is over the mighty waters. The LORD's voice in power, the LORD's voice in beauty, the LORD's voice breaks cedars,

הכנסת ספר תורה

The ארון קודש *is opened. All stand. The* שליח ציבור *takes the* ספר תורה *and says:*

תהלים קמח
יְהַלְלוּ אֶת־שֵׁם יהוה, כִּי־נִשְׂגָּב שְׁמוֹ, לְבַדּוֹ

The קהל *responds:*

הוֹדוֹ עַל־אֶרֶץ וְשָׁמָיִם:
וַיָּרֶם קֶרֶן לְעַמּוֹ
תְּהִלָּה לְכָל־חֲסִידָיו
לִבְנֵי יִשְׂרָאֵל עַם קְרֹבוֹ
הַלְלוּיָהּ:

On a יום טוב *occurring on a weekday say:*

תהלים כד
לְדָוִד מִזְמוֹר, לַיהוה הָאָרֶץ וּמְלוֹאָהּ, תֵּבֵל וְיְשְׁבֵי בָהּ: כִּי־הוּא עַל־יַמִּים יְסָדָהּ, וְעַל־נְהָרוֹת יְכוֹנְנֶהָ: מִי־יַעֲלֶה בְהַר־יהוה, וּמִי־יָקוּם בִּמְקוֹם קָדְשׁוֹ: נְקִי כַפַּיִם וּבַר־לֵבָב, אֲשֶׁר לֹא־נָשָׂא לַשָּׁוְא נַפְשִׁי וְלֹא נִשְׁבַּע לְמִרְמָה: יִשָּׂא בְרָכָה מֵאֵת יהוה, וּצְדָקָה מֵאֱלֹהֵי יִשְׁעוֹ: זֶה דּוֹר דֹּרְשָׁו, מְבַקְשֵׁי פָנֶיךָ, יַעֲקֹב, סֶלָה: שְׂאוּ שְׁעָרִים רָאשֵׁיכֶם, וְהִנָּשְׂאוּ פִּתְחֵי עוֹלָם, וְיָבוֹא מֶלֶךְ הַכָּבוֹד: מִי זֶה מֶלֶךְ הַכָּבוֹד, יהוה עִזּוּז וְגִבּוֹר, יהוה גִּבּוֹר מִלְחָמָה: שְׂאוּ שְׁעָרִים רָאשֵׁיכֶם, וּשְׂאוּ פִּתְחֵי עוֹלָם, וְיָבֹא מֶלֶךְ הַכָּבוֹד: ‹ מִי הוּא זֶה מֶלֶךְ הַכָּבוֹד, יהוה צְבָאוֹת הוּא מֶלֶךְ הַכָּבוֹד, סֶלָה:

On a יום טוב *occurring on* שבת *say:*

תהלים כט
מִזְמוֹר לְדָוִד, הָבוּ לַיהוה בְּנֵי אֵלִים, הָבוּ לַיהוה כָּבוֹד וָעֹז: הָבוּ לַיהוה כְּבוֹד שְׁמוֹ, הִשְׁתַּחֲווּ לַיהוה בְּהַדְרַת־קֹדֶשׁ: קוֹל יהוה עַל־הַמָּיִם, אֵל־הַכָּבוֹד הִרְעִים, יהוה עַל־מַיִם רַבִּים: קוֹל־יהוה בַּכֹּחַ, קוֹל יהוה בֶּהָדָר: קוֹל יהוה שֹׁבֵר אֲרָזִים, וַיְשַׁבֵּר יהוה אֶת־אַרְזֵי הַלְּבָנוֹן: וַיַּרְקִידֵם כְּמוֹ־עֵגֶל, לְבָנוֹן וְשִׂרְיוֹן כְּמוֹ בֶן־רְאֵמִים:

the LORD shatters the cedars of Lebanon. He makes Lebanon skip like a calf, Sirion like a young wild ox. The LORD's voice cleaves flames of fire. ▸ The LORD's voice makes the desert quake, the LORD shakes the desert of Kadesh. The LORD's voice makes hinds calve and strips the forests bare, and in His temple all say: "Glory!" The LORD sat enthroned at the Flood, the LORD sits enthroned as King for ever. The LORD will give strength to His people; the LORD will bless His people with peace.

As the Torah scroll is placed into the Ark, all say:

וּבְנֻחֹה יֹאמַר When the Ark came to rest, Moses would say: "Return, *Num. 10*
O LORD, to the myriad thousands of Israel." Advance, LORD, to Your *Ps. 132*
resting place, You and Your mighty Ark. Your priests are clothed in righteousness, and Your devoted ones sing in joy. For the sake
of Your servant David, do not reject Your anointed one. For I give *Prov. 4*
you good instruction; do not forsake My Torah. It is a tree of life *Prov. 3*
to those who grasp it, and those who uphold it are happy. Its ways
are ways of pleasantness, and all its paths are peace. ▸ Turn us back, *Lam. 5*
O LORD, to You, and we will return. Renew our days as of old.

The Ark is closed.

HALF KADDISH

Leader: יִתְגַּדַּל Magnified and sanctified may His great name be,
in the world He created by His will.
May He establish His kingdom
in your lifetime and in your days,
and in the lifetime of all the house of Israel,
swiftly and soon – and say: Amen.

All: May His great name be blessed for ever and all time.

Leader: Blessed and praised, glorified and exalted,
raised and honored, uplifted and lauded
be the name of the Holy One, blessed be He,
beyond any blessing, song, praise and consolation
uttered in the world – and say: Amen.

קוֹל־יהוה חֹצֵב לַהֲבוֹת אֵשׁ: ◦ קוֹל יהוה יָחִיל מִדְבָּר, יָחִיל יהוה
מִדְבַּר קָדֵשׁ: קוֹל יהוה יְחוֹלֵל אַיָּלוֹת וַיֶּחֱשֹׂף יְעָרוֹת, וּבְהֵיכָלוֹ, כֻּלּוֹ
אֹמֵר כָּבוֹד: יהוה לַמַּבּוּל יָשָׁב, וַיֵּשֶׁב יהוה מֶלֶךְ לְעוֹלָם: יהוה עֹז
לְעַמּוֹ יִתֵּן, יהוה יְבָרֵךְ אֶת־עַמּוֹ בַשָּׁלוֹם:

As the ספר תורה *is placed into the* ארון קודש*, all say:*

וּבְנֻחֹה יֹאמַר, שׁוּבָה יהוה רִבְבוֹת אַלְפֵי יִשְׂרָאֵל: קוּמָה יהוה במדבר י
לִמְנוּחָתֶךָ, אַתָּה וַאֲרוֹן עֻזֶּךָ: כֹּהֲנֶיךָ יִלְבְּשׁוּ־צֶדֶק, וַחֲסִידֶיךָ יְרַנֵּנוּ: תהלים קלב
בַּעֲבוּר דָּוִד עַבְדֶּךָ אַל־תָּשֵׁב פְּנֵי מְשִׁיחֶךָ: כִּי לֶקַח טוֹב נָתַתִּי משלי ד
לָכֶם, תּוֹרָתִי אַל־תַּעֲזֹבוּ: עֵץ־חַיִּים הִיא לַמַּחֲזִיקִים בָּהּ, וְתֹמְכֶיהָ משלי ג
מְאֻשָּׁר: דְּרָכֶיהָ דַרְכֵי־נֹעַם וְכָל־נְתִיבוֹתֶיהָ שָׁלוֹם: ◦ הֲשִׁיבֵנוּ יהוה איכה ה
אֵלֶיךָ וְנָשׁוּבָה, חַדֵּשׁ יָמֵינוּ כְּקֶדֶם:

The ארון קודש *is closed.*

חצי קדיש

ש״ץ: יִתְגַּדַּל וְיִתְקַדַּשׁ שְׁמֵהּ רַבָּא (קהל: אָמֵן)
בְּעָלְמָא דִּי בְרָא כִרְעוּתֵהּ
וְיַמְלִיךְ מַלְכוּתֵהּ
בְּחַיֵּיכוֹן וּבְיוֹמֵיכוֹן וּבְחַיֵּי דְכָל בֵּית יִשְׂרָאֵל
בַּעֲגָלָא וּבִזְמַן קָרִיב, וְאִמְרוּ אָמֵן. (קהל: אָמֵן)

קהל וש״ץ: יְהֵא שְׁמֵהּ רַבָּא מְבָרַךְ לְעָלַם וּלְעָלְמֵי עָלְמַיָּא.

ש״ץ: יִתְבָּרַךְ וְיִשְׁתַּבַּח וְיִתְפָּאַר וְיִתְרוֹמַם וְיִתְנַשֵּׂא
וְיִתְהַדָּר וְיִתְעַלֶּה וְיִתְהַלָּל
שְׁמֵהּ דְּקֻדְשָׁא בְּרִיךְ הוּא (קהל: בְּרִיךְ הוּא)
לְעֵלָּא מִן כָּל בִּרְכָתָא וְשִׁירָתָא, תֻּשְׁבְּחָתָא וְנֶחֱמָתָא
דַּאֲמִירָן בְּעָלְמָא, וְאִמְרוּ אָמֵן. (קהל: אָמֵן)

רשימות

RESHIMOT

RESHIMOT

THE COUNTING OF *BEIT DIN*

In the beginning of *Parashat Behar* (Lev. 25:8–10), the Torah states regarding the jubilee year: "You shall count for yourself seven sabbatical years, seven years, seven times, and the period of the seven sabbatical years shall be for you forty-nine years… And you shall hallow the fiftieth year." Nahmanides, in his commentary on *Parashat Emor* (Lev. 23:15), cites the *Torat Kohanim*: "'You shall count for yourself' – in *beit din*." Nahmanides comments: "I do not know whether this means that *beit din* is obligated to count the years and sabbaticals at the beginning of each year [i.e., to count verbally] and recite a blessing, as we do for *sefirat ha'omer*, or whether this means that *beit din* must take care [to keep track] of the count and sanctify the fiftieth year."

Maimonides, on the other hand, in the beginning of *Hilkhot Shemitah VeYovel*, writes that "It is a positive commandment to count forty-nine years and to sanctify the fiftieth year… and these two mitzvot were given to *beit din* alone." Unlike Nahmanides who is unsure whether counting is a mitzvah or whether *beit din* must merely keep track of the years, Maimonides maintains that it is indeed a mitzvah for *beit din* to count. The view of Maimonides is also shared by Ḥizkuni (beginning of *Behar*); however, Ḥizkuni adds the following comment: "Since here there is only one counting, in *beit din*, there is no need to recite a blessing. But regarding the *omer* where counting is written twice, once in *Parashat Emor* and once in *Parashat Re'eh* – one for *beit din* and one for the public – one must recite a blessing." What is the meaning of this cryptic comment?

To explain the view of Ḥizkuni, we must note a discrepancy between the mitzvah of *sefirat ha'omer* as recorded in *Parashat Emor* and in *Parashat Re'eh*. In *Re'eh*, the verse is written in the singular (שִׁבְעָה שָׁבֻעֹת תִּסְפָּר־לָךְ, "Seven weeks shall you count for yourself" – Deut. 16:9), while in *Emor* it is written in the plural (וּסְפַרְתֶּם לָכֶם, "You shall count for yourselves" – Lev. 23:15). The singular form is used to convey a single obligation upon the entire people, which is implemented by *beit din hagadol* on behalf of the people. The plural, on the other hand, indicates an obligation incumbent upon every individual.

Thus, we find in the *Sifrei* on the verse in *Re'eh*: "'Seven weeks shall you count for yourself' – in *beit din*; and from where do we know [the obligation of] each individual? The verse states: 'You shall count for yourselves' – each individual." According to the *Sifrei*, there are two distinct obligations of *sefirat ha'omer*, one incumbent upon *beit din*, and one incumbent upon each individual. The Vilna Gaon, however, emends the *Sifrei* to read: יכול בבית דין – "I may have thought [the obligation is] in *beit din*." תלמוד לומר וספרתם לכם, לכל אחד ואחד – "Therefore the verse states, 'You shall count for yourselves' – each individual." According to the Gaon, the *Sifrei* rejects the possibility that there is an obligation of *sefirat ha'omer* incumbent upon *beit din*; there is only the obligation of each individual.

Regarding the possibility that there is an obligation of *sefirat ha'omer* incumbent upon *beit din*, we find similarly that the sanctification of the new moon and the intercalation of years (*kiddush haḥodesh ve'ibbur shanim*) depends on *beit din hagadol* (see *Sefer HaMitzvot, aseh* 153, and *Hasagot* of Nahmanides). The Gemara (*Rosh Hashanah* 6b) tells us that Shavuot is not tied to a specific calendar date but to the completion of *sefirat ha'omer*. Thus, just as *beit din* is entrusted with the determination of all other holidays by its authority over the sanctification of months and years, it may be entrusted as well with establishing Shavuot on the basis of *sefirat ha'omer*.

While the Gaon maintains that this possibility is rejected, it seems Ḥizkuni accepts the view of the *Sifrei* without emendation. If so, there are in fact two different mitzvot of *sefirah* derived from two verses, one which applies to *beit din*, and another which applies to individuals. Yet there is a difference between these two obligations. The mitzvah of *beit din* is to count for the purpose of establishing the holiday of Shavuot, while the individual mitzvah is merely to count the days, without the purpose of establishing Shavuot. Accordingly, the mitzvah of each individual is completed upon counting each day, while the mitzvah of *beit din* is only completed retrospectively, upon sanctifying Shavuot.

It would further seem that according to Ḥizkuni, *beit din*'s counting of forty-nine years is a precondition for the jubilee year – only through *beit din*'s counting does the fiftieth year have the status of *yovel* (see *Ḥiddushei R. Ḥayyim HaLevi, Hil. Shemitah VeYovel* 10:5). If so, the counting is a means to sanctifying the fiftieth year, not an end unto itself. The Gemara (*Menaḥot* 42b) states that any mitzvah where the performance

◂ of a particular

of a particular act is not the completion of the mitzvah does not receive a blessing. The counting of *beit din* is not the completion of the mitzvah – both in the case of counting the years to sanctify *yovel* and in the case of *sefirat ha'omer* to sanctify Shavuot, *beit din* counts as a means to an end, not as a freestanding mitzvah. However, in the case of *sefirat ha'omer*, the members of the *beit din* have a dual obligation: They are not only the representatives of the Jewish people whose counting serves to establish Shavuot; they are also individuals for whom the counting is a freestanding mitzvah. Therefore, for *sefirat ha'omer* the members of *beit din* would recite a blessing due to their obligation as individuals. This explains Ḥizkuni's comment: "Since here there is only one counting, in *beit din*, there is no need to recite a blessing. But regarding the *omer* where counting is written twice, once in Parashat Emor and once in *Parashat Re'eh* – one for *beit din* and one for the public – one must recite a blessing." *Beit din* does not recite a blessing on counting years, because the sole obligation is counting as a means to sanctifying *yovel*. But the members of *beit din* do recite a blessing for *sefirat ha'omer*. In this case, their counting fulfills not only their obligation as *beit din* but also their obligation as individuals, and a blessing is recited on the individual obligation because the counting itself is the fulfillment of the mitzvah.

"YOU SHALL COUNT FIFTY DAYS"

Maimonides (*Hil. Temidin U'Musafin* 8:1) writes: ביום חמישים מספירת העומר הוא חג השבועות והוא יום עצרת – "On the fiftieth day of *sefirat ha'omer* is the holiday of Shavuot, the day of Atzeret." What does Maimonides mean by the words "On the fiftieth day of *sefirat ha'omer*"? After all, the counting of the *omer* is completed on the forty-ninth day. It seems that according to Maimonides, Shavuot is not on the day following the completion of the *omer* but is in fact part of the *sefirah*; the fiftieth day of *sefirah* is Shavuot. In fact, this is the simple meaning of the verse as well: עַד מִמָּחֳרַת הַשַּׁבָּת הַשְּׁבִיעִת תִּסְפְּרוּ חֲמִשִּׁים יוֹם וְהִקְרַבְתֶּם מִנְחָה חֲדָשָׁה לַה׳ – "To the day after the seven weeks, you shall count fifty days; and then you shall present a new grain offering to the Lord" (Lev. 23:16). Regarding the counting of the

◂ jubilee

jubilee years, the Torah specifies that the count is forty-nine years (Lev. 25:8), but regarding *sefirat ha'omer* we count fifty days – in that we mark the fiftieth day with the holiday of Shavuot, even though we do not count it verbally, in the manner of the first forty-nine.

Maimonides' view here is in keeping with his view (*Hil. Temidin U'Musafin* 7:24) that the mitzvah of *sefirat ha'omer* remains a biblical obligation even without the offering of the *korban ha'omer*. According to those who maintain that the mitzvah of *sefirah* today is only rabbinic, one cannot say that Shavuot is the fiftieth day of the *omer* – because Shavuot applies even when the mitzvah of *sefirat ha'omer* does not (see, e.g., Nahmanides, Lev. 23:16). But according to Maimonides, Shavuot can always be identified as the fiftieth day of the *omer*.

On the other hand, Rashi (Lev. 23:16) explains the verse "you shall count fifty days" to mean that we count up to fifty but do not count fifty (*velo ad bikhlal*). This is also the explanation of *Tosafot* (*Menaḥot* 65b s.v. *katuv*). Rosh (*Pesaḥim* 10:40) raises the question of why we do not count the fiftieth day and answers that we follow only the verse which requires counting seven weeks; the mention of fifty days is an example of the Torah rounding up by one which, he says, we find elsewhere as well. In contrast to the view of Maimonides, according to Rashi, *Tosafot* and Rosh, the fiftieth day is not part of the mitzvah of *sefirah*.

Netziv (*Haamek Davar*, Lev. 23:15) explains that when the Torah instructs us to count, this refers to a mental count; but when the mitzvah is repeated twice, the additional verse is interpreted to mean that we must count verbally. Regarding the first forty-nine days, the instruction to count is repeated, and therefore we must count them verbally. However, there is only one verse regarding the fiftieth day, and therefore it is sufficient to count it mentally (see also the commentary of R. David Zvi Hoffmann). R. Yitzhak of Volozhin, Netziv's father-in-law (*Peh Kadosh*, ibid.), offers another interpretation: the mitzvah to count the fiftieth day is incumbent upon *beit din* alone, not individuals. According to both Netziv and his father-in-law, there is some obligation to count the fiftieth day, either mentally or by *beit din*. This is similar to Maimonides' view, except that according to Maimonides, the fiftieth day does not require any act of counting other than the observance of Shavuot.

◂ THE *KEDUSHAT*

THE *KEDUSHAT HAYOM* OF SHAVUOT

The Torah does not establish a specific date for Shavuot. The Gemara (*Rosh Hashanah* 6b) notes that Shavuot can fall on the fifth, sixth or seventh of Sivan – depending on whether the months of Nissan and Iyyar contain twenty-nine or thirty days. Instead of being tied to a fixed date, Shavuot is established by *sefirat ha'omer* – counting forty-nine days from Pesaḥ. Thus, Pesaḥ forms the basis for the holiday of Shavuot. The reason for this is that Shavuot is an extension of Pesaḥ. The purpose of the Exodus from Egypt commemorated on Pesaḥ was *mattan Torah* on Shavuot. While the Exodus occurred on Pesaḥ, the goal of the Exodus was only realized on Shavuot.

This was revealed to Moses at the Burning Bush, when God said to him, וְזֶה־לְּךָ הָאוֹת כִּי אָנֹכִי שְׁלַחְתִּיךָ בְּהוֹצִיאֲךָ אֶת־הָעָם מִמִּצְרַיִם תַּעַבְדוּן אֶת־הָאֱלֹהִים עַל הָהָר הַזֶּה – "This is the sign that I have sent you: After you release the people from Egypt, you will serve God on this mountain" (Ex. 3:12). In other words, God told Moses that the purpose of the Exodus would only be realized at *mattan Torah*, and that, at the very moment that the Jews will be freed from Egypt (בְּהוֹצִיאֲךָ אֶת־הָעָם מִמִּצְרַיִם), they should start to count the days leading to *mattan Torah*. The Exodus *per se* was not the most important event. Its importance was only that it was the first step toward *mattan Torah*, תַּעַבְדוּן אֶת־הָאֱלֹהִים עַל הָהָר הַזֶּה.

While the Torah refers to the holiday as Shavuot, the Sages call it by the name Atzeret. The term Atzeret emphasizes that Shavuot is an appendage to Pesaḥ. Rashi (Lev. 23:36) explains the word "Atzeret" to mean to overstay and refrain from going away. Just as Shemini Atzeret is an extension of Sukkot, Shavuot is an extension of Pesaḥ.

This issue was the nub of the controversy between the Sadducees and the Pharisees regarding the timing of Shavuot. The Gemara (*Menaḥot* 65a), citing *Megillat Taanit*, relates that a holiday was established on the days that the Pharisees seized control of the Sanhedrin from the Sadducees and established Shavuot on the fiftieth day following Pesaḥ. *Megillat Taanit* refers to this commemoration as איתותב חגא דשבועיא, "the festival of Shavuot was restored," using the biblical name, Shavuot, and not the rabbinic name, Atzeret. Why here do the Sages depart from their usual name for the holiday?

◄ According to

According to the Sadducees, the verse וּסְפַרְתֶּם לָכֶם מִמָּחֳרַת הַשַּׁבָּת, "You shall count from the next day after the Sabbath" (Lev. 23:15), means that *sefirat ha'omer* always begins on Sunday. They further maintained that this should commence on the Sunday immediately following the start of the harvest. The first day of the harvest changed from year to year depending on the climactic conditions. Accordingly, Shavuot also occurred on a different date each year. Thus, the Sadducees rejected any bond between Pesaḥ and Shavuot.

The Pharisees, on the other hand, argued that מִמָּחֳרַת הַשַּׁבָּת refers to the day after the first day of Pesaḥ. Thus, *sefirat ha'omer* commences on the second day of Pesaḥ, and Pesaḥ and Shavuot are inextricably linked. In order to counter the Sadducee view, the Sages used the term Atzeret to convey the message that this holiday is dependent on and inextricably linked to Pesaḥ. This terminology was instituted immediately after the episode related in *Megillat Taanit*. When the Gemara relates the episode of how the Pharisees defeated the Sadducees, it employs the term חגא דשבועיא, since that was the last time that the holiday was called by this name. Immediately after this victory, the Rabbis began to use the name Atzeret to refer to the holiday.

In the Torah, we find the word Atzeret used with respect to the last day of Sukkot and Pesaḥ (Lev. 23:16; Deut. 16:8). The respective mitzvot associated with these holidays (i.e., dwelling in the sukkah and the obligatory eating of matzah) no longer apply on the last day of each holiday, and therefore the last day of each holiday is termed Atzeret. In other words, Atzeret indicates a *yom tov* which possesses *kedushat hayom* with regard to *issur melakha*, the prohibition of work, but not the performance of any other mitzvah. The Sages used the term Atzeret for Shavuot because it likewise has no specific mitzvot which are characteristic of its *kedushat hayom*, such as sukkah and matzah.

Interestingly, Targum Onkelos (Num. 28:26) translates the word בְּשָׁבֻעֹתֵיכֶם, "on your [festival of] weeks," as בְּעַצְרָתְכוֹן, "on your Atzeret." Apparently, the Targum felt that the Torah's use of the possessive form ("*your* weeks") implies that the weeks which bring about the holiday are not the standard weeks which commence each Sunday but rather weeks which are generated by the Jewish people. This is contrary to the view of the Sadducees who maintained that *sefirat ha'omer* must commence on Sunday and that the seven weeks of counting are the seven natural calendar weeks, not seven-day periods beginning on any day of the week. The Targum's translation thus refutes the view of the Sadducees and emphasizes that the holiday is generated not by ordinary weeks but by *our* weeks, which follow the holiday of Pesaḥ.

THE JEWISH PEOPLE'S CONVERSION AT SINAI

Maimonides (*Hil. Issurei Biah* 13:1,4) writes:

> Israel entered the covenant with three acts: circumcision, immersion, and offering a sacrifice.... Similarly, for [all] future generations, when a gentile desires to enter into the covenant, take shelter under the wings of the Divine Presence, and accept the yoke of the Torah, he must undergo circumcision, immersion, and the offering of a sacrifice.

Maimonides' description is based on the Gemara (*Keritot* 9a) which derives the laws of conversion from the experience of the Jewish people at Sinai. The Vilna Gaon (*Beiur HaGra, Oraḥ Ḥayyim* 490:9) explains that this is the basis for our custom to read *Megillat Rut* on Shavuot – just as *Megillat Rut* describes one conversion, Shavuot commemorates the conversion of the nation.

However, the idea that *mattan Torah* was the Jewish people's conversion seems to stand in contradiction to a statement of Nahmanides in his commentary on the Torah (Lev. 24:10). Nahmanides writes that "from the time that Abraham entered the covenant, they [i.e., his descendants through Isaac and Jacob] were Israelites and were 'not reckoned among the nations.'" According to Nahmanides, following Abraham's circumcision he and his descendants already achieved Jewish status. If so, what was the need for the conversion at Sinai? Ritva (*Ketubot* 11a) addresses this issue and states that, "The seed of Abraham had already been commanded regarding circumcision and were entered into his [Abraham's] covenant from their youth, and this [i.e., the conversion at Sinai] was only the completion of conversion [*gemar gerut*]." How are we to understand this?

We can explain as follows. The concept of conversion is equivalent

◂ to accepting

to accepting the yoke of Torah and mitzvot. Abraham was given one commandment – circumcision – and therefore, in his time only partial conversion was possible. In Egypt, the Jewish people received additional mitzvot (see *Hil. Melakhim* 9:1) but since they did not receive all the mitzvot, full conversion was still impossible. At Sinai when the people received all six hundred and thirteen mitzvot, they required a new act to complete their conversion and be imbued with the full sanctity of the Jewish people. Since the sanctity of the Jewish people derives from Torah and mitzvot, the addition of new mitzvot required a new conversion; the completion of *kedushat Yisrael* could take place only with the revelation of all six hundred and thirteen mitzvot. This is the meaning of the *gemar gerut* that took place at Sinai.

Although we have described the conversion at Sinai as the paradigm of future conversions, it seems that there is one significant difference between the conversion at Sinai and subsequent conversions. In characterizing the offering brought as part of the people's conversion, Maimonides (*Hil. Issurei Biah* 13:3) writes: "Sacrifices [were offered then], as the verse (Ex. 24:5) states: 'And he sent out the youth of the children of Israel and they brought burnt offerings.' They offered them as agents of the entire Jewish people [על ידי כל ישראל הקריבום]." The phrase על ידי כל ישראל הקריבום seems to indicate that these offerings were brought on behalf of the Jewish people as a nation, not as individuals, i.e., as *korbenot tzibbur*. If so, it follows that the conversion of the Jewish people was performed not as a group of individuals but as a single communal conversion. Likewise, the acceptance of the mitzvot (*kabbalat mitzvot*) was performed communally when the people said *naaseh venishma* – "we shall do and we shall heed" (Ex. 24:7) – "as one man, with one heart" (Rashi, Ex. 19:2). The conversion took effect on the nation as a whole at one time.

Based on this, we can resolve a question that arises from the Gemara (*Shabbat* 130a). Commenting on the verse וַיִּשְׁמַע מֹשֶׁה אֶת־הָעָם בֹּכֶה לְמִשְׁפְּחֹתָיו, "Moses heard the people weeping with their families" (Num. 11:10), the Gemara explains that Israel was weeping concerning family matters, for marriages within the family that became forbidden after they accepted the Torah. Yet there is a well-known rule that a convert to Judaism is akin to a newly born infant (*Yevamot* 22a) – meaning that the convert's former family relationships are dissolved. If so, Maharal (*Gur Aryeh*, Gen. 46:10)

◂ notes that

notes that there should have been no prohibited marriages following *mattan Torah,* since all Israel underwent conversion at Sinai.

However, according to the above, we can explain that this rule did not apply to the conversion at Sinai because it was fundamentally distinct from the ordinary form of conversion. Ordinarily, conversion is an individual act, and in such cases the convert gains the status of a newborn. But the conversion at Sinai was not a separate conversion of each individual member of Israel, but a conversion of the entire nation in the aggregate. Since the conversion at Sinai took effect on the whole nation as a single entity, their family relationships persisted.

ACCEPTANCE OF MITZVOT IN CONVERSION

Maimonides, in *Hilkhot Issurei Biah* 13:17, states: "A convert who was not examined or who was not informed about the commandments and the punishments [for transgressing them], but was circumcised and immersed in the presence of three laymen, is deemed a [valid] convert." I once heard from my father and master, of blessed memory, that Maimonides does not mean that a person who converted with the intention of not observing the commandments is deemed a valid convert. Such a notion would subvert the entire concept of conversion and the holiness of Israel, which exhausts itself in our obligation to fulfill God's commandments. Maimonides' position is that the acceptance of the commandments, unlike immersion, does not constitute a distinct act in the process of conversion that would require the presence of a court. Rather, acceptance of the commandments is a defining feature of the conversion process that must be undergone for the sake of fulfilling the commandments. Therefore, if we know that the convert, at the time of immersion, is willing to accept the yoke of the commandments, the immersion effects conversion even though there was no special act of informing the convert about the commandments and his consenting to fulfill them, since the convert intends to live the holy life of an observant Jew.

However, *Tosafot* (*Yevamot* 45b, s.v. *mi lo tavlah*) state that the acceptance of the yoke of the commandments can precede immersion. It would appear that the view of *Tosafot* is that the acceptance of the commandments is a distinct element in the conversion process and, consequently, that the law necessitating the presence of a court refers to the court's presence at the act of acceptance. Only this act of acceptance – and not immersion – requires the presence of the court.

Nahmanides, in his *Ḥiddushim* (on *Yevamot* 45b, s.v. *mi lo tavlah*), states: "Even a male convert who accepted [the commandments] upon himself prior to his being circumcised must once again accept [them] upon himself when he immerses himself." It would seem, at first glance, that according to Nahmanides, there is an act of acceptance of the commandments which takes place at the time of circumcision, and not only at the time of immersion. However, one might suggest that Nahmanides is not referring to a special act of acceptance of the commandments at the time of circumcision, but, rather, is characterizing the general nature of circumcision. Circumcision must be undergone for the sake of obligating oneself to fulfill the commandments. This interpretation of Nahmanides' view is similar to the explanation offered earlier with respect to Maimonides' position. Maimonides, however, is of the opinion that the absence of a distinct act of acceptance of the commandments does not constitute any legal impediment to the validity of the conversion. Nahmanides, on the other hand, agrees with the *Tosafot* that there is a distinct act of acceptance of the commandments and that it requires the presence of a court. However, Nahmanides believes that aside from the distinct act of acceptance, both circumcision and immersion must be undergone for the sake of being obliged to perform the commandments, that is to say, for the sake of conversion.

STANDING FOR THE TEN COMMANDMENTS

On the first day of the holiday of Shavuot, we read the Torah portion about the Revelation at Sinai and the Ten Commandments (*Shulḥan Arukh, Oraḥ Ḥayyim* 494:1). Maimonides (*Teshuvot,* Blau ed., 263) was asked if it is an appropriate custom to specifically stand during the reading of the Ten Commandments. The questioner felt that such a custom should not be allowed, just as the Rabbis themselves (*Berakhot* 12a) dissolved the practice of reading the Ten Commandments along with the

◂ *Shema*

Shema because of heretics who claimed that the Ten Commandments were more important than the rest of the Torah. The questioner felt that anything that places extra emphasis on the Ten Commandments over the rest of the Torah would share the same potential for heresy.

In his response, Maimonides passionately agrees with the questioner and maintains that indeed one should not stand specifically for the reading of the Ten Commandments. Rather, one should sit, as one does during the rest of the Torah reading. Maimonides suspects that standing for the Ten Commandments will possibly lead to a laxity in faith, for one will begin to think that certain sections of the Torah are more important than others. Therefore, Maimonides concludes that this practice should be avoided.

However, despite Maimonides' opinion, the current commonplace custom is to stand during the reading of the Ten Commandments (see *Shaarei Ephraim* 7:37; *Iggerot Moshe, Oraḥ Ḥayyim* 4:22). The question is, why indeed is this our custom? Why do we not follow Maimonides' compelling argument? Furthermore, why is standing for the reading of the Ten Commandments any different from the custom that the Rabbis dissolved of reading the Ten Commandments with the *Shema*?

We can understand our custom of standing for the reading of the Ten Commandments based on the following. The Ten Commandments, unlike other sections of the Torah, have two sets of cantillations, known as *"ta'am taḥton"* and *"ta'am elyon."* The difference between them is as follows: The *ta'am taḥton* divides the Ten Commandments by verses, in the same manner as the rest of the Torah. The *ta'am elyon,* however, divides the Ten Commandments not into units of verses but by commandment. For example, the fourth commandment contains four verses according to *ta'am taḥton* (Ex. 20:7–10), but when using the *ta'am elyon,* it is read as one long verse, being that these four verses comprise just one of the Ten Commandments. Likewise, the fifth through eighth commandments, according to *ta'am taḥton,* are contained in one verse (Ex. 20:12), but when using *ta'am elyon* are read as four separate verses, one verse for each individual commandment.

With this in mind, we can understand the custom of standing for the Ten Commandments. The regular weekly reading of the Torah was instituted in order to fulfill our communal obligation of Torah study. It was specifically designed to fulfill this obligation through the reading of the Written Torah. Consequently, we fulfill this obligation by reading the *pesukim* of the Torah. The Talmud states that we cannot divide a verse in a way that Moses did not divide it (*Megillah* 24a). Therefore, when fulfilling our communal obligation of learning Torah, the Torah must be read in the way that Moses divided it, to constitute reading *pesukim*.

When the Ten Commandments are read with the *ta'am elyon*, by contrast, our goal is not to fulfill our obligation of reading Torah. Rather we are reading the Ten Commandments as a commemoration of what transpired at Mount Sinai, and therefore the reading is divided into commandments (as they were said at Sinai), not into verses.

In many congregations, on the weeks of *Parashat Yitro* and *Va'etḥanan* in which the Ten Commandments are read, they are read with the regular cantillation, *ta'am taḥton* (see *Beiur Halakhah* 494). This is because this reading is part of the regular weekly reading of the Torah in which we are fulfilling our communal obligation of learning Torah, and therefore it must be read with the regular cantillation (*ta'am taḥton*).

However, on Shavuot, everyone has the custom to read the Ten Commandments with the *ta'am elyon*. This is because the reading of the Ten Commandments on Shavuot is not meant to fulfill our communal obligation of learning Torah; rather, the reading is a commemoration of the giving of the Torah at Mount Sinai, and thus we divide the Ten Commandments into the unit of commandments, not into verses (see *Magen Avraham* 494 in the name of Ḥizkuni).

It follows that our current custom to stand during the recitation of the Ten Commandments applies when they are being read with the *ta'am elyon*. This cantillation demonstrates that our reading is a commemoration of what took place at Mount Sinai, and therefore we stand just as the Jewish nation stood around Mount Sinai when receiving the Torah (see Ex. 19:17; Deut. 4:11). Likewise, it would seem that Maimonides' disapproval of standing for the Ten Commandments is when they are being read with the *ta'am taḥton*, which indicates that they are being read as verses of the Torah. One cannot stand for the Ten Commandments when they are read as a particular segment of the Torah, because this would indeed indicate that one ascribes more significance to them than to the rest of the Torah.

◂ When reading

When reading the Ten Commandments with *ta'am elyon,* however, we do not have to be concerned about the appearance of giving primacy to the Ten Commandments. We are not standing due to the content of the Torah reading but rather as a commemoration of what transpired at Mount Sinai. The Ten Commandments are no more sacred than the *parashah* which speaks of Timnah, the concubine of Elifaz (Gen. 36:12), but the Ten Commandments are read not only as a text which is being studied, but as a text which is being promulgated and proclaimed by God Himself.

Judaism developed a very peculiar philosophy of memory, indeed, an ethics of memory. Memory and forgetfulness are subject to ethical determination. Memory is not just the capacity of man to know events which lie in the past. Memory is experiential in nature; one does not simply recollect the past or just remember bygones, but reexperiences that which has been, and quickens events that are seemingly dead.

Many mitzvot are based upon this idea. The Passover seder is, of course, the prime example: "In each generation a person is required to see himself as if he had gone out of Egypt" (Haggadah). Likewise, the reading of the Ten Commandments is not only a didactic performance of *limmud,* study, but a restaging, a dramatic reenacting of *mattan Torah.* That is why people rise when it is read.

THE *BERAKHOT* ON READING THE TORAH

In discussing the laws of *Keriat HaTorah,* Maimonides (*Hilkhot Tefillah* 12:5) writes:

> Each of the readers opens the *sefer Torah,* looks at the place that he is reading, and then says *Barekhu*.... He then recites the blessing, "*Barukh Atah Hashem... asher baḥar banu...* and the entire congregation responds Amen. He then reads until he has completed the reading, closes the *sefer,* and recites the blessing *Barukh Atah Hashem... asher natan lanu*....

It is interesting to note that when writing of the blessing before the Torah reading, Maimonides mentions that "the entire congregation responds Amen." However, Maimonides makes no such comment with regard to the blessing after the Torah reading. How can we explain this difference?

The Talmud (*Berakhot* 21a) cites the verse כִּי שֵׁם ה׳ אֶקְרָא הָבוּ גֹדֶל לֵאלֹקֵינוּ, "When I proclaim the LORD's name, give glory to our God" (Deut. 32:3), as the biblical source for our everyday obligation to recite a blessing upon Torah study. Rashi explains that the words "כִּי שֵׁם ה׳ אֶקְרָא" refer to Moses' blessing God before reciting the song of *Haazinu*; "הָבוּ גֹדֶל לֵאלֹקֵינוּ" – the end of the verse – is Moses' instruction to the people to respond Amen to his blessing. Thus, according to Rashi, the imperative to recite a blessing before Torah study includes in it as well the Amen response to the blessing.

Likewise, in the book of Nehemiah (8:5–6), we find: "And Ezra opened the book in the sight of all the people… and when he opened it, all the people stood up. And Ezra blessed the LORD, the great God. And all the people answered: 'Amen, Amen,' with the lifting up of their hands; and they bowed their heads, and fell down before the LORD with their faces to the ground." Ezra blessed God before reading the Torah, and the people answered Amen. There is no mention of a blessing after the reading of the Torah. It would seem from here that both the blessing before the reading of the Torah and the response of Amen by the people is an integral part of the public reading of the Torah.

In short, the Amen in response to the blessing on the Torah is not the same as the Amen response to all other blessings, but is rather a component of the obligation of *Birkat HaTorah*. In addition, it seems that the blessing before the reading (and the Amen response) is a component of the public reading of the Torah. This is why the verses in Nehemiah describe this blessing. The blessing made after reading the Torah, however, was instituted by the Rabbis as a blessing in its own right, and not as part of the obligation of reading the Torah in public.

When Maimonides writes how the Torah reading is performed, he mentions that the congregation answers Amen to the first blessing because this Amen is not merely the Amen of all *berakhot* but a component of the blessing on the Torah and of the public Torah reading. However, regarding the blessing after the reading of the Torah, Maimonides does

◂ not mention

not mention that the congregation answers Amen because that Amen is not specifically related to the obligation of reading the Torah.

Regarding the blessings on the Torah, we can ask: Are they only the obligation of the one who is called up to read the Torah (the *oleh*), or are they the obligation of the entire congregation, which fulfills its obligation through the *oleh*'s blessing?

The Mishnah (*Megillah* 4:1) tells us that originally, the first *oleh* would make the blessing before reading the Torah, and the final *oleh* would make the blessing after reading the Torah. Eventually, the Rabbis instituted that each and every *oleh laTorah* must make a blessing before and after reading. The Talmud (*Megillah* 21b) explains that this is due to those who enter the synagogue in the middle of the reading, and due to those who leave early. Rashi explains that the concern was that a latecomer would erroneously think that it is not necessary to make a blessing before reading the Torah. Similarly, one who leaves the synagogue early may incorrectly assume that a blessing after reading the Torah is not needed. To avoid this, the Rabbis instituted that every *oleh* should make the blessings before and after reading the Torah.

Meiri, however, explains the reasoning of the Talmud differently. According to Meiri, the Rabbis were concerned that a latecomer would not hear the blessing before the reading of the Torah and will be listening to the Torah reading without having heard its blessing. Similarly, one who leaves early will fail to hear the blessing after the reading of the Torah. It seems according to Meiri that the blessings said upon the Torah reading are the obligation of each and every person in the congregation, and they fulfill this obligation through the *oleh*. Every *oleh* must make the blessings before and after reading the Torah in order to ensure that everyone hears the Torah with its blessings.

Based on the foregoing, it is possible that Maimonides holds that only the blessing before reading the Torah is the obligation of the entire congregation, but the blessing after the reading of the Torah is only the obligation of the *oleh* and not of the entire congregation. Therefore, Maimonides specifies that the entire congregation answers Amen to the blessing before reading of the Torah since through the *oleh* they all fulfill their obligation of this blessing.

BIRKHOT HATORAH AND EMOTIONAL INVOLVEMENT IN TORAH

There are two versions of the first *berakha* that an individual recites prior to Torah study: "*la'asok bedivrei Torah*" is the version of the *Ḥakhmei Ashkenaz*; "*al divrei Torah*" is the version which was quoted by Rif, Maimonides, and most *Ḥakhmei Sepharad*. I cannot see any basic difference as to the motif and theme between the Ashkenazic version and the Sephardic version. *Birkhot HaTorah* are not related to the cognitive act of *talmud Torah*, but rather are associated with the axiological involvement and consecration to Torah. Whether the version of "*la'asok*" or "*al divrei Torah*" is adopted is of no relevance; the net result is that we do not pronounce a blessing concerning the actual study of Torah – "*lilmod divrei Torah*" is not mentioned. What is emphasized is the fascination which *divrei Torah* possess. "*La'asok bedivrei Torah*" means to occupy ourselves, to devote ourselves, to be fascinated. "*Al divrei Torah*" means to be emotionally involved in it, not merely "*lilmod divrei Torah*," the intellectual act of study.

If we should scrutinize the halakhot pertaining to *Birkhot HaTorah*, we would find a few laws which are peculiar to *Birkhot HaTorah*, in contrast to other *birkhot hamitzvot*, which will corroborate our thesis that this *berakha* relates to the emotional component in *talmud Torah*.

The recital of the *berakha* in the morning suffices for the whole day and also for the night study, whereas other *birkhot hamitzvot* are canceled by *hese'aḥ hadaat* (distraction from the act at hand). If I should take off my *tefillin* for a while not intending to put them back soon, and then I change my mind and I want to put the *tefillin* on, it requires another *berakha*. However, reciting *Birkhot HaTorah* in the morning relieves me of the duty of reciting the *berakha* for twenty-four hours.

Tosafot (*Berakhot* 11b) note this difficulty and explain that there is *hese'aḥ hadaat* with regard to other mitzvot but not with regard to Torah for we are duty bound to study all the time. It is difficult to understand the answer. Whether or not one is permitted to interrupt the study is irrelevant concerning the problem of *hese'aḥ hadaat*, as the whole problem revolves around a factual, not an ideal, situation. It is not a question of what he is supposed to do, the question is what he is doing. We have to reckon with the fact that many people interrupt their studies with no intent of resuming them after a short while. This means there is *hese'aḥ hadaat*. Why shouldn't they recite the *Birkat HaTorah* if they are ready to read the Torah after a long intermission during which they haven't even thought of engaging in the study of the Torah? The fact that those people acted not in accordance with the law that requires that a man should never have *hese'aḥ hadaat* should not change the fact the *berakha* has been canceled for reason of *hese'aḥ hadaat*.

However, we understand the answer of *Tosafot* when we realize that *Birkat HaTorah* is related not to the explicit intellectual preoccupation, which is not continuous, but to the emotional consecration and involvement associated with a state of mind, with love for and devotion to the Word – and this involvement is a permanent, continuous experience which cannot be interrupted or canceled. Of course, emotional involvement sometimes is an acute experience, an explosive experience – I think of my great treasure and my heart overflows with love – and sometimes it is a latent experience; however, this love can never be extinguished.

Let us take our relationship to children. There is certainly emotional involvement with children, devotion, but you cannot say the experience is at all times identical. Sometimes it is an acute experience, when I play with the child, when my heart overflows with love for the child, I experience an explosive feeling which demonstrates itself in some external traits, like an expression on my face and so forth. It is an acute experience. And frequently, when the father is in his office or in his shop and his mind is occupied with other matters, it loses its acuteness and explosiveness and turns into a latent feeling. Yet he can never forfeit its greatness and depth.

This is exactly my relationship to Torah. The emotional involvement is a continuous experience, sometimes in an acute stage, sometimes in a latent stage, in an inactive stage. Yes, sometimes the acute experience is sharp with passion, and overabundant feelings, and sometimes, under other circumstances, it is a quiet experience; when the mind is occupied with other matters it loses its acuteness and explosiveness and turns into latent feeling. Yet the father can never forget the child and can never stop loving the child, and this is exactly valid with reference to Torah. The emotional attachment is never broken.

Maimonides actually says that the *Birkhot HaTorah* every day are part of *Birkhot HaShaḥar. Birkhot HaTorah* are a *birkat hodaya* – just as every day one has to recite a *berakha* of "who gives the rooster understanding," every day man has to praise God that He actually involved him and entitled him in this great experience.

Second, many *Rishonim* hold the view that there is no need to recite any passages from the Torah after reciting *Birkhot HaTorah. Tosafot* (*Berakhot* 11b, s.v. *shekvar*) quote the French sages who say there is no need to study *Torah Shebikhtav* or *Torah Shebe'al Peh* following the pronouncement of *Birkhot HaTorah,* in contrast to other *birkhot hamitzvot* which are necessarily related to the subsequent action. For example, if I should say *al netilat lulav* without holding the *lulav,* that would be a *berakha levatala,* blessing in vain. But most of the *Rishonim* think there is no need for *limud haTorah* following *Birkhot HaTorah.* The *berakhot* refer not to the actual performance but to a value judgement, emotional assessment, a mood, a world perspective and the actual study is of no significance and has no bearing upon the validity of *Birkhot HaTorah.*

Third, the *Shulḥan Arukh* (*Oraḥ Ḥayyim* 47:14) ruled that women must say *Birkhot HaTorah.* With regard to *mitzvot aseh shehazman grama,* time-bound commandments, there is a controversy between Maimonides (*Hilkhot Tzitzit* 3:9) and Rabbenu Tam (*Tosafot, Rosh Hashanah* 33a) as to whether women should say a *berakha* or not. Ashkenazim have accepted the viewpoint of Rabbenu Tam and the Rema that women pronounce a *berakha* on all *mitzvot aseh shehazman grama* like *lulav, shofar, sukkah* and so forth. The *Meḥaber,* R. Yosef Karo, however, does not accept the viewpoint of Rabbenu Tam but Maimonides' viewpoint that women must not say a *berakha* over *mitzvot aseh shehazman grama* (*Oraḥ Ḥayyim* 589:6). If they are relieved of the duty, they cannot say "*vetzivanu,* who has obligated us" because there is no "*vetzivanu.*" The Vilna Gaon asks why the *Meḥaber* rules that women recite *Birkhot HaTorah,* since women are actually relieved of the duty of *talmud Torah.* If the *Meḥaber* is of the Maimonidean opinion that whenever there is no duty, the *berakha* is out of place, women should not recite *Birkhot HaTorah* either. The answer is that women recite *Birkhot HaTorah* because women have also witnessed *Ma'amad Har Sinai,* and the Torah says, "Assemble the people, the men and the women and the little ones" (Deut. 31:12). Women are duty bound

◂ to attend

to attend *hakhel* because *hakhel* is not intellectual *limud*; it is more a demonstration of our total commitment to the Torah. Men and women might differ in their respective obligations in intellectual *limud*, but there is no difference between men and women regarding emotional involvement, and that is why women recite *Birkhot HaTorah*.

A total commitment is at first an emotional commitment. The objective which is anticipated is an ideal; the objective which is attained is a value. Torah is a great ideal and a great value. Whatever is realized is a value; whatever I haven't attained is an ideal which has unlimited fascination for me. Torah exerts some supernatural power of fascination upon the human personality in the same manner as God fascinates me and captivates my imagination. I yearn for Him, "As the hart pants after the water brooks, so my soul pants after Thee, O God" (Ps. 42:2). This great, total involvement involves not only the study of Torah but for its ideals to be integrated in my existence and my personality as a value. *Limud Torah* expresses intellectual engagement; *esek bedivrei Torah* expresses emotional involvement or the axiological relationship. *Birkhot HaTorah* are related not to the first aspect but to the second aspect.

COMBINING TORAH STUDY WITH ITS BLESSINGS

At the end of his discussion of the laws of the morning blessings, Maimonides (*Hil. Tefillah* 7:10–11) writes:

> (10) One who rises to study Torah before he recites the *Shema*, whether to study the Written or the Oral Law, should first wash his hands, then recite three blessings, and then study. These [blessings] are: "[Blessed are You…] who has sanctified us with His mitzvot and commanded us concerning the words of Torah"; "Please, LORD, our God, make the words of Your Torah sweet in our mouths and the mouths of Your people, the entire House of Israel. May we, our offspring, and the offspring of Your people, know Your name and occupy ourselves with Your Torah. Blessed are You, LORD, who teaches Torah to His people, Israel"; "Blessed are You, LORD, our God, King of the universe, who has chosen us

◂ from among

> from among all the nations and given us His Torah. Blessed are You, Lord, who gives the Torah."
>
> (11) Every day, one is obligated to recite these three blessings and then read a few words of Torah.

Seemingly, Maimonides repeats himself. He states that one who rises to study must recite three blessings; why then does he repeat that one is obligated to recite these three blessings every day? He has already established that it is forbidden to study without reciting these blessings.

The answer is clear. Maimonides formulated two separate halakhot with regard to *Birkhot HaTorah*. 1) It is forbidden to study Torah without reciting a blessing (or three blessings). 2) There is an obligation to recite these blessings; even if, for example, one is engaged in business or in communal needs and will not be free to study Torah, one is still obligated to recite these blessings. If so, these blessings are distinct from other blessings recited for mitzvot. In all other cases, one who is not performing a mitzvah has no obligation to recite a blessing, but in this case every individual is required to recite *Birkhot HaTorah*, whether or not he can study. Halakhah 10 establishes the first principle, that Torah study requires a blessing and it is forbidden to study without it. Halakhah 11 relates to the second concept, that each individual is required to recite these blessings each day, just as one is obligated to recite the blessings "who has not made me a heathen," "who has not made me a slave," etc., each day.

Furthermore, it seems that each of these halakhot relates to a distinct area of obligation. The first halakhah, that it is prohibited to study Torah without reciting a blessing, corresponds to the prohibition against deriving benefit from this world and performing a mitzvah without a blessing. Fundamentally, this halakhah is one of receiving permission (a *mattir*); the blessing is akin to an act of redemption, as the Gemara states regarding *berakhot* on food (*Berakhot* 35a).

According to Maimonides, mitzvot too require a *mattir* in the form of a blessing; performing a mitzvah without a blessing is included in the prohibition of benefitting from the world without a *berakha*. This emerges from *Hilkhot Berakhot* 1:2–3: "The Rabbis ordained that we recite blessings before partaking of any food … Anyone who derives benefit without reciting a blessing is considered as if he committed sacrilege … Just as

◂ Just as

we recite blessings for pleasures, so do we recite blessings for each mitzvah before fulfilling it." Thus, one who studies Torah without reciting a blessing has benefitted from God's Torah without permission, an act of sacrilege. In fact, the first blessing is identical to the *birkhot hamitzvot* in its structure and form; the formula of the blessing, "who has sanctified us with His mitzvot and commanded us," is consistent with that of every blessing on a mitzvah.

The second halakhah, that one is obligated to recite these blessings every day, is rooted not in the laws of *berakhot* but in the mitzvah of *talmud Torah*. Within this framework, there is a specific fulfillment and obligation to study the Written or Oral Torah and to bless the Almighty who granted us His Torah. One is obligated to study after reciting these blessings; the fulfillment occurs not in the recitation of the blessings *per se* but in the Torah study. Together, the blessings and the study form one entity, "Torah study with its blessings." The primary thrust of this obligation is the Torah study – study which requires the accompaniment of *berakhot*. According to Maimonides, the requirement to study after the *berakhot* is not due to the general halakhah that one may not interrupt between a *berakha* and the performance of a mitzvah, but rather it is because the obligation is not centered on the *berakha* but on Torah study with a *berakha*. Every day, one is obligated to study Torah together with a *berakha*.

This duality emerges from the Talmudic discussion as well. Maimonides' first halakhah, "One who rises to study Torah before he recites the *Shema*," is based on a statement of Rav Yehudah in the name of Shmuel (*Berakhot* 11b). Elsewhere (21a), we find another statement of Rav Yehudah, in the name of Rav: "From where in the Torah is the blessing before Torah study derived? As it is stated: 'When I proclaim the LORD's name, give glory to our God' (Deut. 32:3)." It seems that these two statements reflect two principles. From the verse "When I proclaim the LORD's name, give glory to our God," we derive the obligation to combine Torah study with its blessings. Nahmanides, following the straightforward meaning of the Talmud, rules that *Birkhot HaTorah* are a biblical requirement (*Hasagot* on *Sefer HaMitzvot, Mitzvot Aseh SheShakheḥan HaRav,* 15). It seems that he too does not limit the obligation to merely reciting the blessings but includes within it study as well; together they form one fulfillment. Rav Yehudah in the name of Shmuel (11b) comes to teach us

◂ a different

a different law, namely that it is prohibited to study without a blessing. We can prove that these two *sugyot* are distinct halakhot: The prohibition against studying without a blessing is merely rabbinic, just as benefitting from the world without a blessing is only a rabbinic prohibition. Yet, according to Nahmanides, the statement of Rav Yehudah in the name of Rav (21a) explicates a biblical law. Additionally, the passage in *Berakhot* 21a continues with a statement of R. Yoḥanan who derives an obligation to recite a blessing after Torah study. Obviously, a blessing after study cannot serve as a *mattir*; this requirement relates not to studying without a *berakha* but to the positive fulfillment of combining Torah study with a blessing. If so, it stands to reason that the *berakha* prior to study discussed in that passage also relates to this fulfillment. We see that these two *sugyot* address two different subjects: one, the prohibition against study without a blessing, which is certainly only rabbinic, and two, the combination of Torah and *berakha* which, according to several *Rishonim* and the plain meaning of the Talmud, is a biblical obligation.

The obligation to combine Torah and its blessings, rooted in the verse "When I proclaim the LORD's name, give glory to our God," certainly applies to the public Torah reading. Reading the Torah portion of the day constitutes *talmud Torah*, and the framework of the reading and blessings creates a joint entity of Torah study and praise. This is explicit in Nehemiah (8:5–6): "And Ezra opened the book in the sight of all the people… And Ezra blessed the LORD, the great God. And all the people answered: 'Amen, Amen,' with the lifting up of their hands; and they bowed their heads, and fell down before the LORD with their faces to the ground." We see that the communal reading requires offering praise and thanksgiving to God, apparently on the basis of the verse "When I proclaim the LORD's name, give glory to our God."

The Gemara (*Megillah* 23b) includes *Keriat HaTorah* within the category of *devarim shebikedushah*, "matters of holiness" which require a quorum of ten men, based on the verse "I will be sanctified in the midst of the children of Israel" (Lev. 22:32). Seemingly, the Gemara is difficult. We understand that reciting *Barekhu* and *Ḥazarat HaShatz* are considered *devarim shebikedushah*, but why is *Keriat HaTorah* included in this category?

The solution is simple. The Gemara refers not only to the reading itself but to the recitation of *Barekhu* before the reading, which is obviously a

◂ *davar*

davar shebikedushah. The institution of the public reading by Ezra included not only the reading but the reading combined with the sanctification of God's name. This supports the view of those *poskim* who maintain that the congregation does not fulfill its obligation through the reading alone but must hear the reading as well as *Barekhu*. Both, the offering of praise and the reading, constitute the complete fulfillment of communal study, *talmud Torah berabbim*.

In Nehemiah, we find a source for this combination with regard to the public reading of *Torah shebikhtav*, but we find this combination with regard to *Torah shebe'al peh* as well. This is the institution of *Kaddish DeRabbanan*, or in the words of the Talmud, *yehei shemeh rabbah de'aggadeta* (*Sotah* 49a). Rashi (ibid.) explains that every Shabbat, the public would gather to hear the preacher's sermon and afterward they would recite this prayer – thus realizing both "Torah and sanctification of God's name." It seems that this too stems from the verse "When I proclaim the LORD's name, give glory to our God," and from the verses in Nehemiah.

Does this concept apply as well to an individual's Torah study? Perhaps it is the case that while an individual cannot recite *Barekhu*, and therefore cannot fulfill the verse in Nehemiah in its entirety, nevertheless the fundamental halakhah is not uprooted, and the obligation to offer praise and thanksgiving remains. An individual too must "give glory" to God when he studies Torah – but he does so not with *Barekhu* but with the *Birkhot HaTorah* which parallel those recited during the public reading. However, it seems that the basis for an individual's combining of Torah and praise into one entity is to be found in another halakhah, which will shed light as well on the concept of the public Torah reading.

We find in the Gemara (*Berakhot* 8a):

> Rava said to Rafram bar Pappa: Let the Master tell us some of those outstanding statements that you said in the name of Rav Ḥisda with regard to matters of the synagogue. He said to him, Rav Ḥisda said as follows: What is the meaning of the verse: "The LORD loves the gates of Zion [*Tziyyon*] more than all the sanctuaries [*mishkenot*] of Jacob" (Ps. 87:2)? This means that the LORD loves the gates distinguished [*metzuyanim*] through

◂ the study

> the study of halakhah more than the synagogues and study halls. And this is [expressed in] that which Rabbi Ḥiyya bar Ami said in the name of Ulla: Since the day the Temple was destroyed, the Holy One, Blessed be He, has in His world only the four cubits of halakhah. Abaye said: At first, I studied in the house and prayed in the synagogue. Once I heard what Rabbi Ḥiyya bar Ami said in the name of Ulla, since the day the Temple was destroyed, the Holy One, Blessed be He, has in His world only the four cubits of halakhah alone, I pray only where I study.

Talmidei Rabbenu Yonah explain that the "gates distinguished through the study of halakhah" does not refer to study halls; these "gates" are preferred over synagogues and study halls as well. Rather, this refers to a place where Torah is taught in public and from which rulings are issued (*beit havaad*). By contrast, Maimonides (*Hil. Tefillah* 8:3) writes: "A *beit hamidrash* is greater than a synagogue, and the great sages, although they had many synagogues in their cities, would pray only in the place where they studied Torah." Apparently, Maimonides' text of the Talmud included only the words "more than the synagogues," not "and study halls."

However, if so, why did Abaye change his place of prayer only upon hearing what Rabbi Ḥiyya bar Ami said in the name of Ulla? The question of the relative status of a synagogue versus a study hall is debated by R. Yehoshua b. Levi and R. Yoḥanan (*Megillah* 26b–27a) with regard to whether one can transform a synagogue into a study hall or vice versa. If Abaye held that a study hall has greater sanctity, he should have prayed there from the start, and if he held that a synagogue has greater sanctity, why did he change his place of prayer to the *beit midrash*?

Again, the answer is clear. The discussion in *Megillah* regarding which has greater sanctity has no connection whatsoever to establishing the place of prayer. Even if a *beit midrash* has greater sanctity, it may be that prayer should take place in a synagogue. Each place is sanctified and dedicated to its purpose and its mitzvah. A synagogue is set aside for the mitzvah of prayer, and a *beit midrash* for Torah; thus, prayer should be conducted in its place, the synagogue, and there is no advantage to praying in a *beit midrash*, which is dedicated to another mitzvah. The whole creation of the *beit midrash* is for Torah study, not prayer. Regarding

◂ the halakhah

the halakhah of changing one to another, the fact that a *beit midrash* has greater sanctity tells us that it cannot be transformed into a synagogue, but this has nothing to do with it being a place of prayer.

Thus we can derive nothing about the place of prayer from the dispute between R. Yehoshua b. Levi and R. Yoḥanan. Rav Ḥisda and R. Ḥiyya bar Ami in the name of Ulla introduced an entirely different concept. A *beit midrash* is dedicated not only to the mitzvah of Torah study but to the mitzvah of prayer as well – and, in fact, its status as a place of prayer exceeds that of a synagogue. This is how Rav Ḥisda interpreted the verse "The Lord loves the gates of Zion [*Tziyyon*] more than all the sanctuaries [*mishkenot*] of Jacob" – the verse equates *batei midrash*, the gates distinguished through the study of halakhah, with the Temple in Zion, and it equates the other sanctuaries – such as Shiloh, Nov, and Givon – with synagogues. Just as the Temple in Jerusalem did not lack the sanctity of the other sanctuaries – it had the same sanctity to a greater degree – so does the *beit midrash* contain within it the sanctity of the synagogue – to a greater degree.

We can explain this as follows. Maimonides (*Sefer HaMitzvot, aseh* 5) cites the *Sifrei* which explains the words "to serve Him with all your heart" (Deut. 11:13) in two ways: "to serve Him – this is prayer; to serve Him – this is study." Through Torah study, one fulfills the imperative of worship of the heart just as one fulfills it through prayer. Thus, we see that Torah and *tefillah* merge into a unified mitzvah of *avodah shebelev*. We can further explain that *talmud Torah* itself constitutes a fulfillment of prayer; one who studies Torah worships God with his heart and soul. What is worship of the heart if not prayer?

This understanding – that Torah study is considered an outpouring of the heart, supplication and plea, song and praise – is found throughout Scripture and the sayings of the Sages. This also explains King David's request that reciting Psalms be considered like the study of *Negaim* and *Ohalot*. Why didn't he request that the supplication of Psalms be considered like any other mitzvah – charity, acts of kindness, offering sacrifices, etc.? The answer is that the praises of Psalms and Torah study share the same foundation of *avodah shebelev*; David requested that the value of the *avodah shebelev* of his Psalms equal that of the worship contained in *talmud Torah*.

◂ This is why

This is why there is a unique fulfillment in the combination of Torah and *tefillah*. The complete fulfillment of *avodah shebelev* takes place when one combines study with prayer, Torah with supplication, the meditation of the heart in the depths of halakhah with the introspection and outpouring of the heart. The halakhah which obligates merging Torah study with its *berakhot* is founded on the principle of the unified fulfillment of *avodah shebelev* contained in Torah and *tefillah*.

THE CROWN OF TORAH

Maimonides (*Hil. Talmud Torah* 3:13) writes:

> Although it is a mitzvah to study during the day and at night, one acquires most of his wisdom only at night. Therefore, a person who desires to merit the crown of Torah should be careful with all his nights, not wasting even one on sleep, eating, drinking, talk, or the like. Rather, [he should devote them] to the study of Torah and words of wisdom. Our Sages declared: The song of Torah is only at night, as the verse [Lam. 2:19] states: "Arise, cry out in the night..." And anyone who occupies himself with Torah study at night will have a strand of favor extended over him during the day, as the verse [Ps. 42:9] states: "By day the LORD will command His lovingkindness, and in the night His song shall be with me, even a prayer unto the God of my life."

Maimonides' words are difficult on several fronts. 1) If "one acquires most of his wisdom only at night," we would expect that nighttime would have precedence over day regarding *talmud Torah* – yet this is certainly not the case, as the verse וְהָגִיתָ בּוֹ יוֹמָם וָלַיְלָה, "You shall meditate therein day and night" (Josh. 1:8), equates them. 2) What is the meaning of the statement "one acquires most of his wisdom only at night"? Why can one not acquire most of his wisdom through daytime study? If one toils over the Torah during the day, will he not amass much wisdom? After all, toil is what determines the outcome – as the Sages taught, "If a person says to you: I have labored and not found success, do not believe him" (*Megillah* 6b). 3) Maimonides begins by discussing "most of his wisdom" but concludes

◂ with "the crown

with "the crown of Torah": "Therefore, a person who desires to merit the crown of Torah should be careful with all his nights, not wasting even one on sleep, eating, drinking," etc. What do these terms mean, and what is the relationship between them and Torah knowledge in general? 4) In *Hilkhot Talmud Torah* 1:8, Maimonides writes: "Every Jew is under an obligation to study Torah; poor or rich, in sound health or in pain, in the vigor of youth or very old and feeble... all are under the obligation to set aside a definite period during the day and at night for the study of Torah, as it is said, 'You shall meditate therein day and night.'" Why does Maimonides not emphasize here that one can acquire most of his wisdom only at night? Why does he wait until the end of chapter three to inform us of the unique quality of nighttime study?

To grasp the root of the matter, we must understand what our Sages (*Avot DeRabbi Natan* 41:1) intended in saying, "There are three crowns: the crown of Torah, the crown of priesthood, and the crown of kingship." What is the commonality between priesthood (*kehunah*), kingship, and Torah, which seemingly have no logical connection? And what does the concept of a crown contribute?

The common denominator of *kehunah* and kingship is that these crowns are attained through anointment with the anointing oil, *shemen hamishḥah*: both the *kohen gadol* and the king bear the title "anointed by God," *meshiḥei Hashem*. Anointment results in the sanctification of the individual; being chosen as the *kohen gadol* or king brings about an inner sanctity which awakens a hidden strength in the person. A *kohen gadol* attains lasting *kedushat haguf*, bodily sanctity, through the anointment, and likewise, one chosen as king undergoes a personal transformation of added sanctity accompanied by expanded awareness and inspiration. In a word, the personality is elevated; as Samuel said to Saul (I Sam. 10:6): "And the spirit of the LORD will come mightily upon you, and you shall prophesy with them, and shall be turned into another man." A spark of prophesy is contained in kingship and *kehunah*; Maimonides describes the prophet as follows (*Hilkhot Yesodei HaTorah* 7:1):

> At the moment that the spirit rests upon him, his soul merges with the level of angels called *ishim*, and he is transformed into a different person. He will recognize that he is not the same as he was before but has risen above the level of other men of wisdom,

◂ as was said

> as was said about Saul: "and you shall prophesy with them, and shall be turned into another man."

A similar phenomenon applies to *kehunah* and kingship. Regarding a *kohen gadol,* Maimonides states explicitly that receiving the response to a request of the *Urim VeTumim* is akin to prophesy (*Hil. Klei HaMikdash* 10:11): "Immediately, the divine spirit envelops the *kohen* and he peers at the *Ḥoshen* and sees in it through prophetic vision." Likewise, regarding a king: the anointment sanctifies him and elevates him to an august and exalted level; he becomes a *meshiaḥ Hashem.*

In this light, we can understand the concept of "*keter Torah*" as one of the three crowns with which Israel was crowned. The "crown" means the elevation and enhancement of an individual. The Torah purifies, sanctifies and bestows beauty upon a person, as we find in Proverbs (4:8): "Extol her, and she will exalt you; she will bring you honor when you embrace her." Through Torah study, one merits not only Torah knowledge and wisdom but also personal sanctity and purity. Coarseness vanishes and, in its place, comes sensitivity. Superficiality is replaced by depth of thought. Through the Torah, a new personality is forged. Man's spirit is broadened, his ethical awareness heightened. He is crowned with kingship and those who see him "behold a king in his beauty" (Isa. 33:17). The three crowns stand for the elevation and sanctification of those crowned with them. And the greatest is the crown of Torah, which elevates and purifies more than anointing oil. About this crown is said, "By Me kings reign, and rulers decree justice. By Me princes rule, and nobles, even all the judges of the earth" (Prov. 8:15–16).

This principle is reflected as well in the text of our blessings. Every day we recite the blessing "who has not made me a heathen," which apparently refers to the election of Israel, *beḥirat Yisrael;* if one recited "who has made me an Israelite" he has fulfilled his obligation (see *Magen Avraham* 46:9 and the *Otzar HaTefillot* commentary on this blessing). If so, we must ask why in the framework of *Birkhot HaTorah* we again recite the blessing "who has chosen us from among all the nations."

The answer is simple. There are two elections: 1) the election of the Patriarchs, based on the promise to Abraham (Gen. 17:7), "And I will establish My covenant between Me and you and your seed after you in their generations for an everlasting covenant, to be a God to you, and to your seed after you"; 2) the election of Israel at Sinai, proclaimed in the verse (Ex. 19:5–6), "you shall be My own treasure from among all peoples… And you shall be to Me a kingdom of priests, and a holy nation." The first blessing corresponds to the election of the *Avot*. But in the context of *Birkhot HaTorah* we recite an additional blessing for the second election, which is tied exclusively to *mattan Torah* and the sanctity of the Torah, to the identification of *Knesset Yisrael* with the Torah, and the elevation that takes place, through individuals' sanctification, by its study. In other words, the latter election is tied to the crown of Torah, and we recite a second blessing because Israel has been crowned with it. The crown of Torah is the purification of one's personality, and Israel's election is the same unique quality of sanctification. The unique *segulah* quality of every Jew is strengthened by Torah study. *Talmud Torah* thus adds a new dimension to the election of Israel, and therefore we recite another blessing corresponding to this added dimension within the framework of *Birkhot HaTorah*.

In truth, there are not many sanctities of Israel; there is one sanctity with different levels. What we call *keter kehunah* or *keter malkhut* is an intensification of *kedushat Yisrael*. Kingship and *kehunah* are not independent sanctities but higher rungs on the ladder of *kedushat Yisrael*. The sanctity of Israel is threefold, as reflected in the words "And you shall be to Me a kingdom of priests and a holy nation": 1) "kingdom"; 2) "of priests"; 3) "and a holy nation." However, the foundation for all these sanctities is the crown of Torah, from which the whole character of Israel's election draws; therefore, the crown of Torah rises above those of *kehunah* and *malkhut*. One who studies Torah broadens and deepens *beḥirat Yisrael* and *kedushat Yisrael*, and this is the most radiant and lustrous crown.

Regarding Torah study at night, we find (*Yalkut Shimoni*, Prov. 31:6): "R. Yoḥanan said: the song of Torah [*rinah shel Torah*] is only at night, as is said 'Arise, cry out in the night' (Lam. 2:19); Resh Lakish said: both at day and at night, as is said 'You shall meditate therein day and night' (Josh. 1:8)." According to Maimonides, it would seem, there is no dispute between R. Yoḥanan and Resh Lakish; each view complements the other. Regarding the mitzvah of *talmud Torah*, there is no difference between day and night. Since the mitzvah of "and teach them to your children" (Deut. 11:19) was explained to Joshua as "You shall meditate therein day and night," we cannot give preference to one time over the other. This is the position of Resh Lakish. R. Yoḥanan adds that even so, the song of Torah is only at night. What is the meaning of *rinah shel Torah*?

Maimonides apparently translates the term *rinah shel Torah* as *rov ḥokhmato,* and this term he identifies with *keter Torah*. We encounter the term *rov ḥokhmato* as well in the context of respect for one's teacher. The respect due to one's master teacher, *rav muvhak,* parallels that due to one's father, and *rav muvhak* is defined as the one from whom one gained *rov ḥokhmato* (*Hil. Talmud Torah* 5:9).

It seems clear that *rov ḥokhmato* does not mean a majority of wisdom by quantity, measured by the number of pages of Talmud that one studied with his teacher. I use myself as an example. I have had only one master teacher, and that is my father. I have no doubt that I gained most of my wisdom from him and that I am obligated to respect him as both a father and as my master teacher. However, if I calculate the amount that I studied with him in comparison to the amount that I studied on my own, I would come to the conclusion that I have learned more on my own than what we studied together. Nevertheless, I have not a shadow of a doubt that I received most of my wisdom from him. The term *rov ḥokhmato* should be understood to mean "one's primary wisdom." My father taught me to stand on my feet, gave me the keys to understand the Oral Law, showed me the path and provided me with the methodology to discern and comprehend, to study and teach. Whether I studied with him five hundred folios or six hundred does not matter. What matters and determines the relation of master and student is that the teacher provides the method and approach, shows the way. Even when I study *Eruvin,* which I did not with my father, his image stands before me and guides me through this complex and difficult tractate. It is clear as day that the term *rov ḥokhmato* refers to what we call "*lomdus*" – how to engage in the back-and-forth of halakhah, discuss the words of *Ḥazal* and *Rishonim,* and garner from them precious gems.

Since Maimonides apparently identified *rov ḥokhmato* with *keter Torah,* it emerges that this ability is a component of *keter Torah*. When the Torah is absorbed within a person and sanctifies him, it sheds a brilliant light and opens new gates of understanding. One gains not only a store of wisdom but also discernment and depth, the power to innovate and create. The development of these strengths is an outgrowth of receiving a crown resembling that of the *kohen gadol* upon whose head and eyes is poured anointing oil, so that he can see what is hidden from the eyes of ordinary men and comprehend that which is concealed from commoners. The ability to innovate within the Oral Law is one of the gifts God has granted the individual who merits the crown of Torah. This gift is bestowed primarily upon one who studies at night.

I would like to take a step further. The unique property of night relates not to the fulfillment of Torah study per se but to Torah study as worship of the heart. It is impossible for the mitzvah of study at night to be greater than during the day because the verse "You shall meditate therein day and night" equates the obligations of day and night. The purpose of study is to amass knowledge in order to keep and fulfill the mitzvot, "that you may learn them, and keep, and do them" (Deut. 5:1); with regard to this obligation there is no distinction between different times of day.

However, with regard to the *avodah shebelev* of Torah, which is based on the verse "'worship Him' – through study" (*Sifrei,* quoted in *Sefer Ha-Mitzvot, aseh* 5), there is a distinction between different times – here, night has an advantage over day. Thus, we understand Maimonides' words: "Although it is a mitzvah to study during the day and at night" – because of the mitzvah "You shall meditate therein day and night," nevertheless, "one acquires most of his wisdom," and gains the crown of Torah, only at night. The uniqueness of nighttime study is found in the worship of the heart achieved through *talmud Torah*. "Arise, cry out in the night," the song of Torah – this means *avodah shebelev*. "And in the night His song shall be with me, even a prayer unto the God of my life" – again, this means study as worship. Maimonides delayed the halakhah giving preference to the night until chapter three because in the first two chapters, night has no advantage over day – there Maimonides is discussing the mitzvah of "You shall meditate therein day and night." Only in chapter three, where Maimonides introduces the concept of the crown of Torah, which is based on the divine worship embedded in Torah, does he cite the statements of the Sages regarding night, for night has a special bond to divine worship, as we find (Ps. 134:1): "Behold, bless the Lord, all you servants of the Lord, who stand by night in the house of the Lord" – servants of the Lord, who stand by night.

◄ TORAH

TORAH STUDY AND TRANSMITTING THE SINAI EXPERIENCE

The Talmud (*Kiddushin* 30a) states:

> Rabbi Yehoshua ben Levi says: Anyone who teaches his son's son Torah, the verse ascribes him credit as though he received it from Mount Sinai, as it is stated: "But make them known to your sons and to your sons' sons," and juxtaposed to it is the phrase in the verse: "the day when you stood before the LORD your God in Horeb" (Deut. 4:9–10).

It seems from the Talmud that there is, in a certain respect, an advantage to teaching Torah to one's grandson which exceeds teaching Torah to one's son. It is only with regard to teaching one's grandson that the Talmud attributes the quality of it being as if one received the Torah from Sinai, not with regard to teaching one's son.

However, it is interesting to note that Maimonides does not give any accolade to one who teaches his grandson Torah. Maimonides simply writes (*Hil. Talmud Torah* 1:2) that just as one is obligated to teach his son Torah, he is also obligated to teach his grandson, as the verse states, "You shall make known to your sons and to your sons' sons." In fact, Maimonides writes that the obligation to teach Torah to one's son precedes the obligation of teaching Torah to one's grandson. Maimonides explains that the reason the Torah specifies that there is an obligation to teach both sons and grandsons is because the obligation of one's son comes before the obligation of one's grandson (*ibid.* 1:2–3). Maimonides does not mention any advantage at all to teaching one's grandson, despite the aforementioned Talmudic passage. How can we reconcile Maimonides with the Talmud?

In Maimonides' count of the six hundred and thirteen commandments, the eleventh positive commandment is the mitzvah of studying and teaching Torah. Nahmanides, in his list of mitzvot which he believes Maimonides omitted (*lo taaseh* 2), comments that Maimonides omitted the prohibition to forget what transpired at Mount Sinai: שנמנענו שלא נשכח מעמד הר סיני ולא נסיר אותו מדעתנו אבל יהיו עינינו ולבנו שם כל הימים – "We were forbidden to forget standing at Mount Sinai and to remove [this event] from our thoughts, but our eyes and our heart shall be there perpetually."

◂ This mitzvah

This mitzvah obligates us, Nahmanides writes, to forever transmit what transpired at Mount Sinai to our children and grandchildren, as stated in the verse, "make them known to your sons and your sons' sons." Nahmanides then asks on himself from the Gemara in *Kiddushin* (30a): Seemingly, the Gemara interprets this verse not as part of a new mitzvah to transmit the event of Mount Sinai but as part of the mitzvah to teach Torah – the verse "make them known to your sons and your sons' sons" extends the mitzvah of *talmud Torah* to one's grandsons, but it is not a new mitzvah. Nahmanides explains that this is no contradiction to his view: כי לימוד אמונת התורה הוא הלימוד בתורה – "for teaching faith in the Torah is itself the teaching of the Torah."

It is clear from the words of Nahmanides that the obligation of teaching Torah to one's children contains two aspects. There is an obligation to teach the Torah, derived from the verse "and teach them to your children" (Deut. 11:19), and there is an additional obligation of transmitting our faith in the Torah, derived from the verse "But make them known to your sons and to your son's sons ... the day that you stood before God at Horeb." By teaching Torah to one's sons and grandsons, one fulfills both obligations, because, as Nahmanides writes, "teaching faith in the Torah is itself the teaching of the Torah."

Maimonides may also accept these two distinct aspects, but he maintains that both the actual study of Torah and transmitting what transpired at Sinai are included in the positive commandment of teaching Torah. Regarding the aspect of the mitzvah derived from the verse "and teach them to your children," Maimonides writes that one's son takes precedence over his grandson. However, the Talmudic statement regarding the advantage of teaching Torah to one's grandson relates not to the aspect of teaching Torah but to transmitting the event of Sinai. When it comes to relaying our faith in the Torah, teaching one's grandchild uniquely possesses the status of "it is as though he received it from Mount Sinai." When it comes to connecting the past with the future, the greater the generational divide, the greater the act of transmission. In bridging the gap to Sinai, the grandfather has a closer bond than the father. Maimonides accepts this statement, but it is not the subject of his discussion; the subject under discussion by Maimonides is the aspect of teaching Torah derived from "and teach them to your children."

◀ *KEVI'AT*

KEVI'AT ITIM LATORAH

At the beginning of *Hilkhot Talmud Torah,* Maimonides writes as follows:

> Laws concerning *talmud Torah* comprise two affirmative precepts, the first being to study the Torah... But it is the duty of the father to teach his young son Torah... If a son has not been taught by his father, it is his duty, as soon as he realizes his deficiencies, to acquire knowledge for himself, as it is said, "That you may learn them and observe to do them" (Deut. 5:1). And so too you will find that study in all cases takes precedence over practice since study leads to practice... (*Hilkhot Talmud Torah,* headnote and 1:1, 3).
>
> If a man wishes to learn Torah and has a son who needs instruction, his own requirements are to be satisfied first. But if his son has better capacity and greater ability to grasp what he learns, then the son's education takes precedence. Still, though his son takes precedence, the father must not wholly neglect the study of Torah. For, just as it is incumbent on him to teach his son, so is he under obligation to obtain instruction for himself. A man should always study the Torah and then marry... (*Hilkhot Talmud Torah* 1:4,5).

It is obvious that Maimonides has stated the case of *talmud Torah* in clear unequivocal terms. One is duty bound to study for himself and to teach Torah to others. In view of the above, halakhah 8 comes to us quite as a surprise:

> Every Jew is under an obligation to study Torah whether he is poor or rich, in sound health or in pain, in the vigor of youth or very old and feeble. Even a man so poor that he is maintained by charity and goes begging from door to door, as also a man with a wife and children to support, are all under the obligation to set aside a definite period during the day and at night for the study of Torah, as it is said, "You shalt meditate therein day and night" (Josh. 1:8) (*Hilkhot Talmud Torah* 1:8).

The question which comes immediately to the fore is a simple one: Why was it necessary for Maimonides to duplicate? He has already defined the mitzvah of *talmud Torah* in the previous seven paragraphs, parts of which I quoted before. Why repetition and redundancy?

Apparently, Maimonides speaks of two distinctive performances. In the first seven paragraphs he deals with the performance of acquiring knowledge, of training the mind in the methodology of Torah, in interpretation, exposition and conceptual analysis, precise application, *et cetera.* In paragraph 8, Maimonides speaks of an entirely different duty. One is under obligation to set aside a definite time for the study of Torah. The general precept of *talmud Torah* is not concerned with programming, with arrangements in terms of a fixed schedule. Whether one is systematic or disorganized is irrelevant. What counts is the result: the amount of knowledge one acquires, the development of intellectual prowess, the exercise of talents. Decisive is the scholarship one masters, at both levels, quantitative and qualitative. The method he may have employed is unimportant. He might have studied in spurts at random without setting up a program. The relevant question is: *what* did he accomplish, not *how* did he accomplish. However, in halakhah 8 emphasis is placed upon the "how," upon the way in which he studies. Halakhah 8 is out to achieve orderliness. It wants that the process of *talmud Torah* be systematic, well organized, that definite hours be set aside, and that the tightly organized schedule be kept at all costs. Tardiness, procrastination, delay, and change are considered a grave violation even though the loss was recouped later by devoting to study an equivalent number of hours.

As a matter of fact, *Tosafot* (*Sanhedrin* 7a, *s.v. ela,* citing *Shabbat* 31a) imply that on the day of judgment one is interrogated about two things in respect to *talmud Torah:* whether or not he was engaged in the study of Torah; and whether or not *kavata itim laTorah,* whether he set up and kept a fixed schedule for *talmud Torah.*

At best, the law pertaining to *kevi'at itim,* establishing specifically fixed times and dates, is *prima facie* enigmatic. The question is simple. Why is it necessary to set aside definite hours? What difference does it make how one studies as long as he puts in long hours and as long as the results are good? In respect to other mitzvot no rules have ever been formulated about regularity and orderedness. Why should *talmud Torah* be different from other mitzvot? Why is a person compelled to answer two questions pertaining to *talmud Torah* on the day of judgment? One question is concerned with the "what," the other with the "how."

At a second glance, it begins to dawn upon us that what appeared at first as incomprehensible reflects an exalted idea which aspires to transcend intellectual formalism and rise to a sublime drama of faith. In this drama we will see presented, under veils, the adventures of restless man, adult and child. Apparently, *talmud Torah* is a dual activity. At one level, the mind is preoccupied with the study of Torah. As such, it is a regular intellectual performance which fits into the framework of the classical formula of learning. At this level, the relationship prevailing between Jew and Torah can be compared to, or rather equated with, the universal subject-object encounter which takes place in any intellectual performance. In essence, the encounter is purely functional, and, using Martin Buber's jargon, exhausts itself in "I" facing "it," which means the absence of relationship.

At the second level, *talmud Torah* becomes a total performance claiming the whole of the personality, and it cannot, as a total performance, be pressed into the classical formula of learning as an I-it confrontation. It is rather, to use again a Buberian phrase, an I-thou relationship. *Talmud Torah* is not just acquisition of knowledge but a personal meeting of the Jew with the Torah. At this level, the Jew cannot just walk into the *beit hamidrash* unannounced and unexpected and study Torah in his leisure time. As long as the Torah is an it, an object, one can act vis-a-vis an "it" at random; the scientist opens up the door of the laboratory, walks in and picks up the test tube. If the Torah, however, is a "thou," one must arrange a meeting, make a date with her. Otherwise she will not wait for him.

The Jew has a rendezvous with the Torah. Maimonides placed enormous emphasis upon the sanctity of this rendezvous, the significance of keeping the engagement. Neither pain (*ba'al yissurin*), nor hunger or abject poverty (*ani*), nor the dreariness and desolation of old age (*zaken*), nor the aggressive excitement of youth can serve as an apology for breaking the engagement with the Torah. If an hour was designated, the appointment made, the meeting arranged, no excuse is good enough to disappoint the Torah. Any delay, no matter how potent the reason was, is a violation of the precept of *vehagita bo yomam valailah* (Josh. 1:8), studying Torah day and night. Punctuality and promptness concerning the rendezvous a Jew has with the Torah are a prime prerequisite. After all, the command of *vehagita bo yomam valailah,* to engage in the study of Torah at night and day, was addressed to Joshua who was the commander of the armed forces, the king, the chief justice and the successor of Moses. He certainly was a busy man.

The question arises again. Why is it important that the Jew have an engagement with the Torah? What is in general the gist of the idea that the Jew-Torah relationship is an I-thou rather than an I-it encounter? One may say the Torah is a book, a discipline, a doctrine, a Law, a method that I can master, but not a living person whom I must meet. Is the whole halakhah of *kevi'at itim* pure imagery, a flight of human fantasy, an allegory, a mystical vision which recedes fast with the daybreak of reality, or is it something more than all these things? I believe the second alternative is true.

It is self-evident that the halakhic emphasis upon a rendezvous with the Torah and the significance of punctuality and promptness in keeping this rendezvous are to be understood as referring to someone else who trails behind the Torah, namely the *Shekhinah.* God, the *Ribbono Shel Olam,* in this case disguised as Mother *Shekhinah,* never separated Herself from Her daughter; veiled in humble anonymity, She accompanies Her daughter princess, the Torah. She is present wherever Her princess happens to be. Can one meet the Mother *Shekhinah* alone without having a date with Her daughter? No! Whoever is eager to invite Mother *Shekhinah* must first set up a meeting with Her daughter, the princess. She always accompanies her; she is the princess's mother, the princess's friend and the princess's chaperone, who does not leave her out of sight. By dating the daughter, one dates the mother as well. "Moses received the Torah from Sinai" (*Avot* 1:1). The Mishnah does not say "*HaKadosh Barukh Hu* gave the Torah to Moses at Sinai." Why? Because Torah and *Shekhinah* are inseparable. The *Shekhinah* never divorced Herself from the Torah. The latter is still *Torat Hashem,* Her word, Her beloved princess. They never parted company. She lets Moses and Her chosen community share in the great adventure, in the wonderful unitive love affair of *Shekhinah* and *Torat Yisrael.* "When two sit together and engage in Torah, God's *Shekhinah* rests upon them" (*Berakhot* 6a).

◂ The mitzvah

The mitzvah of *talmud Torah* begins as an intellectual activity which requires exertion, concentration, absorption, a trained logical mind. The aim of this activity is acquisition of knowledge. However, once the activity is initiated it turns into a great total experience of meeting *Shekhinah*, of having a rendezvous with God. The Jew studying Torah is like a traveler who, within sight of the initial goal, stops to take a breath and then continues with new strength upon his endless journey toward an unknown destination. Knowledge alone, at first very much desired, does not satisfy any more; he is in love with the *Shekhinah*.

In this context another problem is resolved. Have all Jews an equal share in Torah, or is the share proportionate to the accomplishment, to the amount of knowledge one possesses? On the one hand, we know the singular importance we ascribe to *talmud Torah*. On the other hand, we also know what Moses proclaimed: "*Torah tzivah lanu Moshe, morashah kehillat Yaakov*" (Deut. 33:4). The whole congregation of Jacob owns the Torah – the scholar and the ignorant have the same rights and prerogatives! The process of learning Torah is both esoteric and exoteric. At the esoteric level the brilliant mind accomplishes more, the dull – less. This cannot be helped. No process of democratization can change the character of education from esoteric into exoteric. There is an aristocracy of the brains, an institution which Congress cannot abolish – an intellectual gesture is esoteric. However, when we come upon the second aspect of *talmud Torah* – as a rendezvous with the *Shekhinah*, as a meeting with God – the act of *talmud Torah* becomes exoteric and completely democratized.

Let me explain: when Maimonides enumerated various kinds of situations in which one must, in spite of staggering difficulties, comply with his fixed Torah schedule, he has indirectly conveyed a new idea, namely, the experiential component of *talmud Torah*. The feeling of the presence of the *Shekhinah* is determined not by accomplishment but by effort. The act itself is redemptive, hallowing and inspiring, regardless of who is engaged in it, be he a genius, be he a dull person; if *talmud Torah* even at the experiential level had an esoteric character – the worth being determined by achievement – how could Maimonides warn us against delay? If results count, a change of time may be beneficial. It may raise the quality of the performance. A person who is hungry or in pain

◂ cannot concentrate

cannot concentrate. The time he spends in study is a total waste. And yet Maimonides insists that the engagement be kept. Let us ask ourselves: What is the use of study without obtaining the regular benefits of the intellectual exercise? Wouldn't it be more profitable to postpone the "date" for a short period of time and resume the study of Torah after all physical handicaps have disappeared? The answer to this question was given already, and it is terse and clear.

In respect to the rendezvous with the *Shekhinah* through the study of Torah, centrality has been assigned to the effort; the results are of marginal significance. The worth of the meeting between man and *Shekhinah* is determined by the sincerity of the commitment, by the intensity of the dedication, by the warmth of the encounter, by the love and passion of the God-questing individual, and not by the brilliance of the performance. The *gaon* and the dull person, the great mind and the simpleton, share in the redemptive hallowing experience in accordance with the effort – "*lefum tzaara agra*, according to the labor is the reward" (*Avot* 5:26).

THE CONVERSION OF THE WIVES OF SAMSON AND SOLOMON

By Rav Ahron Soloveichik

Maimonides (*Hil. Issurei Biah* 13:14–17) writes:

> Let it not enter your mind that Samson, savior of Israel, or King Solomon, who is called "friend of God," married non-Jewish women who remained gentiles; rather, the explanation is as follows: The proper mitzvah when a male or female comes to convert is that we investigate whether he wants to enter our faith for financial benefit or to gain authority or due to fear. [Likewise,] for a male, we investigate whether he has set his eyes on a Jewish woman, and for a female, we investigate whether she has set her eyes on a Jewish bachelor. If we do not find any ulterior motive, we notify them of the weight of the Torah's yoke and how difficult it is for the commoners to keep it so that they will part. If they

accept and do not part, and we see that their conversion is out of love, we accept them, as the verse (Ruth 1:18) states, "Naomi saw that Ruth was determined to come with her, and she spoke to her no more."

Therefore, throughout the days of David and Solomon, Jewish courts did not accept converts – in the days of David, because maybe they came to convert out of fear, and in the days of Solomon, because maybe they came to convert for the dominion and the good and wealth which the Jewish people possessed. For anyone who converts because of one of the empty things of this world is not a righteous convert. Nevertheless, there were many who converted in the days of David and Solomon in the presence of laymen [i.e., not before a proper court], and the Sanhedrin treated them with concern: They did not reject them, since they had immersed themselves, and they did not draw them near until they saw what became of them.

And since Solomon converted women and married them, and likewise Samson converted and married [Delilah], and it is known that they converted for an ulterior motive and [therefore] their conversion was not in accordance with the court, Scripture considers it as if they were gentiles and that they remained forbidden. Furthermore, their ultimate [conduct] revealed their initial [intent], for they worshipped their idols and built altars for them....

A convert who was not investigated or was not notified of the mitzvot and penalties, who [nevertheless] was circumcised and immersed before three laymen, is a convert, even if it is known that he converted for an ulterior reason – since he circumcised and immersed himself, he has left the category of the gentiles, and we treat him with concern until his righteousness is made clear. Even if he returns to idolatry, he is treated like an apostate Jew whose betrothal is valid. It is a mitzvah to return a lost object to him; once he has immersed himself, he is considered a Jew. This is why Samson and Solomon kept their wives, even though their secret had been revealed.

◂ This passage

This passage requires explanation: Maimonides states that we cannot entertain the thought that Samson or Solomon married gentile women, and so their wives must have converted, but subsequently he writes that the ultimate actions of these women revealed their initial intent, and therefore Scripture treats them as gentiles who remain forbidden. If so, doesn't this mean that their conversion was invalid, and that Samson and Solomon did marry gentile women? Although Maimonides writes that Scripture treats them *as if* they were gentiles, and not that they actually were, the question remains: Why were these not simply invalid conversions, which would mean that the wives of Samson and Solomon were in fact gentiles?

To understand this, let us begin with the Gemara (*Yevamot* 46a) which cites a dispute about what is necessary for conversion:

> The Sages taught: A convert who was circumcised but did not immerse, R. Eliezer says this is a convert, as so we found with our forefathers [following the Exodus] that they were circumcised but were not immersed. One who immersed but was not circumcised, R. Yehoshua says this is a convert, as so we found with our foremothers that they immersed but were not circumcised. And the Rabbis say: Whether he immersed but was not circumcised or whether he was circumcised but did not immerse, he is not a convert until he is circumcised and immerses.

It seems clear that although R. Yehoshua maintains that immersion by itself effects conversion, he agrees that circumcision is a necessary part of conversion, and not merely because every male Jew must be circumcised. Likewise, it seems clear that although R. Eliezer holds that circumcision by itself makes a convert, he nevertheless agrees that immersion is necessary. The dispute between R. Eliezer and R. Yehoshua is merely whether lack of circumcision or immersion prevents the conversion from taking effect, but all agree that these are, ab initio (*lekhatḥila*), necessary components of conversion on a biblical level.

The Gemara (*Keritot* 9a) mentions a third component of conversion: *hartzaat damim*, i.e., the convert must offer an animal sacrifice. When the

Temple was standing, the bringing of a sacrifice was necessary to allow a convert to marry a Jew (see *Shita Mekubetzet, Keritot* 8b). Even though a convert who did not bring a sacrifice already possessed the sanctity of Israel with regard to all other laws, it nevertheless remained forbidden for such a convert to marry a Jew. It seems that the same would be true according to R. Eliezer regarding a convert who was circumcised but did not immerse himself, and according to R. Yehoshua regarding a convert who immersed himself but was not circumcised – although they each respectively hold that this is a convert and he has the status of a Jew for all other laws, he remains forbidden to marry a Jew. How are we to understand this idea?

Apparently, we must distinguish between the act of conversion itself and those things which are requirements of conversion, without which the convert cannot marry into the Jewish people. According to the Rabbis – the third opinion in *Yevamot* 46a above – both circumcision and immersion are necessary to effect conversion; *hartzaat damim*, however, is not part of the conversion itself, but in the time of the Temple the convert cannot marry into the Jewish people without it. In short, there are requirements beyond those that effect conversion, and without fulfilling them the convert cannot marry into the Jewish people. This is true of bringing a sacrifice according to the Rabbis, of circumcision according to R. Yehoshua, and of immersion according to R. Eliezer.

Turning to the acceptance of the mitzvot: Is this part of the conversion itself or is it an additional requirement which is incumbent upon a convert? According to *Tosafot*, the Mordekhai and the Rosh, accepting the mitzvot is the most fundamental aspect of conversion itself – *Tosafot* (*Yevamot* 45b and *Kiddushin* 62b), the Rosh (*Yevamot* 4:31), and the Mordekhai (*Yevamot* §36) write that a *beit din* of three is required ideally for all parts of the conversion – circumcision, immersion, and the acceptance of mitzvot – but if the *beit din* was present only for the acceptance of mitzvot, the conversion is valid. According to this view, the acceptance of mitzvot is the essence of conversion. However, according to Maimonides, the *beit din* is necessary for immersion (and it would seem for circumcision), but the acceptance of mitzvot is akin to the requirement to bring a sacrifice in the times of the Temple: A convert was required to bring a sacrifice before marrying into the Jewish people but it does not prevent his conversion from taking effect.

◂ We can

We can now understand Maimonides' view regarding the wives of Samson and Solomon. If one converts and accepts the yoke of mitzvot, but after accepting the mitzvot he continues to act as he did before conversion, his acceptance is viewed as mere words and does not count. For his acceptance to be deemed valid, he must actually change his behavior and become dedicated to keeping the mitzvot. Regarding Pharaoh's daughter, who married Solomon, and Delilah, who married Samson, since their acceptance of mitzvot did not change their behavior, it was clearly mere words and not effective. They were therefore not allowed to marry into the Jewish people and were lacking a component of the sanctity of Israel with regard to marriage. This is the meaning of Maimonides' words, "Let it not enter your mind that Samson... or King Solomon... married non-Jewish women who remained gentiles." They did not marry actual gentiles, but they did sin in that the women they married were not full converts and were forbidden to marry into the Jewish people.

However, Maimonides' view remains difficult. At the end of halakhah 17, he writes that "this is why Samson and Solomon kept their wives, even though their secret had been revealed." If these women were not full converts and marriage to them was prohibited, why did the Jewish court not compel them to divorce, even though these women were not actual gentiles? We can explain this as follows: Maimonides holds that even if the initial acceptance of mitzvot was insincere and therefore invalid, if subsequently the convert does begin to keep the mitzvot, the initial acceptance is retroactively validated. According to Maimonides, Samson and Solomon kept their wives even though they continued to worship idols and did not change their practice because they were confident that in the end their wives would abandon their idolatry and embrace the mitzvot, in which case they would retroactively be full converts. *Beit din* did not force them to divorce because they too did not know whether they would change with time, and therefore they allowed Samson and Solomon to rely on their certainty. This is akin to the case in *Ketubot* 22b, where the Gemara allows a woman to remain married, even when there are contradictory witnesses about her previous husband's death, because she states that she is certain that her previous husband has died.